NO PANIC!
HOW TO ADOPT AN OLDER CHILD

NO PANIC! HOW TO ADOPT AN OLDER CHILD

by Bethany M. Gardiner, M.D.

sticky
tape
press

2014

Published by Sticky Tape Press
5349 228th Avenue SE, Issaquah, WA, 98029
www.stickytapepress.com

Copyright ©2012 by Bethany Gardiner

All rights reserved.

No part of this book may be reproduced, stored in a retrieval system, or transmitted by any means, electronic, mechanical, photocopying, recording, or otherwise, without written permission from the copyright holder.

Distributed by River Grove Books

For information or special discounts for bulk purchases, please contact River Grove Books at PO Box 91869, Austin, TX 78709, 512.891.6100.

Cover art: Kateryna Datsun
Layout Design: Roman Solonynka
Editor: Matthew Perry

Cataloging-in-Publication data is available.

Library of Congress Control Number: 2013958044

98765432

ISBN: 978-0-9830420-2-0

Printed in the United States of America

First Edition

DEDICATION

To my husband, my partner and protector; to my daughter, whose quiet strength always inspires me; to my oldest son, whose penchant for logic makes me reexamine everything; and of course, to my new son who has taught me the true meaning of love.

Contents

Acknowledgements 13
Introduction 15

Getting Started **17**

No Panic—At Least Not Yet 19
International vs. Domestic Adoption 31
Adopting an Older Child 41
The Great Paperwork Chase 49
Money Matters 59
Great Expectations 67

Worlds Apart **73**

1: Let's start at the very beginning 75
2: Oh the things we have yet to learn 78
3: Till we meet again 79
4: A whirlwind week 81
5: The "talk" and our first goodbye 83
6: Penny pinchers 85
7: What's that? I can't understand you 87
8: Off to a grand start—maybe not 89
9: You can't win—no matter what 91
10: The doctor is in 93
11: Halfway done is as just begun 95
12: Just one more thing 97
13: At last we speak 98
14: Keeping our cool 99

15: Count to ten	101
16: Finally, eagle scout!	102
17: Christmas wishes	103
18: Yippee—no more paperwork!	104
19: Time to panic	105
20: Time to worry	106
21: We don't live in a cardboard box—honest	108
22: Sitting on pins and needles	110
23: Eight days and counting	111
24: Mortician or spy? You decide.	113
25: Four days until flight	115
26: Last night in the USA	116

Getting Closer — 117

Traveling Overseas for an Adoption	119
Bonding and Attachment	135
Let's Talk	147

Worlds Collide — 157

27: Day 1—Kiev	159
28: Reflections in the dawn	162
29: Day 2—Kiev	163
30: Day 3—Kiev—rain, rain, go away	165
31: Day 4—Kiev to Donetsk	167
32: Day 5—Donetsk to Mariupol	170
33: Day 6—Mariupol	174
34: Day 7—Mariupol—paperwork moving along nicely	176
35: Day 8—Mariupol—relaxing and visiting	179
36: Day 9—Mariupol—happy orthodox Easter	182

37: Day 10—Beautiful spring day	184
38: More day 10	186
39: Day 11—Mariupol—What's in a name?	187
40: Day 12—Last day in Mariupol for now	189
41: Day 13—Mariupol to Kiev	192
42: Day 14—Kiev to London	194
43: Day 15—London—happy birthday Amanda	195
44: Day 16—London—shop 'til you drop	196
45: Day 17—London	198
46: Day 18—London—rain again!	199
47: Day 19—Just tripping along	200
48: Day 20—London to Mariupol	202
49: Day 21—Our day in court	203
50: Day 21—Addendum	208
51: Day 22—Mariupol	209
52: Day 23—Sad news from home	212
53: The rest of day 23	214
54: Day 24—Taxi troubles	216
55: Day 25—Tomorrow never comes	219
56: Day 26—A very humbling day	222
57: More Day 26—Get ready to need more hankies	226
58: Day 27—American embassy part 1	228
59: Day 27—Part 2	232
60: Day 28—Goodbye John and Amanda	233
61: Day 29—Goodbye to A1	237
62: Day 30—Everything is done!	240
63: Day 31—Leaving tomorrow	243
64: Home at last	245

Finally Home	**251**
Easing the Transition	253
Managing Emotions	261
Developmental Stages	269
Becoming One	**279**
65: Settling in	281
66: Happy Mother's Day everyone!	284
67: School begins	288
68: Sore muscles and tickle fights	290
69: A thought on language	293
70: Jealousy and building trust	295
71: Major breakthrough	297
72: Mommy flips out	299
73: Daddy flips out	301
74: Nothing like a mopey teenager	304
75: A day in the life of Alex's stomach	305
76: Yikes—help me out!	306
77: First family vacation	307
78: Last day of vacation	311
79: Talk about ruining a good thing	312
80: Things calm down	314
81: The good (science experiments) and the bad (my cellphone)	317
82: Setting a few boundaries	320
83: Our first fight	322
84: Sickness hits	324
85: The dam breaks	326
86: Mom is out of reserves	328

87: Mental health day	330
88: Epic parenting fail	331
89: San Francisco and a love/hate list	333
90: My heart breaks	336
91: Things look up	339
92: Silver medalist at Nationals!	341
93: Eight weeks as a family of five	343
94: Trying not to be cynical	345
95: No rest for the weary	348
96: Internal conflicts	350
97: All good things come to an end	352

A New Normal Life — **355**

Getting Your Life Back—Not!	357
Becoming a Family	363
Getting Help	371
Epilogue	381
References	387
About the Author	389

Acknowledgements

Recently, as the children and I were studying sociology this past year, I became aware of just how interdependent and connected we are as human beings. This being said, the journey of adopting an older child showed me just how true this was. Our family wouldn't have been able to accomplish everything we have been able to without the immense help and support of so many. Of course, our facilitators, David and Sasha, the hosting program coordinator, Rob, and all the other personnel that helped the actual adoption were important, as were the other families we knew going through the same process. But so were all the other people that I only had a fleeting interaction with but who helped so much, from the bank tellers that searched out new money, to the postal employees who patiently processed our many envelopes, to the immigration officials who smiled as Alex got his citizenship papers. It is the compilation of everyone who has touched our family's lives on this journey that I would like to thank and send my heartfelt gratitude. Neither Alex nor we were on this journey alone, there were so many rooting for us along the way, it was bound to turn out all right!

Introduction

I received a bit of advice a couple of years ago and amazingly I decided to heed it. Usually I take advice from others poorly, if at all. I wish I could say it is because I am incredibly talented and gifted and rarely need redirection or corrections, but the truth is closer to the fact that I am incredibly stubborn and tend to think I am always right. But for whatever reason, I was open to this particular piece of advice and really took it to heart.

Our family was beginning the process to adopt a teenage boy from Ukraine and in conversation with a friend, she mentioned that she herself had adopted internationally many years ago. The circumstances were different, as she had adopted an infant and was actually living in the same country as the infant at the time, but we did have the international adoption in common. She mentioned to me how important it was to chronicle every step of the journey to adoption, giving several reasons for her statement, saying, "It will mean a great deal to him one day when he starts to question, as all adoptees do, your choice of him, his previous life, and how to move forward. It will also surprise both of you when times get rough, how much love you had for him even before he came to live with you, and at times, you will both need to be reminded of that."

This piece of advice really resonated with me and felt right. Most of the other pieces of advice I have received and information I sought out, however well-intentioned, just didn't seem to make sense for our family. There are so many different paths that lead families to adoption and there's a lot of difference between adopting internationally and domestically and between adopting an infant and an older child, that much advice just doesn't apply.

So taking this piece of advice to heart, I started a blog called Dearest Dema to chronicle our adoption. I decided to write the blog in a series of letters as my ideas just seemed to flow better that way. There was so much that I wanted to communicate to our new son and so much that I wanted to share. I also figured when he learned to read English, he would enjoy reading them. However, as I was writing the blog, I realized I was learning so much about myself, my family, and children in particular. And remember, with my background as a board-certified pediatrician, I thought I already knew all about children. So this book grew out of all of these disparate places: a desire to give Dema a past with us, sharing of information with others, chronicling how much our family was learning and changing, and showing other families what our experience was like to empower them to take the information and change it and grow it to fit their situations.

I hope everyone will laugh and cry along with me as I show you the good and not so good of adopting a teenager. It was a momentous year that finally brought Dema to us and I hope to spread knowledge and awareness about the adoption of teenagers and to share with others what an incredible experience it is. Everyone has a unique family situation and just as no two children are the same, no two adoptions will be similar, but hopefully our story will inspire you and there will be common elements that you can draw upon in your own journey.

So on that note — here we go.

PART ONE:

GETTING STARTED

No Panic — At Least Not Yet

Just being in the same room with a teenager can be upsetting, what with mood swings, hormonal surges, and attitudes, bringing some people to their knees, but adopting one, on purpose? Really? I know what is going through your mind as you read this, that I need some sort of professional help, or at the very least, a hard conk on the head, but trust me, there is no need to panic. Adopting a teenager can be a wonderful, rewarding experience that will complete your family in the best way possible.

In the beginning, as my husband and I were contemplating adding to our family, we thought only of dealing with an infant, one that I could call our very own, raise from day one, imprint with (in my own mind) all of our wonderful and unsurpassed parenting skills, knowledge, and superior abilities. Add into that the fact that I already had two teenagers at home and while they are wonderful kids, they are still, well, teenagers. They have moods, hormonal swings in personality, the absolute certainty that my husband and I are incompetent, and the knowledge that they know everything that there is to know in the world. Ok, after writing this, even I am starting to panic, just a little, at the picture I am painting. But not to be deterred even with this knowledge, that is just what we did. We adopted a fourteen-year-old boy from Ukraine.

To be honest, we had not set out intending to adopt a teenager. My husband and I had toyed with the idea of adoption in the past after infertility and difficult pregnancy issues had declared me unable to procreate any more, but as we had two biological children at the time aged twelve and fifteen, we were happy and satisfied. We had briefly thought about adoption, but were scared to start a process of which we knew nothing about. We did also briefly investigate the state foster system but we told that because we attachment parented and homeschooled, we were not ideal candidates to foster/adopt. So, with that rejection and a pile of uncertainty, we were not really looking specifically to add to our family, but at the same time, we were not opposed to the idea. But before I delve too much into our own story, let me back up for a minute here.

You will find that so much in adoption depends on individual circumstances; any advice or information you receive or seek out will need to be run through the filter of your family. I want you, the reader, to feel empowered to make decisions that are right for your family and circumstances, even if they are contradictory to other advice you have received or the opinion of so-called 'experts.' I don't want you ignoring others and charging ahead based only on your own internal ideas and wishes, but understanding the need for flexibility and interpretation based upon your own family and circumstances.

So given this, I need to introduce you to our family first. Understanding who we are will allow you to gain a deeper understanding of our circumstances and be able to adapt what I am describing to your unique situation. After all, there really isn't any right or wrong in adoption, just love and acceptance and what feels right in your heart.

First, John, my husband. He is the CFO of a large software company and is somewhat of a workaholic. He is the common sense part of the equation, always providing the voice of reason and practicality. However, he is fun-loving, extroverted, and willing to have any new experience that he can. He enjoys outdoor activities and is very involved as a dad and caregiver.

Next is G4, our oldest son. He is John also, but since he is the fourth, the nickname G4 just sort of stuck to him. He has been a challenge to parent as he is quite gifted, and in fact started college when he was fourteen. He is currently a junior in college pursuing a degree in molecular biology and thinking that he knows everything—the sad thing is that he usually does about any topic that is being discussed. At just about every party or social gathering we go to, you can find him in the middle of a group of intellectuals having a debate on anything from early man to quantum physics.

Then, we have Amanda, my perfect child. She has not given me a moment of difficulty. She is easy-going and pleasant, always eager to please. She is a competitive little creature though, always wanting to win. She is very into Taekwondo, taking her training very seriously, and competes at the national level. She loves music, creative writing, and is also a social bug.

Next there is me, Bethany. I am a pediatrician who changed careers to writing many years ago to stay home and homeschool my kids. I am somewhat opposite of my husband. I am an emotional creature, worried about feelings and matters of the heart more than more pragmatic matters. I fell in love with the philosophy of attachment parenting when I first heard of it, being a philosophy of meeting children's needs first and foremost, no babysitters, no crying it out, and being a constant parental presence. I attachment parented my first two children and felt this method fit my personality very well. I am not a morning person, or really very organized, but I do try. But you will get to know me better as you read this book, so for now I won't spoil your impressions with the bald truth.

And finally, there is our new child, Alex. You will see that we go through several different names here throughout the book. He started out as Dema to us, then when we learned we had spelled it incorrectly, he becomes Dima. In the end, he turns into Alex, as he changed his name with our adoption of him. I will try to refer to him by the name by which we associated with him at the time, so just understand that Dema, Dima, and Alex are all the same person. I really don't want to say too much about him now, as I want him to unfold to you much as he did to us. That is part of the fun and mystery of it all. In the beginning, we really didn't know him either!

So now that you have been introduced to the major characters in our story, let's continue with some practical information about adoption.

Considering Adoption

I suspect that most of you reading this have already decided on adoption as an option for your family. Whether you are single, fed up with infertility issues, or just wanting to add to your existing family, you have decided that adoption is for you. And while I know that you are just wanting to get started, there are discussions that need to be had first.

The more work done up front, the easier the journey will ultimately be. There are so many facets that go into the actual decision to adopt. Let's go through some of the most common ones that need to be considered, but remember, every family is different and you will need to customize to fit your particular situation.

The first thing I want to cover is back to the actual consideration of adoption. The most important question that you need to answer is, do you have a missing piece that you need to find to complete your family? If the answer is yes, then probably adoption is for you. If the answer is no, then maybe you need to rethink. As a good friend said to us, "Do not adopt because you want to rescue a child or do good deeds. This will not be enough to sustain the relationship. Adopt only if you think that this child or children were truly meant to be yours and a part of your family."

I know that we felt strongly that there was a missing piece to our family. We didn't feel complete, but as to how to fill that hole, we weren't quite sure. Ultimately, adoption provided us the chance to fulfill our dreams, but in the beginning, we weren't that committed to it as the only solution to our family.

The initial phase of considering adoption is only that, the initial phase. The rest of your life with your new child once you have them at home is really where you need to put your mind. I know this isn't easy when you are contemplating taking this journey, as it is easy to get caught up in the process. Excitement and pressures, both internal and external, will be pushing you forward, but it is important to step back a little and slow down. I look at adoption a little like learning a new job, giving birth to a baby, or any other major life change. You can plan and hope and pray, but nothing really turns out exactly like you plan in advance. The nice thing is that usually it turns out a lot better, but certainly different than you had planned.

If you really want a child but feel that your family or situation is complete and whole already, there are alternatives that are not as permanent, where you can form attachments with children, help, and in a way rescue children from bad situations, without taking on the complete responsibilities of adoption.

You can volunteer with the Big Brothers Big Sisters organization to mentor a young child or teen that needs your help. This is a good way to learn how to talk to and interact with a sometimes recalcitrant youth whom you don't know. Also, many of these children come from difficult home situations that might mirror some of the problems a future adopted child might have experienced.

For many of us that have led privileged lives, we are new to the abuse and neglect that some children face on a daily basis. Learning about it and dealing with it is a powerful tool that will help you in the future if you do adopt a neglected or abused child. Many times people feel sorry for the child, and try to rush in and correct the situation immediately, unknowingly causing more harm than good. Facing some of these problems and becoming comfortable with them will allow you to be able to deal with them intellectually and when developmentally appropriate and not just react on an emotional level with overcompensation.

Besides Big Brothers Big Sisters, there are other ways to grow closer with a child and help out. There are opportunities such as Court Appointed Special Advocates. These are individuals who assist the court and the Department of Child Welfare with cases. You are an advocate for the child first and foremost, while working with all the parties, the courts, the family, social workers etc., to find the best situation for the involved child. No special background is required, the training that is needed will be provided by the state. Anyone who is interested in helping a child can volunteer. Each state will have slightly different systems, but the basic function is the same. In this program, you will have the opportunity to not only get to know a child, but become familiar with the system that exists around them, including the family dynamics. Again, this type of knowledge is invaluable in helping you understand and build a picture of a child's past if you pursue adoption.

I have discussed some national and state programs, but there are a host of other ways you can help children on a local level. Check into your local homeless shelter or Food and Care Coalition. There are many times volunteer positions available working with children in which help is desperately needed. There are a host of programs on the local level working with at-risk moms and their newborns. There are also opportunities through local schools to mentor or counsel children with special needs. So, just about any situation with children you might have envisioned yourself being involved with by adoption, can be investigated with volunteer opportunities first.

Also, if you want to adopt in the future but are scared about some of the situations you might encounter and want to gain some experience, there are ways to accomplish this, like getting involved as I described above.

NO PANIC!

I want to adopt, but how, when I am scared to death of issues I would face that I don't know how to deal with?

Put aside the actual adoption for a little while and familiarize yourself with some of the issues you might be facing with adoption. You can read books about adoption and child development, follow blogs, get out and talk to people who work with children and especially underserved populations of children, and then volunteer. Then once you have information, it won't seem so scary.

Along the lines of volunteering directly with children, there are countless other ways you can help out and at the same time arm yourself with knowledge about children's issues. While you will not have the benefit of one-on-one contact with a child, you will be able to feel good about helping children in need. You can help with organizing toy drives, coat drives, school supply drives, etc. You can write letters and emails to policy makers on issues of child welfare, you can donate to organizations, and generally raise awareness on children's issues. This can even extend out of traditional children's areas, to issues which lead to at-risk children, such as teen pregnancy, substance abuse, poverty, and lack of education, which cause many parents to lose their children to the system. Any of these will help fulfill your desires to help out, and will have the added bonus of giving you information and knowledge about at-risk children, and the issues they face.

However, abuse and neglect aren't the only issues you could possibly face with an adoption of an older child. One of the most challenging aspects of our particular adoption was that Alex grew up in Ukraine and spoke no English in the beginning. For us, the fact that we had hosted an exchange student years before from Ukraine made us feel a little more comfortable with the language barrier.

If you are interested in learning about what it would be like to adopt from a foreign country and deal with language and cultural barriers, exchange students are a good way to test the waters so to speak. There are programs from a variety of countries that span a variety of time commitments, from short summer experiences of a few weeks, to full summers or semesters, and some even that offer full year exchange programs. They vary in the type of financial support you are expected to provide for the child and in some particulars of travel and schooling, but all are essentially giving you the opportunity to host a child from another country in your home.

The experience will not be quite the same as an international adoption as these children are usually quite proficient in English and have intact supportive families at home, but there will still be a language barrier as book proficiency is not the same as fluency and dealing with cultural issues will be the same as you would experience with adoption. Exchange programs can be rewarding experiences for both parties involved.

There are also usually mission works that are organized by churches or various philanthropic organizations that can allow you time in a foreign country working with locals and children. While this will be far different from adopting, it can serve to familiarize yourself with a population and the issues they are facing.

Any of these ideas I mentioned, among others, are great ways to familiarize yourself with children and the unique social issues that surround them. As I mentioned before the experience you gain will pay you back a thousand-fold as you navigate through the adoption process and then integrate a new family member into your household. Research and knowledge are great ways to demystify and prepare you.

Looking back on my adoption experience, my background as a pediatrician was immensely helpful. I was used to dealing with social workers, situations of abuse and neglect, and was familiar with the ramifications in children's behavior and development. My previous training allowed me to recognize a little faster when Alex needed intervention and to distinguish it from when it was just a normal teenager thing. I was able to understand his developmental stages a little easier and tolerate them with less frustration.

Mostly though, I don't want to scare off anyone who doesn't have specialized training in children. I do think that it is helpful however if you don't have this advantage, it can easily be addressed with research and reading and the presence of an adequate support system after the adoption.

NO PANIC!

Help! I have no specialized training in children and in fact have very little experience dealing with them. How can I ever adopt a child?

While previous experience makes some people's life a little easier, you *can* adopt, and just as successfully as anyone else. You will have to put a little more work in up front with reading and research, but it will not affect your outcome in the long run. The important point to note here is that everyone needs to be informed and aware of the special issues faced by adopted older children and be ready to deal with them either by themselves, or with the help of a professional. The only wrong thing is to ignore problems and not seek help.

Hopefully, I have given you some ideas of how to prepare yourself for the decision and a way to assuage some of your concerns and worries that might be present. But don't forget the most powerful tool is to talk to people. Even if you don't know any that have adopted personally, you can reach out over the internet and make contacts.

There are many organizations dedicated to children's issues and more specifically adoption. For example, FRUA is a national organization dedicated to families that have or are considering adoption from Russia and former Russian countries. They have forums, blogs, local chapters, and a myriad of other resources available. There are many organizations like this that focus on adoption from just one country or area of the world. Along these same lines, www.adoption.com has discussion forums and specific sites for people that are just getting started. There is no excuse for not googling adoption and starting to read, and once you do, reaching out to others.

Spending the time researching and gathering knowledge beforehand will make you a stronger candidate for adoption and a more capable one. While it may seem like an emotional decision now, trust me, it will only get worse and in the heat of the moment, you will not be wanting to listen to others, only follow your own heart.

Making the Decision

After going through the above process of figuring out whether adoption is the right decision for you, you have to actually make the commitment and move forward. Later on, I will cover in more detail the specifics of our situation, but for now, I want to empower you to consider your own unique scenario. After we met Dema, we had an easy time of knowing that we wanted to add him to our family, but the actual final decision to adopt him, we did not take lightly. John and I had several serious discussions as we walked through the scenario of adding another member to our family.

I will give you a list of questions we asked ourselves while we were going through the decision-making process. These were just a few of the questions we asked ourselves, but I can imagine that there are many others that could come up.

---

1. What would be the effect on our two biologicalal children of another child in the family?
2. Financially, could we afford the adoption process and the ensuing costs of educating, feeding, clothing, and entertaining another person?
3. How would the culture and language differences affect us and Dema?
4. How could we be sure that Dema wanted to be with us?
5. Could we complete the necessary paperwork and agree to signing con-

tracts and working with another country where we had very little control and very little transparency?
6. How would we handle it if Dema never really accepted us or was never able to live up to our expectations?
7. Practically, a family of four is different from five with respect to cars, hotel rooms, even tables at restaurants. Could we handle the extra person?
8. What would happen if there were barriers to getting Dema? How would we deal with it?
9. Could I (Bethany) handle the stress of homeschooling Dema with another child, G4, in college at a young age and needing a lot of support and Amanda's intense taekwondo competition schedule?
10. Would this be the right decision for our family?
11. Would this be the right decision for the child, to take them away from their country, language, and culture?

This is a short list that we started with, and it led to great conversations and debates within the family. John had more reservations than I did; remember, he is a much more practical person than I am. He was appropriately asking the questions while I was more interested in matters of the heart, but it was good to have a balance. Adoption is a serious matter and needs to have all sides considered.

We asked these questions first between the two of us, and then branched out to ask Amanda and G4. We knew that we had the final say so in the adoption, but they are part of the family and would be dealing with a new sibling. Because of this, we needed to make sure that they were on board with the decision as well. They would have to share the resources of the family with another person and would sometimes not be able to get their needs met because of him. John and I wanted to be sure they understood this. We knew they wouldn't be happy with it at times, but if they at least understood the process and reasons why it would happen, it would maybe take the sting out of it a little. We were lucky, with G4 and Amanda at the ages they are, fifteen and twelve, they were able to fully understand and be involved in the process, whereas I can imagine it would be different if you had little ones to consider. But regardless of your other family members' ages and circumstances, I think that as full a disclosure as possible of the realistic side of adoption before the process begins will help set expectations.

We also eventually asked Dema himself, after looking within the family. As he was old enough to understand what was going on and the implications of adoption, we felt it was only fair to get his buy in on the process. After all, if he had not wanted to be adopted, we would have respected that decision and backed off, no matter how hard it would have been to do so.

All in all, after answering all these questions and more, we decided that Dema was the one for us! Ultimately it came down to the fact that we had always wanted more children and were not able to have any more. Here was a wonderful child that I had already fallen in love with the moment I met him, with the rest of the family not far behind, needing a forever home, and we had room in our hearts and life for him. I think it was somewhat of a forgone conclusion, but I caution everyone—go through the motions of asking the tough questions anyway. You can learn a lot about yourself while answering them, and any self-insight will help as you navigate the journey in front of you.

International vs. Domestic Adoption

So, here we are. You have considered adoption, decided it is for you, made the decision and are now at the point of moving forward. But at this point, there is yet another decision to be made: do you try to adopt domestically or internationally? What are the benefits of each and what are their drawbacks? Why do some people chose one way over another? These are complicated questions and I will guide you through the process as best as I can, but always remember, your own family situation is the most important deciding factor.

First to consider, are there reasons why an international adoption would make sense for you? Do you have family members or a strong heritage in another country? Are there other reasons for an international consideration, such as language, expertise, travel, etc.? Or are there binding reasons for a domestic adoption? Do you have a situation of a family member that needs to have their child adopted? Do you personally know or have close contacts in a situation where there is an available child? Are you opposed to the idea of a possible interracial or intercultural adoption for any reason?

Sometimes these are tough questions to ask yourself. In today's society of political correctness, many people feel it is unseemly to ask some of these questions, but for the sake of your future child, you need to. There could be bona fide reasons why an interracial or intercultural adoption wouldn't work in your family, and you need to be honest with yourself. The last thing you want to do is to unknowingly proceed with an adoption that will have even more of an uphill battle than is already the case.

All adoptions have similarities and common ground, but the differences between international and domestic adoption are huge in some respects and should be considered first. First, let's talk how the fact of getting another country's government involved really complicates the adoption scenario.

In fact when I first drafted this book, the Russian government temporarily banned adoptions to the US, more as a political maneuver to protest the US's ban on travel and financial restrictions by human rights abusers in the Russian government than anything else, but this is an example of how fast things can change. This came out of the blue and obviously totally disrupted many families efforts to adopt. While the reasons cited by the Russian government were some deaths that had occurred among adopted children (as of yet, no Child Protective Services investigations have uncovered anything), it was a political tactic to force US lawmakers to rethink some of their policies. It shows how much the machinations of governments, ours not excepted, can cause issues for adopting families. Hopefully this will be resolved in the future to allow adoptions to the US to continue from Russia, but as of now, we are still awaiting a resolution.

Next consideration in the case of an international adoption, you have to be OK with the fact that if you get an older child, they will likely not speak English and may always have an accent. They might grow up looking quite different and be always easily identifiable as adopted. Are you ready to handle this?

NO PANIC!

I am worried enough about adoption without having to worry about people looking at me and an adopted child and always wondering, "Am I the real mom?" What do I do?

You need to honestly assess your feelings on this subject. While maybe a taboo topic, not everyone is able to invite scrutiny and questions that outsiders will ask. Seeing an obvious interracial adoption for example will forever label you as "the adoptive mom" in a stranger's mind before you even open your mouth. If you are worried about this aspect of adoption, talk to your partner and family about it. Making sure you have comebacks and coping mechanisms in place before the issues arise will help. But if ultimately you decided that it is an issue that you can't handle, pat yourself on the back for realizing it now, not later. This is only one of several issues you will face while going through the adoption process and the more open and honest you are with yourself, the better the outcome will be.

Domestic versus international adoptions also vary considerably when talking about the age of an adopted child. In the case of infants, there is a significant wait domestically but they are available, whereas infants are not usually available internationally. As of writing this book, I know that China and Ethiopia still allow infant adoptions, but they are some of the few countries that still do. Unfortunately, I can't provide up-to-date information about international adoptions because it changes so quickly. The best way is to keep checking the news and embassy websites of the involved countries.

The situation with older children, over the age of five, is far different from infants. There are vast numbers of older children available for adoption both domestically and internationally. And the sad fact of the matter is that as children age, the number available for adoption soars and their chances of getting adopted takes a nose dive dramatically. So here is one place where international and domestic adoptions converge, there are far more older children available than younger ones. The adoption statistics are dismal for children over the age of five whether you are talking about domestic or international adoptions. The latest report from the US State Department showed only sixteen percent of international adoptions were in the age five and over category with the numbers dropping to only three percent in the thirteen and over category. For domestic adoptions, the numbers were better but not too drastically different with four percent of adoptions taking place over the age of five and approximately nine percent of adoptions occurring in the thirteen-to-seventeen year age group. These numbers are skewed slightly as they don't reflect the average wait of two years that children in domestic adoptions are in foster care with their adoptive families before the adoption is finalized. But the final conclusion is the same no matter how you slice and dice the data: adoption statistics for children over the age of five are scary in their low numbers in any country.

The next consideration to think about is the way that displaced children are handled by their country. Most international countries still have orphanages, while the USA doesn't anymore. Domestically, older children usually have been in a series of foster homes for a long while, some maybe good, some maybe not so good. On average, children in the foster system that were adopted waited three years for adoption, and over fifty-five percent have been in three or more foster homes before permanent placement. And these are the lucky ones that have found homes. Each year over 29,000 children turn eighteen and age out of the foster system. This means that they are on their own without financial or familial support. They will have to find a place to live and a way to support themselves on their own. Of those children that age out, twenty-five percent do not have a high school diploma, and follow-up studies have found that only six percent ever earn a two- or four-year college degree. These are damning statistics, but don't feel that there is any great difference in the statistics with foreign countries. They have just as many kids that age out of orphanages and their futures are if anything, more bleak.

The foster system in America is based on the fact that children need families and that the relationship with the biologicalal parents needs to be preserved almost at all costs. We don't have orphanages here any more, with the last ones being phased out in the 60's. Children are now cared for in temporary foster homes with the state supervising. Many times there can be messy relationships with birth parents or other family members and adoption doesn't usually proceed immediately. Because of the way the system is set up, usually you foster first, even with the intent to adopt, and go through the process while the child is with you. This can be a complicating factor as the child will delay bonding until they know things are permanent. However, this could have benefits, giving you and the child a chance to get to know each other without the pressure of permanence and to gradually integrate into the family.

The presence of biological relatives can also be a double-edged sword. It can be positive, grounding the child with some familiar interactions and preserving a part of their past that you can't provide. However, it could be painful for the child to be reminded of what was lost to them and painful for you as a constant reminder that you were not always there for the child, even creating a sense of not being a real parent.

International adoptions can remove the biologicalal relative interactions, because even if they are alive and involved, there is only so much you can do several continents away, and thankfully, out of sight is often out of mind. It also removes the concern about fostering a child before adoption. In an international case, the child is yours without any red tape or qualifications once you land in America. It is finalized and there is no going back by you or others.

However, as mentioned before, there are other concerns in international adoptions, such as culture and language. You probably will have not the issues of family to deal with, but will substitute issues of difficulty communicating and difficulty bridging the culture gap at least initially. These can be overcome, but they can be extra problems on top of the universal issues that are present in any adoption.

Also, the international scenario means that you will not have had as much time, if any, to get to know the child before adoption as they are in a different country. Usually when wanting to adopt internationally, you complete the paperwork, fly to the country once approved, and then are shown a dossier of available children. You pick one or more based on pictures and history and then go meet the child/children, spending a few days in the orphanage visiting with them to decide if you all are a match as a family. There are some ways around this problem of a lack of time with the child by the use of a hosting program. A hosting program is an organized trip usually coordinated by a philanthropic organization stateside that will bring over children to spend about three or four weeks in the US from an orphanage. This will give families a chance to meet with and get to know the children in their future setting. It will allow the children also to get an idea of what the family functions like and for both parties to figure out if it is a good fit.

The hosting program that we participated in was a chance to get to meet our future son and learn a little about him before we moved forward with the adoption, but the time we spent with him was really inadequate to get to know him fully. It was somewhat of an awkward time as we were on our best behavior trying to convince him that we would be a good family for him and he was on his best behavior trying to convince us that he would be a good fit for us. But at least it was something. We were able to interact with him "on our turf" so to speak and get an idea of how he would fit into the family.

Unfortunately, there are many people that don't have the benefit of a hosting program to meet their future children before going to the country to adopt. In fact the majority of people that adopt internationally don't participate in such a program. They are expensive and require a lot of planning to execute them. Also, younger children may not be able to travel as easily.

Without the hosting program, you will have a different scenario as you have all the attendant difficulties of the adoption process while trying to make a decision about whether your family and the child are a good match in a foreign country under duress. Meeting a prospective child while traveling overseas and having time constraints on you can be stressful, but there are many that do it very successfully.

If you are interested in hosting a child through a hosting program, you will have to seek one out. There is no central registration place to find one, so the internet and word of mouth will be your best tools to find one.

NO PANIC!

I would love to host a child but am confused about how to get involved.

There are many resources for finding a hosting program. First, let the computer do the work by googling hosting programs for orphans. This will hit on a lot of programs. Also, contacting a local adoption agency and asking for hosting programs in the area is helpful. Not all of the programs operate every year and many are locally based programs only, but persevere! You will find one. If you are still not able to locate one, contact local churches and ask if they are affiliates in any orphan programs.

People who have adopted internationally before could also be resources, even if they didn't host, they probably have heard of a program before. And if you can't find one, you can always help sponsor one. There are many agencies that have relationships with orphanages in other countries that could help you set one up.

Domestic Adoptions—Where to Start?

If you have decided that domestic adoption is the right choice, then start with your state's Department of Children and Families. Even if you are considering a private adoption, they will have a plethora of resources available for you, from recommendations of agencies, to parenting classes, to post-adoption support groups. Then you can make the decision whether to go forward with a private adoption versus through the state foster system. If an infant is your primary choice, then private adoption is probably the best way to go, but for older children, the state foster system is fine. Again the internet is a great resource, allowing you to connect with others that have adopted and find information and available resources.

International Adoptions—Where to Start?

When considering international adoption, you have to think about which country to choose from. Each one has its own different rules and regulations. Some work with agencies and some don't. Also, some are Hague certified (meaning they follow certain international guidelines) and some are non-Hague, meaning they set their own rules. These guidelines are meant to protect both the children and the adopting families and ensure that there are no opportunities for exploitation. The US State Department offers the Hague certification to adoption agencies in America and keeps an up-to-date list on their website. This is not meant to scare you off of non-Hague countries (after all Ukraine isn't and we chose to move forward) but just to inform you of all the possibilities out there.

I wish that I could detail more in depth the pros and cons of each country and their individual requirements, but the rules change so frequently that it would be impossible. In this case, the internet will be your best resource for up-to-date information. Usually each country will have a website that gives their rules and regulations for international adoption in English. It is important to pay attention to these rules as some require parents to be married, or under a certain age, whereas others don't.

I would start with researching the embassy of the country you are interested in. They mostly all have English websites through their consulate on American soil. I have also found that the embassies are very helpful either on the phone or by email. We contacted both the American embassy in Kiev and the Ukrainian embassy here in America prior to moving forward with the adoption and were pleasantly surprised by the quick responses we got.

Adoption Agencies and Other Supportive Personnel

Regardless of which way you choose to go, however, you will need legal and official help while going through the adoption process. Domestically, this could come in the form of a great social worker, a supportive attorney, or an independent adoption agency. Internationally, you will need an agency that is familiar with the country you are working with and has experience in that country. Even if you have ties to the country in question, you will still need help. Navigating a foreign country can be frustrating and difficult and add to that layers of governmental bureaucracy, you can see why you need some help. Also, you will be focused on the adoption and the child, having someone else manage the mundane paperwork will free you up to spend time with your child.

The international agency should have people stateside to help you on this end and also people on the ground in the foreign country to help you when you are over there. This is key, as familiarity with the country and its government is invaluable when working through the adoption process.

When looking at adoption agencies and/or attorneys, it is important to check them out. Start with talking with the agency and asking for references. Of course, these will be biased—the company will only give you happy, satisfied references, but you can still learn information from these. Make sure you call them and ask for a good time to talk to them. You will want to take your time on the call and want to make sure they have the time to talk to you as well. Or better yet, are there local references so that you could talk to them in person? Prepare a set of questions ahead of time to ask, but also listen carefully. There might be issues that come up when you talk that you hadn't considered before.

NO PANIC!

What questions should I ask when checking references?

You won't be able to ask everyone all of the questions you have probably, but if you keep a list, it will help organize you. Here are some possibilities to start you off.

1. How did you decide on this particular agency/lawyer/social worker?
2. Who recommended them to you?
3. Can you describe a little about your personal scenario if you feel comfortable?
4. Were they clear with you in the beginning about expectations, costs, timelines, etc.?
5. Who did you primarily work with?
6. Did you have any problems?
7. If yes, what were they and were they resolved?
8. What type of support were you offered before, during, and after the adoption process?
9. Would you use this agency again or recommend it to a close friend?

After contacting references, move onto other sources. Talk to friends and family that have adopted and ask them for their recommendations. Do an internet search; technology can be so helpful in this age of instant information. Contact the state regulating agencies, as often there is a state certification system for adoption agencies. They are usually under the jurisdiction of the Office of Consumer Affairs, but it could be done on a local level as well.

You probably will uncover some unhappy people in this process, but look at the unhappiness objectively. Adoption is a very emotional process and if you have been invested in a child and something happened to stop the adoption, you are going to be upset and search for someone to blame, and often that is the agency. There could be a legitimate concern though, so dig a little deeper. It pays to understand exactly what went wrong in these cases so you are better prepared for when you might have some problems. Hopefully, you won't, but knowing in advance potential problems can maybe help you avoid them.

Finally, read any contracts you sign carefully and maybe even get them reviewed independently. There is a lot of money (we will get into more detail later, but probably between $10,000 and $40,000) and a lot of emotion at stake here and you want to feel good about the decision from the beginning and feel that you have your interests protected as much as possible. There is no way to really mitigate all the problems that might occur in your adoption, but hopefully, you will be able to identify possible problem areas before they become problems.

Adopting an Older Child

Because most adoptions occur in the age range under two years of age, when people think of adoption, they think of an infant or very small child. However, I want to show you the other side of adoption, that of an older child. Whether it is an elementary school aged child or a teenager, as I showed before, the statistics for adoption of this age group are dismal. There are far too many children of this age category than families that want them and this is a sad fact that exists both domestically and internationally.

But I think we are moving a little too fast here. There are so many things that need to be considered in any adoption. Before we start with a detailed discussion about adopting older children, let's look at some child development and parenting facts and see how they impact adoption for any age.

Nature Vs. Nurture

As a pediatrician, I can attest that there are two parts of parenting, nature and nurture. There are two camps in which experts reside in with regards to the nature versus nurture debate, kind of like which came first, the chicken or the egg. Everyone has their own opinion as to which is more important, the nature that is given to the child at birth by genetics, or the nurture provided by their environment.

But without getting into a debate about which is more important, let's just accept that they are both important as they both affect the future of your child. The nature part, no adoptive parent can change; biological parents trump us on that one. We simply have to accept the hardwiring that the child comes with and work with it. This is especially true when it comes to inherited physical characteristics, but science is just beginning to unravel and understand the genetic component of less tangible things like personality. So while, adoptive parents can't change the genetic makeup of their child, understanding it will of course help dealing with any resultant issues. And again, this is where knowledge comes in: the more you know about your child's family history, the more capable you will be to meet the challenges from that history, whether they be good or bad.

For example, if you know that your child's family had a history of substance abuse, then you will be more clued into looking for evidence of addictive tendencies in your child's personality. Or maybe even before you see these tendencies, you might start a campaign of minimizing exposure to certain subjects or experiences until a child is more fully developed. Or what about a child that had a family history of ADHD (Attention Deficit Hyperactivity Disorder)? With that knowledge, you might seek out a different type of classroom environment, or even think about teaching the child coping strategies before there is even anything noticed in school.

NO PANIC!

What if I can't get any information about my child's birth parents or family situations?

Many times you won't be able to get adequate or even any information about your child's background. While this information would be most helpful and make your life a whole lot easier, without it, you can do just as well. It just means that you will have to be a little more vigilant and proactive as you will not have any guides. And this is probably good for families that can even get a lot of information or have had full disclosure. Always be open and expecting of everything, then when it doesn't happen — you can breathe a sigh of relief. Just remember the old proverb, an ounce of prevention is worth a pound of cure.

Regardless though of what your child's genetic background has in store for you, there is nothing you can do to change it. And I think there is some freedom in that knowledge. There is also nothing you can do about which genes your biological children inherit either (or at least not yet with our medical technology) so while you might feel a large rift between adoptive parents and biological parents, it really isn't there. All parents whether adoptive or biological must play with the hand they are dealt in their children so to speak and while having some knowledge can help up front, in the long run, everything evens out. But just being aware that you might be surprised will go a long way to relieving some of your anxieties.

There has also been recent new evidence that certain behavioral characteristics that we thought were very heritable or coded for in the genes, might not be as heritable as we initially thought. A new technique of looking at the genetic code, Genome-wide Complex Trait Analysis, suggests that there is less correlation with the genome and certain behavioral problems like autism, hyperactivity, and conduct disorder than was previously supposed. This is good information for those of us that want to feel more in control and not feel like so many things are predetermined about our adopted children; however, it doesn't really change the end result. If your child has a diagnosis, it doesn't really matter where it came from, just how to deal with it. There are some hard-wired facts about your adopted child that you won't be able to change regardless of whether they are inherited or have come about *de novo* in your child.

The other half of your child's makeup comes from what the caregivers give, the nurture part. And while everyone is always talking about the importance of early childhood experiences, and I don't want to detract from the importance of these, the nurturing provided at any age is key. If you doubt this, just think for a moment of a child that you have heard about that has "gone bad." We all have a story like this of a neighbor's child or relative's child or a coworker's child that used to be "such a nice child," and now as a teenager is having problems with the law, substance abuse, or personal problems. Now some of these might honestly come from genetic predispositions, but some of these problems come from improper nurturing in the later teenage years. Teenagers are difficult creatures at best and need to be nurtured as much as small children, just in a different way. Many parents think that once pre-teens and teens are more independent, they don't need as much direction and help in life, and nothing could be farther from the truth.

People of all ages need to feel connected and valued, and the more connected and valued they feel, the more they will want to contribute back to society and others. While the nurturing does tend to change from routine care such as feeding and diaper changes of the infant years to carpooling and advice later on, it is no less important to allow a teen to commiserate on an embarrassing moment or worry about what to wear before a social event, or pick a course of study in school. Not only does this type of nurturing help them feel valued and important, but it allows you to model behavior that will allow the child to start to figure out how to live on their own.

So while the age at which your child is at adoption will allow you different amounts of nurturing that you can provide to them, it doesn't necessarily mean that your nurturing is less important or valued for their eventual success in life. Adoption of an infant or a younger child is much different than adoption of an older child, simply giving you more time to provide the nurturing. Being able to affect the entire part of the nurture experience for a child can be a powerful parenting tool for you, but again any amount of nurturing that you can provide will make a tremendous impact on the child.

I recently had a discussion with a fellow mom in my homeschooling group who was adopted at the age of sixteen through the foster system. She relayed to me that having an adult take an interest in her life and her future was the single most important thing she remembered about childhood. She had been in a series of foster homes and when she found this last one, knew she had found a home. Her five children now call this woman Nana and she to this day will relate to how important this individual was to her future, even though she only spent less than two years with her foster mom before leaving out on her own.

However, when you bring a child into your family with part of the nurture already done by someone else, there can be issues that you need to be able to understand and embrace. This can be quite difficult as at times it might be in direct conflict with the nurturing that you would have provided if given the chance. Nurturing by someone else, even if for only a few years can make the child not fit as tightly into your family unit as you had imagined it. And this holds true for any kind of family unit, whether you already have other children or not. Some of these differences are good and broadening, and some are not so good.

How can you embrace this fact and build off of it? How can you accept the boundaries you have been given of years that you have to affect versus those that were already affected for you by others? These boundaries will be different with the age of the child in question. Adopting a seven or eight year old for example will give you a different boundary of many more years to influence your child than that of a fifteen year old. This is an important question to ask yourself as you need to be able to embrace the nurturing by others and then build on top of it to complete the parenting experience.

I found that the easiest way to do this was to consciously release myself of expectations regarding the previous nurturing my child had received. When an issue arose that harkened back to Alex's time before our family, I would adopt a questioning mode and investigate it, getting as much information as I could get, without being judgmental. After all, there was nothing I could do to change it at the point I was at, so criticizing would just be counterproductive and divisive. Finding out as much information as I could allowed me to understand better the type of nurturing he had received and gave me a better insight into his personality.

The more I knew, the more empowered I felt. This is a nice way to counteract the feelings of helplessness that often arise in adoptions when you just don't know where to go next. It also helped me to get over the fact that it was not me that provided the nurturing, which is not as easy at is sounds. I think I actually went through a grieving period in the beginning of the adoption for the time that was lost to me with my new child. I can never get back the time that he was not with me; all I can do is make the most of the time going forward.

Knowledge is power, and this is nowhere more evident than in these situations. Knowing more about the environment that a child was exposed to before joining your family allows you to decide how to best build upon those experiences and provide the nurturing that you want to. After all, you will be the one to tie up the loose ends so to speak and send the child off to adulthood, so your contributions are the most important.

Also, knowing what type of nurturing and environment your child was exposed to and the quality of the nurturing can make a difference in your parenting. Children that have been socialized into a functional family unit will have different needs than those that have been in a dysfunctional family unit or those that have been institutionalized. Children that are accustomed to the give and take of a family won't need that reinforcement but will need help finding their place in your family. Those children who don't understand family dynamics will need help simply understanding how a normal family works before they can even think about their place in one.

These are not reasons to scare anyone away from older children as the issues are not always bad. These children tend to be adaptable and flexible having learned how to navigate situations already without putting extra burden on your shoulders. They often also have learned a degree of self-reliance which is helpful when you need focus on another family member, or even yourself for a while.

However, realistically since the reason many of these children are available is because of abuse or neglect with their biological family, there will probably be many hurdles to overcome. You first have to be willing to accept this, then you have to be willing to peel away the layers of the hurt and pain that can occur on both sides as you start nurturing your way. Building up the nurturing your way will shave rough edges and create connections that will allow this child to fit into the puzzle woven already by your family. And, you have to compress all this into an artificially short time and keep your sanity and the rest of your family happy too!

It will take some time to accept these differences with your older child and move forward. The importance of recognizing the existence of these issues from the very beginning before you start out can't be emphasized enough. Just verbalizing an understanding will help your intelligent, rational brain start preparing your emotional, irrational heart for what is coming. However, the exciting and good part of building upon what already exists is that you have a starting point already. There is a lot of uncertainty in parenting and many biological parents of infants and teens feel overwhelmed and scared. With an adopted older child, you will have the edges filled in already, but watching the child take your nurturing and internalize it can be the most fulfilling part of being a parent.

Considering an Older Child

What are the good things about adopting an older child? Now that I have you quaking in your boots about the scary, why would people want to invite a teen into their homes?

Well, I can tell you there are many reasons. The first is somewhat pedantic, but there are no diapers, midnight feedings, car seats, or playdates on playgrounds. Also, there is some measure of comfort in being able to communicate with a child. As an older child, they can verbalize needs and frustrations and be a partner with you. You can engage them on a different level than you can engage an infant, which is pretty much only as a caregiver.

You can learn so much from older children; you can learn from them as much as you will want to teach them. You will find your life changing in a wonderful way as you embrace the good differences they have brought you. With our family, the cultural richness that was brought to us from Ukraine by Alex crept into our everyday life. We now have many Russian words, new foods that we routinely eat, and new routines that are now a part of us.

In fact, the phrase 'no panic' is just one such new thing that our son brought to us. He noticed that at times, I would lose it and start to fuss and panic. Whether it was the fact that I had not accomplished as much school work with the kids that day, or the fact that the laundry was piling up, or whether the house was a mess; there are any number of reasons that I would freak out. And this was usually accompanied by me fussing at the children and ineffectually running around the house cataloging all of the ways I was a deficient caregiver and mother. He would grab me by the shoulders and say, "No panic Mom." I would then at that point laugh and realize what I was doing. Now any time someone starts complaining, the nearest person within earshot will yell out, "No panic," leaving us all laughing and smiling.

And finally, the best reason to consider the adoption of an older child, is the simple fact that there are more of them than there are families to take them. Again, I want to reiterate the fact that you shouldn't be on a charity mission, you are looking for the child that should have been yours naturally, but couldn't have for whatever reason. But don't look only at little ones, your child could be a lovely teenager that really needs a forever family. Bottom line, there are a lot of wonderful kids out there waiting for their forever families and one of them might be yours.

Keeping an Open Mind
The most important quality to have when adopting is patience and second most is flexibility. Patience because there are so many factors out of your hands and flexibility which will allow you to take advantage of the best opportunities. People who automatically rule out certain children based upon certain qualities such as race, age, and country of origin could possibly be missing their forever child. Now obviously you will have to narrow down your field at some point; you can't consider every available child in the world, and there might be good reasons to narrow down and weed out certain categories. Maybe you are not in a position to nurture an older child, or maybe you can't deal with a language barrier. These are all important considerations that need to be taken into account and you need to be honest with yourself. You need to possess a great deal of self-insight to be successful in adoption and the process of acquiring this self-insight will point you in certain directions. But there is always a great deal of change in the adoption journey and being open-minded and as flexible as possible will allow you the best experiences and the best chance of success.

The Great Paperwork Chase

Wow, we have covered a lot of ground the first few chapters mostly dealing with esoteric emotional and life-changing decisions. It is time to detour a bit and talk about a topic that is mundane in the extreme but one that can make or break an adoption. I know it seems excessive to devote an entire chapter to paperwork, but holy cow, it was a long and arduous process for us and I suspect for many other families as well.

The point of all the paperwork is to compile a dossier of your family that contains all the information needed by the approving agency, whether that be a foreign government or a state agency. This dossier will contain absolutely everything about you and will basically be a paper snapshot of your family and its suitability for adoption. It will include a lot of personal information including financial information, so it is wise to make sure that everyone handling the papers understands that this is confidential and shouldn't be shared with anyone that doesn't need access.

I guess I shouldn't scare you off too much from the paperwork, as the difficulty really depends on how good a record keeper you are and how complicated your life is. By record keeper, I mean, do you have the extra copies of your marriage license that were given to you? Do you have your taxes done on time every year? Do you have a good system for keeping paperwork organized? By how complicated your life is, I mean, have you moved a lot? Do you have a divorce or remarriage in the past? Have you ever lived overseas? I will show you why the answers to these questions are so important.

The complicated life answer is what made the paperwork process so hard for us; we have lived all over the US and after several moves, I couldn't put my hands on many of the documents that were needed. And then getting duplicates was a difficult process as well.

But regardless of what challenges you face, organization is key at this point. You need to make sure that you keep on top of this. Find a place or folder that is undisturbed and keep all your papers in that one spot faithfully. Also, put one person in charge of the papers. It will be important to make sure that one person is directing the process and knows the status of everything. You will feel like a circus performer with many balls in the air trying to juggle them all simultaneously but that is still better than trying to coordinate your juggling with someone else stepping in here and there.

So once you have appointed a point person for the paperwork process, next you need to get with whoever your facilitator is, whether that is a formal adoption facilitator, an agency, or a lawyer, and get the big overview of what is needed in the dossier. But remember, not everything is done at once. You can take it in small bites. Also, don't worry about taking notes or trying to start on the paperwork at first, just listen to what is needed and absorb it. Ask for any checklists or recommended ways to proceed. Many people have gone before you and usually your agency or facilitator will have tips and tricks they can pass on from other families in similar circumstances. Often they will have a sample timeline of things for you to pursue, but don't get too caught up in the details yet. I will cover timelines later in the chapter, but there are some other things to think about first before an accurate timeline can even be established.

Once you understood the scope of what is needed, then you can start with taking notes and making stacks of papers, etc. in your quest to get everything done. Each entity that you could possibly adopt from will have different requirements; a private adoption, foster to adopt, or international will all have slightly different paperwork needs to approve you for adoption, so I will cover the basics here, but be sure to check the specifics that relate to your adoption.

How to Deal with Red Flags

I want to digress here for a bit and discuss things in your background or life that could slow down your adoption. Hopefully you won't have any of these, but if they are there, find out about them early and try to deal with them before they become any more difficult. Don't be afraid of full disclosure to your agency or facilitator. You will need their support and trust just as you need to trust them. An open and honest relationship from the beginning is the best way to go.

So, what kind of things am I talking about here? Well, for example, a dear family that we met as we were adopting was trying to adopt a sibling group of three when on the mom's criminal background check came back a forgotten misdemeanor charge from her college days, years before. It was insignificant in her mind, there was no further legal action or jail time, so it had just been forgotten about. Unfortunately, this was enough to render them ineligible for adoption from a particular foreign country as they found after submitting their dossier the first time, so they had to start the lengthy expunging process. However, if they has started the process before they had submitted, it would have sailed through. Also, they noticed that on the second submission of their dossier, it was a much slower process as if they had been singled out for extra attention.

Another family had an incorrect spelling of a name on the marriage license that wasn't noticed so when they went to get a notary to notarize it for inclusion in the dossier, it was refused. Their entire dossier submission was held up as they had to go back to the state agency for marriage licenses and get it corrected. And yet another family had a dad that was an American citizen but had been born in another country and wasn't able to prove it as his parents had never completed the citizenship paperwork for him when they moved to the US when he was a baby. He had an American passport which had been sufficient for everything, from school enrollment to employment, until the requirements for the adoption dossier from a foreign government actually needed the citizenship papers from UCIS.

All of these instances can be mitigated, but if not caught early enough and corrected before your dossier is submitted could result in at worst your paperwork being thrown out and the adoption denied or at best a delay of weeks or months. And in this case because this could have devastating consequences, it pays to be thorough up front and try to take care of any possible problems before they are recorded on your paperwork.

Any bureaucracy wants to be able to check off the requirements of its services without any exceptions, and any foreign government or state foster system is no different. It's kind of like this: on forms there are spaces to check a box yes or no and if the answer is yes, there is always the statement, "Please explain below or attach explanations." And these bureaucracies want the answers to be no and not need any attached explanations. Now sometimes these can't be avoided, but the less of them, the better.

NO PANIC!

Will a divorce or other family issues cause a problem for adoption in the future?

Divorces are commonplace as are remarriages and blended families. Even things that you might feel are deal breakers for adoption aren't. You just need to be open and up front about them from the beginning and let you adoption team help you. Trying to hide something will only make it worse and potentially cause problems.

I will take you through each of the common components of the dossier, explaining the steps and the processes that are involved in each. As I said before, each entity will have different requirements, so you will have to customize this to fit your circumstances, but I can help walk you through the more common ones.

Home Study

The first step in adoption paperwork is getting the home study done. This is a most important step as it is an independent opinion of your fitness for adoption. It is conducted by an outside agency, sometimes the state, that will make a recommendation of how many children and what ages you can accommodate. This is a very difficult step to go through as you are basically putting yourself out there to be judged fit by another person. A licensed social worker will conduct the interview and the actual form, amount of time, and cost it can take will vary from person to person, but expect about a month from beginning to end and anywhere from $600–$1000.

The agency or facilitator you are working with should recommend an agency to use for a home study, but if they don't, there are resources to help you find one. Each state will conduct home studies through their Department of Children and Families. These will be slightly cheaper, but will take far longer as there is always a backlog of work for their social workers. They also contract out to private agencies, so if the wait is too long, feel free to get their recommendations for a private agency or social worker to work with you.

While the home study should be an unbiased look at your ability to adopt and therefore shouldn't be prepared for per se, there are some things that you can do ahead of time to facilitate the study and make it easier. The first thing you should do, is one that you have already started doing, and that is researching adoptions and parenting. You might even want to consider some pre-adoption classes. These are offered by a variety of private sources but are also always offered for free through the state department of children and families. They might even be required of you if you are doing a domestic adoption through the foster system.

These classes will give you the vocabulary of adoption and will highlight some of the most important themes that adoption entails. This will serve not only to make you appear more informed and erudite about the process you are going through, but will also pinpoint areas of interest for you to research further.

An alternative to classes or even a supplement is reading books and other sources, such as online articles and blogs. These also can introduce you to topics that might be brought up during the home study. Just familiarizing yourself with the terms will help you in answering questions and will allow you to appear composed and prepared.

The home study will comprise several different parts. The first will concern simply biographical information about you and your family. This includes your ages, income, whether you own or rent your home, number of other children or family members living in your home and any previous marriages that still have an impact in your life. It is best to be simple and straightforward with the answers to these questions. You want to give accurate and correct information, but there is no need to go into details. For example, if you have relatives that visit, even if frequently, there is no need to mention them here. No need to bring up family disagreements, embarrassing moments, or any other mundane information that is not flattering to you or your family or relevant to the adoption process.

Each spouse will then be interviewed separately and then together and each member of the family will be interviewed with a series of questions that will judge their attitudes toward an impending adoption and their ability to cope with it. For you and your spouse/partner, I will share a list of common questions, but you should not limit yourself to thinking about just these.

---

1. What led you to consider adoption?
2. What type of parenting style do you have/ hope to have?
3. What preparations have you made with respect to learning about adoption?
4. How will you handle discipline issues?
5. Do you have a support system for you?
6. What specific post-adoption services have you lined up such as counseling?
7. What if a sibling is unexpectedly found or what if other circumstances change in the adoption?
8. What do your extended family and friends think of the adoption?
9. If considering an intercultural/interracial adoption, what issues are you concerned about and how will you face them?
10. What are your provisions for childcare?
11. How do your immediate family members feel about the adoption?
12. How will your life be impacted with the adoption, both good and bad?
13. Is your spouse just as supportive of adoption as you are?
14. How do you and your spouse/other children handle disagreements?

While this seems like these are very personal and intrusive questions to answer, remember that the social worker is trying to get a picture of how your family works and how an adopted child or children will fit in. They are trying as best they can to ensure that you will provide a safe and loving environment for a child that most probably has faced hardships in their past, so they are trying to cover any contingency that might arise. Nobody ever wants a disrupted adoption, meaning one in which the adoptive family legally undoes the adoption, and carefully vetting the family first will hopefully mitigate this possibility.

So be prepared for intrusive and possibly offensive questions, but understand where the social worker is coming from when they are asked. If there are problems, or things that you feel uncomfortable discussing, then you need to state that clearly and nicely. For example if you and your spouse have had problems in the past and you don't want to discuss them, if the social worker asks, just reply that you are uncomfortable discussing the topic, but that you and your spouse have worked things out and then detail the ways in which the adoption will not affect this and how you all have taken steps to separate this from the adoption. Hopefully this approach will be enough to assuage the social worker. Just remember, be honest, open, composed, and calm. These are the main qualities that are prized and will go a long way to judging your fitness to adopt.

Once the individual and group interviews are done, the social worker will ask to see your home. They are not there to judge your efficiency as a maid or housecleaner, but at the same time general cleanliness and order are indicative of an organized life. So, clean up and put clutter away, but don't worry about a white glove test. If you are looking at a younger child, you will need to have safety locks on cabinets, outlet covers, and general safety measures. If you are looking at older children you will need to demonstrate a space that is theirs, their own bed, places for their things, etc. Children don't need their own rooms, but they will need their own beds and spaces. You don't have to have purchased everything that you might need, but you will have to have shown that you are ready. Sometimes foster to adopt placements can happen quickly and you won't have time to pick up necessary items.

So now that you have been interviewed and your home inspected, what next? Well, the report will have to be typed up by the social worker and then reviewed by you for any mistakes or corrections. As part of this step, the social worker will need to verify your residence (home loan if you own a home, or lease agreement if you rent) and your income. So you will need copies of tax returns and other papers for them, in addition to the ones that will be a part of your dossier as a whole.

At the end of the home study you will see an official recommendation, which will hopefully be that the adoption is recommended and approved. If it is not, you should have had conversations before this point and have been given steps to correct the issues. But, look at the recommendation carefully, as it will be very specific. We were interested in one child who was thirteen at the time and our recommendation stated, "This family is approved to adopt a teenage boy or girl between the ages of twelve to fifteen." While this is what we wanted, our facilitator pointed out, what if the adoption process took longer and he was sixteen? What if we found a sibling that needed to be adopted to and was younger? In these cases, the home study would have to be redone at considerable time and expense, so the best thing is to over estimate your needs. Get a wide age range approved and make sure it covers multiple children of any gender. This way, you at least will be covered in your home study if something unusual happens in the adoption process.

Once you have reviewed the home study and found it to be correct, request many copies of the report and many copies of the social worker's license. You will need these to be a part of your dossier paperwork and if you have to submit multiple times, you will need more than one copy.

Supporting Papers

For your dossier, you will need a host of "supporting documents" for lack of a better term. They include notarized copies of your marriage certificate, criminal background checks from the states you have lived in for the past 7 years, copies of your driver's license, copies of your passports if it is an international adoption, among others.

As I mentioned earlier, if you have moved around, this step will take longer, as you will need to send away for copies of some of these documents and then need to wait for them. If you have lived in one place, your job will be marginally easier, but will not be a walk in the park, I assure you.

You and your spouse or partner will need to be available during work hours for many of these things to be done, such as the fingerprinting at your local police station. It is helpful if one of you has a full schedule to even take a half day off of work to accomplish these things. You can save them up and try to do everything at once that can only be done during work hours.

As you work your way through these papers, it is helpful to have a system of organization for keeping track of what is finished, pending, and not started yet. I think my life would have been a lot easier if I had one master schedule that showed everything that needed to be done and when it was to be received by. I ended up with an Excel spreadsheet by the end, but no one had told me ahead of time how important a system of organization was, which would have saved me a lot of time and confusion.

With a good system, when you have to send off for things, you can easily see where they are in the pipeline. I would suggest that a spreadsheet on your computer would be the best way to go, even going so far as to scan documents in as they are received, but have a system, whatever you might choose.

The next piece of advice I have for adopting parents, is to make friends with a notary. A notary is a state certified person who is able to verify the legitimacy and accuracy of documents. Every piece of paper in an adoption dossier needs to be authenticated that it is true and accurate and a notary is the best way to accomplish this. Every document needs to notarized; even the copies of the passports needed to accompanied by a notarized statement saying that they were exact and unaltered copies of the originals.

I can't stress finding a nice notary enough, as you will be seeing them a lot. And even after you think everything is done, if there are any changes to your dossier, everything will need to be re-notarized. You will be shelling out a lot of money on this process, so if you can locate someone who will do it for free, you will save a ton of money. Many work places will have a notary that you can use, so both you and/or your spouse should check in your offices. If not, maybe a parent, relative, or close friend has a notary that could help out. Check through your church, neighborhood, or any other circle of friends to see is someone is a notary. Once they are found and agree to help, shower them with small gifts. Believe me, you will receive far more than you give in this process.

Now, because we were undertaking an international adoption, we had to get everything that was notarized (which was every scrap of paper) also apostilled. This is a fancy seal from the state capital that gives international certification to the notary signature. This is just an extra step required by foreign governments in order to ensure the accuracy and truthfulness of the documents they receive from adoptive parents. Now we are lucky, living only about an hour away from the state capital, so we could drive the documents up to be apostilled, but if you live further away, you are stuck having to send them by mail, adding extra days onto your timeline and costs in postage.

Timeline

Now that I have brought up the timeline, I feel compelled to mention a few words about that as well. In the beginning, we had a timeline in mind about when we could expect all of the adoption to be done and expect to be a complete family, but of course, everything takes longer than expected. We had artificially broken it down into several areas; the paperwork, the waiting for document approval from the Ukrainian government, and the trip over the Ukraine.

The first estimate you make of your timeline will never be the final date unless you are very, very lucky. While the timeline is helpful for keeping you motivated and on top of things, don't let it discourage you when you don't meet your deadlines. When you see those dates slipping by, just realize that it is no fault of your own, simply the cost of doing business. So take a deep breath and exhale, things will work out in the end. I think we are our own toughest critics; probably some of the dates in your timeline were unrealistic. Remember, it is for motivation, not a hard and fast set of dates that have to be met or else!

Money Matters

Once you have decided to adopt, figured out which agency to use, and confronted details, you need to figure out how to pay for it. There are going to be costs associated with any adoption, whether they are directly out of pocket or not. Not only will you have a new child that will require clothes, food, and toys, you will have hidden costs such as missed days of work, extra insurance copays to get your medical exams done, and postage to get documents back and forth to where they are needed. All of these costs need to be considered when looking at the cost of adoption. The main difference between having a child biologicalally and adopting will be highlighted here. With having a child, all the expenses are there but they are spread out over time. In adoption, they hit all at once and can feel painful to swallow.

Domestic vs. International

The costs of domestic adoption are somewhat lower, but not as much lower as you think. Private adoptions can cost as much as $15,000 and even up to $40,000 depending on a number of factors, such as degree of support for birth mother. Adopting through the foster system is much cheaper, but fees and other expenses can amount to as much as $4,000. Even on the occasion when there are no fees like the fingerprinting from the police station, there are the hidden expenses I mentioned earlier such as gas and travel time to and from the location and lost revenue from hours of work.

For an international adoption, the costs are somewhat more expensive because you are now dealing with a foreign country and have travel expenses among other things. The fees seem somewhat exorbitant at first (for us the total would run about $40,000), but you will get used to the idea. After all, as I mentioned earlier, if you had raised biological children from birth, you would have spent all that and more, it is just artificially compressed into a few months!

NO PANIC!

The idea of spending this much money has me almost paralyzed. How can I overcome this?

Let's look at the costs of a biological child and break those down over eighteen years. Several sources have put the average first year expenses of a child at around $12,000. This would include the medical bills, clothing, diapers, etc. The USDA complied statistics and reported in 2010 that the average middle income family can expect to spend about $250,000 on a child in the first eighteen years, not including college. So take a few deep breaths and realize that the adoption fees are equal to the first couple of years that you would have spent on a biological child and then from there, you are just like any other parent.

Fees are variable depending on who you talk to and what services are included, but for an international adoption you could be looking at anywhere from $10,000 to $35,000 for a single child and upwards of $50,000 for a sibling group.

There are so many variables though when talking about adoption expenses that it is impossible to generalize, your case could be drastically different. There are differences by country, number of children, and even region of country you are adopting from. There are sometimes differences between healthy children and those with special needs. I don't want to scare people off, so researching your particular situation is important and asking questions of others that have adopted and of your agency as well, who will be able to give you more specific details related to your case.

Financing Adoption

We were lucky, just being able to take money out of savings to pay for our adoption, but many don't have the amount needed just sitting around. We had a savings account that we had started many years before that was separate from our retirement and college savings accounts. This account was just for extra money whether that meant a new car some day or a new house downpayment, etc. We never really specified exactly what it was to be used for, but we knew it was for something important that we wanted. When the chance came up to adopt Dema, we knew this was a perfect use for the money in this account. And since we had been working on the adoption for a while, by the time it actually came to taking the money out to pay for the adoption expenses, it seemed natural (even if it suddenly made us really poor!).

Many people though haven't started savings accounts as we did. Don't let this deter you too much, it is never too late to start if you have some time. Of course, you shouldn't be cavalier about money, but there are ways to raise the needed funds.

Fund Raisers

We have met several people who have successfully raised funds for the entire needed amount for their adoption. It takes a lot of work and effort, but it can pay big rewards. People have bake sales, yard sales, and sponsored events like dinner dances. There are however, some activities that are more successful than others and a few basic premises that need to be followed for assurances of success.

First, you need to make sure that you line up publicity for your event. You will need to have more than just friends and family to raise a lot of money, so make sure you have other resources you can tap into, whether that is a church community, work force, or other groups. You will need to get local media involved where appropriate and other resources even if it as simple as posting an event on Craig's List, such as a garage sale.

The second thing to consider is the fact that the less effort others need to make the better. Some things like garage sales, bake sales, and other events, require that people show up. With the busy schedules that many families keep nowadays, you might be hard pressed to get the number of people that are needed to make significant amounts of money. Not impossible, just a little harder. This is easier if you have been in a community for a while, are well-known, and have more connections. But if you don't, don't despair. There are alternatives where people can still donate without relying on their time as much.

In this same way, you can also sometimes get more out of people from in kind services than cash. This helps when you want to do something like an online or silent auction. Many times businesses will donate significant services that you can auction off to help raise money, whereas they might be more reluctant to donate cash. You can also set up a tax-free donation charity that people or companies can donate to directly.

You can also ask for donations of things you will need with the adoption and might be able to reduce your out of pocket expenses that way. For example, you might find someone who travels frequently that could donate frequent flier miles to help pay for airline tickets overseas. Maybe some could buy some of the clothes you will need for your child, donate medical or dental services, or various other things you need to consider in the overall costs.

It can be hard to ask for donations or money, especially if you are shy or feel very self-sufficient. But realize that after all, it really isn't just for you, there is a child at stake. Imagine the child is already yours, then it makes the asking much easier. Don't feel bad about asking everyone and anyone. You can unabashedly hit up friends and family.

Other Sources

Besides raising money yourself, there are other sources that you can tap into to find money to finance your adoption. For example, there are tax credits for adoption. There are certain qualifications of income that must be met, but these can also be helpful in planning out your budget. These federal tax credits can apply to both domestic and international adoptions. Some states will also give tax credits for adoption expenses, so check your specific state tax code.

These credits can be useful, but won't be available until the adoption is finalized and you have filed that next year's return, so understand that they won't help with any up front fees that you will owe. However, they can help with the expenses that you will incur with a new family member in the house.

Sometimes businesses will reimburse employees for adoption costs. You will need to check with your employee benefits coordinator to find out the specifics of the plan, but it is usually in the neighborhood of a couple of thousand dollars. Many times you will need to submit invoices for fees and expenses, so make sure to keep detailed records and copies of the receipts for your expenditures.

In addition to these sources, there are many state and federal agencies that can help as well depending on your particular situation. Certain special needs children could qualify for grants or help from need-specific organizations, as well as general funds that can offer subsidies or low cost loans. These are somewhat more difficult to find, as they are specifically directed at special needs, but they should not be overlooked in your search for help with the funding of your adoption.

And even if you haven't been able to find a grant or help from a need-specific organization, it doesn't hurt to ask. Many times there are funds available that people don't ask for. Don't be shy about asking!

Another resort could be a short term loan for the adoption expenses. There are philanthropic organizations that offer these at low cost to help fund you. Be careful though that you factor in the repayment of the loan when you look at your long-term expenses, as after the adoption you will have expenses related to your family before plus one. However, this could be another resource to getting the chunk of money up front.

A final place to look for help is a withdrawal or loan against savings plans like a 401K, college saving funds, or flex spending accounts. Each of these will have its ups and downs, like fees that will be incurred or penalties, but they represent another source of funding for you.

How to Ask for Help

I have touched on the fact that you shouldn't be shy about asking for help and in this particular case money. This is a key point in adoption, don't ever be shy about asking for help, as you will probably need it at some point in the process. There will be times when you will say to yourself, "What have I done?" and you need to be able to share that feeling and ask for help getting over the stage you are in that left you feeling like that. And here is an excellent place to learn that skill if you don't already possess it, and that is asking for financial help.

However, there are good and bad ways of asking for help, and some are more successful than others. The best way to start out asking is to be able to clearly articulate exactly what you are doing and why you are asking for help. It might seem nice to be able to say, "Oh, just whatever you can spare would be great," but realistically, you will get more if you can be specific. At the same time, you need to be able to indicate that you will accept anything that is offered, as even the tiniest help will be greatly appreciated.

I recommend writing a letter early on in the adoption process that details the specifics of your circumstances. Introduce yourself and your family, explain the adoption and your motivations, and then specifically address the financial needs that you have resulting from the adoption.

I know that in our case, we met several families who were fundraising to adopt from the same orphanage in Ukraine. I read a letter done by one family that started off by introducing their family, then went on to discuss the dismal statistics faced by orphaned children in that country and what happened to children that aged out of the system. This was masterful as it personalized the effort and drew the reader into their story. Then the pitch for funds was made.

These letters can use multiple purposes. They can be customized and sent to local media outlets as you are advertising specific fundraising efforts. They can be sent to friends and co-workers explaining what you are doing, and can even be sent to charitable organizations requesting funds and grants.

Keep some copies of the letter on you as you never know when you will run across a possible funding source. The more you put yourself out there, the more chance you have at success.

Final Thoughts on Money

Money can be a terrible stumbling block for many people considering adoption. I know that in our family, my husband was very concerned about the outlay of that amount of cash from our savings. I, of course, was the more emotional one, just wanting my son at any cost. My husband was very resistant to the idea that we were taking a child from an orphanage that had not been spoken for, and yet we were paying an arm and a leg in the process.

While this is a hard reality to swallow, there are a lot of people and agencies involved in the process that need to be compensated, some more deserving than others. There are all the checkpoints and safeguards in place to assure everyone involved that you will be a good adoptive family, there are the agencies and interpreters, and facilitators, lawyers, etc, that all make their living from adoptions, and finally there are the incentives (bribes) that need to be paid (applies to international adoptions only and then only some countries). So when you look at it this way, as a business of sorts, the expenses make more sense. It is a slimy, nefarious business, making money off of this population of children, but without the help of these agencies and people, you wouldn't have a chance at your forever child.

We talked a lot about money and made sure that my husband was OK with spending our savings and I was understanding of what it meant to our financial future. But in the end, the money paled in comparison to everything else about the adoption. It seemed so big in the beginning but turned out so small later on.

Make sure you talk to your facilitator, your agency, or whoever is your liaison in the adoption process. They have gone through this many times with many families and will have a ton of resources and advice for you. And not to sound cavalier, but you will find a way. It might take longer and take more effort, but when kids are meant to be yours, it will work out.

Also, keep a list of people that help you in the process of adoption, whether it is through money, time, or other services. It will feel good when you finally welcome your new child to be able to send them a picture or occasional update on your life. After all, they invested in it and deserve to hear how their efforts helped everything to work out.

Leave no stone unturned in your effort to find help. Be creative and inventive—it will pay off!

Great Expectations

At this point, you have carefully considered your choice of adoption, decided to adopt, researched agencies, carefully and thoughtfully prepared your paperwork, figured out how to pay for it, and now are anxiously awaiting the placement of your child or children. You have meticulously notarized and prepared documents. You have fundraised, saved pennies, and budgeted your way to insanity. You have already gone through stages of giddiness when things have gone well and deep depression when things have not gone well. You have taken classes, read books, become an expert on adoption blogs, and could almost teach a parenting course yourself with all the knowledge you have accumulated.

Now what? — Patience

But now what? I know that I have focused a lot on the mundane parts of the process like finding agencies, paperwork, and contracts. However, as you will see, this consumed our life for months. It was never-ending and frustrating and slow, all adjectives that I don't deal well with. I was angry that our time was slipping away and we weren't even finished with the first step of the process. It seemed at times that we were no closer to getting our child and in fact, further away than when we hosted him!

I was obsessed with getting Dema by his birthday in January. I really didn't want him to have another one celebrated without his forever family, but as the dates were slipping by, I realized that I was going to have to accept the fact that this might not be possible.

So that brings me to the point of this, patience. You have to learn patience to be able to survive the adoption process, especially the international process. There are so many parts of this that are out of your control that it really doesn't pay to worry about them. Just do your best and leave the rest to others. We were lucky to have a great stateside facilitator that would listen to me complain and commiserate with me when the paperwork got hard and onerous.

NO PANIC!

Help! I am not patient or especially good about waiting for things in life. How am I going to manage this part of adoption?

Patience can be learned. Practice makes perfect and you will have plenty of chances for practice. But even if you don't want to learn, there are ways to manage. You have time on your hands that was previously used in getting ready for the adoption, but now things are in the hands of others and you are waiting. So use this time. Research the country you are adopting from, continue researching adoption issues, continue to reach out and connect with others that have adopted. There is no reason to stop these tactics once the initial phase is over and you are waiting.

As I mentioned above, don't stop researching and learning about adoption. The more you can do before your child arrives the better because once your child is with you, there won't be a lot of extra time on your hands.

As well, sometimes this is a great time to back off the adoption ride you have been on. Since you are in a waiting period, relax and maybe engage in some activities that you haven't had time to do with all the frantic fundraising and paperwork you have been doing. Reconnect with your spouse, take some date nights, maybe even work on some home improvement projects. This might sound trite, but you really won't have time to do these sort of things when you are busy with your new child.

The Importance of Support

Having someone to share your frustrations with was really key for me. Friends and family that are not adopting can empathize, but really have no clue as to what you are going through. It helps to have a friend that is going through the same process or has already been through it to help you deal with the emotions and the ups and downs. This will be the first of many times that I will say this, but trust me, it is true. I can't emphasize the importance of a good support system. I became close to many of the families that hosted children at the same time we did and it helped to make a phone or email contact every once in a while to catch up with how their process was going along. Everyone is different, and even though some families were having to wait for long periods of time for their children to become available for adoption, they still were able to understand the stress of waiting and the paperwork. We even had a couple of potluck dinners for everyone to get together in person and share stories and experiences. It was just a great way to realize that we were not alone in this process and in ways, had it much easier than others.

Whatever support system you use, whether it is faith based or something else, make sure you have it in place as you go through the first phase of the adoption. You will need it through the other phases. And this will be a good time to test the support system you have. Sharing your impatience at this juncture will allow you to more easily navigate this period and look forward to the next steps.

Managing Your Expectations

All the preparation in the world is not enough, I have learned, and that is really all you have been able to do so far—prepare. This was a hard time for me because I am not much on preparation and all about learning and working as I experience things. But I do see now how important this whole process was to us. It helped us take a dream and understand what was necessary to turn it into reality.

But while we were waiting, it was hard not to imagine what our future life would be like, and we were not alone. Everyone going through this same process will experience these same things. During this whole process you have built up expectations in your mind of what your child will be like and what your life with them will be like. You have imagined sharing birthdays and holidays, introducing them to your friends and family, and sharing idyllic family moments together. Even if you are a pragmatic and realistic person, you will probably not be envisioning fights, discipline issues, or behavior problems.

Unfortunately, these expectations can be harmful to your interactions with your new child. You will unconsciously be basing your evaluation of them and their behavior against the norms you have built into your mind. Even if you try consciously not to do this, it will be almost impossible. I have seen this very problem derail many successful adoptions and cause much heartache in both the families and children.

So how do you not let these expectations interfere? What can you do? Well, the first thing is to indulge yourself at this stage. Imagine all you want. Play out scenarios in your mind and daydream about what your ideal family will be like.

Don't feel embarrassed or shy about it, after all you have been dreaming of it for a while, so share this with your spouse or partner and enjoy this phase. But do imagine various scenarios. Imagine extremes of life. Start with scenarios that are close to you.

If you love the outdoors, imagine life with a child who will revel in sharing hikes, state parks, and other outdoorsy activities. Imagine taking them to your favorite places and having them love them as much as you do. Or if you are a bookworm, imagine them discovering one of your favorite books and sharing with them again the wonder you felt when you first read it. If you enjoy cooking, imagine the fun of shopping for, cooking, and then eating together an exotic meal of new foods. If you love snuggling, imagine cuddling up with your new child in front of a fireplace watching a favorite movie.

Knock yourself out with these. Then turn around and imagine alternative scenarios. What if you are in love with the outdoors and you have a child that *hates* physical activity and wants to stay in all the time? What if your child thinks reading is akin to running their fingernails down a chalkboard? What if your imaginative cooking self ends up with a child that only will eat mac and cheese and out of box at that? What if your child hates cuddling and won't let you physically interact? How will you reconcile that? Imagine compromises in activities and imagine dealing with your disappointment.

Just keep doing this. I know it sounds juvenile, but it works. It is impossible not to imagine what life will be like, so just make sure you imagine all different kinds of lives. This way, when you learn your child, you won't be surprised. And this is important to realize, that at this point, you really don't know your child. Even if you had the chance to meet them, they are still largely unknown to you. And this is the fun part. Uncovering the person inside your new family member is an exciting and wonderful thing to do.

It will take time to learn about them and their likes, dislikes, and personalities. Imagining different scenarios will help stop you from locking into any one specific scenario and be more open to others that are more likely. It will help you manage your expectations overall and be more receptive to differences that you will encounter. Nothing can be more upsetting in life than things not going your way, so trying not to have *one* way that you imagine your child, will help you. And remember, flexibility and love will see you through places you didn't think you could navigate.

Life Goes On

And now the hardest thing to swallow in the early phases of the adoption process, the fact that life goes on and life stops for no one. Getting ready to actually welcome a child is the most exciting thing in the world! I know that for me, it was hard to believe that these first phases of paperwork and waiting were drawing to a close and that we were getting closer to having a new son. I was so consumed in those final days leading up to the trip to Ukraine with all the details and the excitement of finally getting Dema.

But, while I was focusing on the adoption and its process, life was slowly marching on around me. It was so hard to stop and try to live a normal life. I had my work with my writing and speaking engagements that were still happening. I was in the middle of my second book as well and wasn't devoting nearly enough time to that. And there were all of the other little details of day to day life that seemed so petty and irritating to deal with when I was contemplating a life-changing addition to our family.

John was helpful during this time, keeping me grounded in real life. He made sure that life went on and that I still was the wife and mother that I always had been before all this happened. This is another constant struggle that I have faced, keeping myself properly focused on everything at once, and not focusing solely on Dema. It was hard, because there were so many times that I wanted to do nothing but focus on him, but the whole family still needed me, and by meeting everyone's needs not just the needs of Dema, I could more effectively attach everyone to each other.

I mentioned previously that I was writing letters to Dema chronicling some of the things that had been happening with us while he was half a world away. I found these letters so cathartic to write. I found that when I was having trouble dealing with the emotions or timing of all of this, just articulating my feelings on paper was enough. Even if you have a good support system, it is helpful to articulate things for yourself without the pressure of feedback like a conversation might provide. There were times that I wanted the world to stop and say, "Wait, I am going to have something momentous happen here. Can't you all see that and respect it?" However, conversely, at the same time, I felt a little guilty that I wasn't able to focus on the rest of my life the way I had been before all this started. There was some anguish as I resented the changes and at the same time welcomed them. There are complicated feelings present that are hard to explain. I know it seems like my emotions were all over the place and to be honest with you, they were. Hopefully as you read these letters, you will understand where we were as a family, anxiously awaiting a new arrival, sure it would never happen soon enough, and worried about all aspects of the adoption. Looking back, this was the beginning of the emotional roller coaster of adoption. So strap yourself in—it doesn't slow down for a while!

PART TWO:

WORLDS APART

1: Let's start at the very beginning

Dearest Dema,

I know I am starting this a couple of weeks late, but so much has happened since you left that I really haven't had time. I will first go back a few weeks in time to catch you up on things that were occurring while you were here in America but didn't know. So to start at the very beginning...

"Dema, come heeee-eeere!" rang out across the playground. Rob yelled and motioned wildly at some kids in the distance, too far off for me to make out. In a few minutes I saw a boy in a pair of rolled up jeans and red t-shirt pull up on a scooter. There you were. You smiled, my heart went flippity-flop, and that was the moment I knew—you were my child. You were quiet but not too shy, polite but not overly so.

So how did I come to be at this park, meeting you and falling instantaneously in love? I had received an email over my homeschooling email loop announcing the presence of a hosting program in the area for some Ukrainian children who were from an orphanage. They were here on a cultural exchange program and were looking for families to host them during their visit. I turned to my husband after reading the email and asked him if we could host a child. After all, we had hosted an exchange student from Ukraine eight years previously for an entire year and had had a wonderful time with the whole experience. In fact, we still keep in touch with Alex and his family, have been to Ukraine to visit him, and consider him a permanent part of our family. We call and Skype each other as often as his schedule permits.

Anyway, John said why not, so the next day I called Rob Jolley, the local contact for the hosting program, and the day after that, found myself sitting on a bench with Amanda on one side and G4 on the other in a playground smiling at you, unable to say anything but hello in Russian. You spoke to Rob for a few seconds and then sped off, scootering around, having a good time. Rob then called over several other children who were in need of a hosting family as well, and while they were just as charming and sweet, my kids and I looked at each other and all connected emotionally with a glance. We knew you were the one. Now of course was the question of how to execute the whole matter!

That day we went to a local aquarium with the whole group of hosted children and their host families. We had a good time, but found it hard to interact with you. You were here, there, everywhere, and we first got a good idea as to your energetic character. You loved being in groups (usually as the leader!) and were very social. G4 came up with an appropriate analogy—that trying to keep track of you was like trying to hold on to smoke. Unfortunately, without access to a translator, all we could do was grin stupidly at you as we all wandered around the aquarium. I think we probably scared you a little bit!

That evening, I spoke to John about the experience and told him that I had met a wonderful little boy that I thought would be fun to host. Ok, not little, you were thirteen at the time, but to me, you were my baby boy. I called Rob and was invited the following weekend to a social at a local park where all the children would be with the director of the orphanage and translators present. So anxiously we all waited several days until Saturday.

We went to the park and felt a little out of place as most of the other families had already been hosting children and were all connected. I realized we had come in late and started to panic a little that maybe we would not be able to host and connect with you. It doesn't help either that I am too shy in group situations to be noticed. And as usual you were never to be found. Every time that I found you in one place and went to get my husband to say hello, I would turn around and found you gone—off in another direction! You certainly are an active boy! I think John was starting to think I was making up your existence. But finally I convinced him that the grey blur on the bike that kept racing back and forth was in fact you.

Anyway, we finally managed to snag a translator and the assistant director of the orphanage. We told her that we had met you several days ago and were interested in hosting you. She gave us some of your background and her hopes for your future and then expertly corralled you as you zipped by us. Poor guy, you looked so bored! After all, what is more fun—racing around on a bike or standing and talking to the weird strangers that had done nothing but grin stupidly at you when they met you. We talked a little and then as evidenced by your squirming, you wanted to go back to playing. We let you go and after conferring with everyone, I extended the invitation to host you for your remaining time in America.

No promises were given, and my anxiety started to mount as I saw several other families talking throughout the evening to you. Naturally I wanted the best for you, but I really, really felt that would be us — now remember at this point all we had done was say hello and talk through a translator for ten minutes! I was hoping the you wouldn't like the other families and would want to try us out! Isn't that evil? But I really wanted you! We left the park a few hours later with hopeful hearts that something would be worked out.

So, I guess I will end your first letter here, Dema. Just never, ever forget how much we wanted you from the very beginning! I wasn't before, but I am now a big believer in love at first sight now — you are the perfect evidence of it.

Love,
Bethany

2: Oh the things we have yet to learn

Dearest Dema,

    We are now two weeks after you went back to Ukraine after the hosting program ended and I had prepared the next installment of these letters but the funniest thing happened tonight that I know will bring a smile to your face and I just couldn't resist telling. You taught us something and if only we could have capitalized on it!

    So to continue with our story tonight—as you know we don't have TV at home, so every time we go on vacation, the TV is a very exciting part of the trip. Well, we are in Seattle now in our motorhome and of course the cable TV is hooked up. G4 was flipping around the stations as I was making dinner and happened across the game show "Jeopardy." We enjoy watching it when we can and love to see how many answers we can get right. Anyway, the last daily double (trust me, you'll understand when you watch the show) was a question about video games. Now, we all groaned because the only games we play are rated E for everyone and are family games—like Wii Sports or MarioKart. While we like them, we do understand that they represent an extremely small portion of the video game market. As we heard the category, the kids groaned and said if only Dema were here—he would probably know.

    We were remembering the first day you were with us when you were a little disappointed with our video game offerings. So we took you to GameStop and you chose several games that you wanted, none of which we had ever heard of. Ok, back to my story... The double jeopardy question that was asked was, "What version of Call of Duty sold 5.6 million copies in the first twenty-four hours when released last year?" (Or something like that). We all squealed and shouted, "Black Ops!" We all know this one since that was one of your favorite games to play, and we are keeping it safe for you on your return.

    So, if we had been competing on Jeopardy, thanks to you—we would have won a lot of money!

Love,
Bethany

3: Till we meet again

Dearest Dema,

So now, we are back to the story of us hosting you. The day after the park meeting, I got a phone call from Rob saying that indeed they would be bringing you that evening after dinner to stay with us for the rest of your visit! We were so excited. Panic ensued in the house as we cleaned it from top to bottom. We scoured everything, then went to work preparing a room for you.

Amanda was upset because the guest room we were going to give you to stay in had a "girly" looking comforter and window treatment. So, John had to switch the window covering from another bedroom and I had to remake the bed with more "manly" accoutrements. We moved a squashy chair into the room along with a nightstand and then ran around the house finding knickknacks to make the room look homey. Amanda donated a clock and her favorite blue Lava lamp, G4 a hex bug game, John a poster of a rugby team, and I set up some Legos of a Ferrari car on the bookcase.

We were done by about five pm and then sat around for the next three hours because I wouldn't let anyone walk on the carpet that had freshly vacuumed carpet marks on it. Everyone kept fussing at me that I was being ridiculous, but I was insistent on putting our best foot forward and that meant a clean, freshly vacuumed carpet, and how could people tell that it was freshly vacuumed if there weren't any carpet marks on it? G4 and Amanda were so anxious, they could barely sit still. We occupied our time with learning the Russian phrases for 'good evening' and 'how are you,' of which everyone including me promptly forgot in the excitement of your arrival.

Finally, there was a knock at the door. Rob and his daughter Zhenia were there, along with the assistant director of the orphanage, her translator, and you bringing up the rear looking very angry and put out. As we came to find out, you had first been hosted for a week with a family that did not offer adoption. Then you were moved around and ended up with a family that had no intention of adopting, but you didn't really know that. This second family had a bunch of teenage boys and lived in a neighborhood where there was a bunch more teenage boys—in short—an ideal scenario for you. There was no shortage of bikes, video games, skateboards, etc. to keep you busy, along with an endless supply of thirteen-year-old boys just like you.

So, here you were, plucked out of this second family where you were having fun and then brought over to us. No wonder you looked so angry and scared. Dema, I will never forget how you looked sitting on the couch—so small and frightened and angry all at once. I wanted to run over and tell you it would be okay and not to worry about anything, but of course, as usual, all we could do was smile, say hello in Russian, and sit there grinning at you. Maybe you were getting the telepathic messages of welcome and love—but based upon your facial expressions—I don't think so!

Well, it was late after everyone left and Amanda and G4 showed you your room and where to drop your few bags of stuff. There was a little playtime but pretty much off to bed after that. I will end here with the thought that I was so happy to have you in our house that night. I was excited and thankful that you were with us and couldn't wait to get to know you better.

Love,
Bethany

4: A WHIRLWIND WEEK

Dearest Dema,

    I am going to fast forward through the next week, after all, you were with us so you won't need any remembrances. Just suffice it to say, we had the best time with you all week. The hosting program had activities scheduled every day for the kids, English lessons in the morning and outings in the afternoons. There were zoo visits, museums, amusement parks and the like. It actually was pretty exhausting. Thankfully, you only wanted to participate in a few of the activities, but I made sure that G4, Amanda, and I went with you whenever possible.

    I felt bad though that on one occasion I had to duck out and let you go by yourself. I had been asked to appear in a local ABC station show promoting my book about homeschooling and I couldn't cancel it. I really felt bad, I knew we had so little time together, but I knew that the outing would be more fun than sitting and watching me get interviewed. After the interview, we went out to lunch and then spent the afternoon just relaxing and catching up on housework. But we really missed you; already the house felt empty without you.

    You came back really late and I was frantic over the hours we lost together. But you seemed happy about the day and I am glad you had a chance to enjoy yourself. While you were gone that evening, John and I had a chance to talk about adopting you and decide to go forward with it, if you wanted to. We talked about the various issues, like the financial impact of another child, the impact on our two children, and the problems with language and culture, but we knew that you were meant to be in our family. Sure, there would be struggles, but we really wanted you as our son, and were willing to do anything to make it happen. We decided to get a translator over the next evening to talk to you and see if you wanted to be part of our family as much as we wanted you to be.

    During the week we spent together, there were some challenges — we discovered pretty quickly that you didn't like being told what to do and you initially used the language barrier to circumvent us, but we were on to that pretty quick. But with humor and perseverance, we all had a wonderful time and felt you fit in so well. It was like we had always had three children. You were certainly as messy as our others and as cranky in the mornings! You were as picky an eater as our kids too, one night scraping your plate and asking for more salad, the next, turning up your nose at it. But there was never a problem with Cokes and donuts . . . hmm . . . I am going to have to address this habit of too few veggies when you come back.

I really felt all week that you were part of our family. You fit in well and seemed at ease with us. I know that we were on our best behavior and that you were too, but under all that, it seemed that we were very compatible people. It was easy for all of us to imagine you as a permanent fixture.

Love,
Bethany

5: "The talk" and our first goodbye

Dearest Dema,

All too soon, it was Monday morning and we had to drive you to the airport. I had already cried packing your bags the night before and I was worried that I would break down completely when time came to say goodbye. I think we were all sad to contemplate having to let you go back home.

We had already had "the talk" with you several nights before, where we had offered to you to become a part of our family. We had invited over the coordinator of the hosting program along with a translator. We started out by giving you a little present, a small iPod shuffle with some of your favorite music on it and then assuring you that we wanted you in our family and that we had grown to care for and love you in the brief time that we had been together. We explained a little about our lives, that we move around a lot, we homeschool, and that education and hard work were important to us. You were quiet through all of this looking again very small and pensive.

We told you that we didn't need an answer right away, but that we wanted you to think about it. After a short while of talking to the translator (and boy did it drive me crazy not to be able to understand what you were saying), you had indicated that you wanted to be a part of our family, but I am never quite a hundred percent sure what is being communicated and if there are any caveats or nuances I am not aware of. My one regret is the way in which we sat and talked during this. You were seated away from everyone at a chair without any seating nearby. I should have gone over to you and kneeled at your feet and held your hand, but I wasn't sure how much you would have liked this. I know now that it would have been OK, but I didn't know then that you welcomed physical contact. I was itching to hug you, but was worried that you might reject me.

We sincerely hope we were able to communicate the depth of our feelings for you and how much you were wanted. There was also that minuscule concern that something would go wrong and we would never see you again. After all, the decision to adopt you was the easy part: now two governments and masses of paperwork and monetary expenditures were standing in between you and us.

Anyway, all too soon, it was time to take you to the airport. It was a scene of mass confusion, with tearful goodbyes from all the hosting families, and kids running everywhere, but before I could blink my eyes, it was over and you were gone—back on your way to Ukraine.

The car ride home was awful, it was way too quiet! It took us three or four days to stop looking for you. It was at least three days before I could bear to go into your room, and at that, all I could do was make your bed—I didn't have the heart to strip the sheets off yet. As of my writing this—two weeks later—I still haven't.

So Dema, we are slowly catching up to the present, but we still have some ways to go. Here seems like a good place to end this letter so, remember, we love you and can't wait to see you again.

Love,
Bethany

6: Penny pinchers

Dearest Dema,

I am sure there will be many frustrating moments and low points as we try to finalize the adoption, but this last week will linger in my memory as one of those low points. Once you were gone, the paperwork started...

John and I had to sign the adoption agreement and get the first payment off. I signed the agreement, and took it into his office for him to sign. I thought he had signed it and sent it off and therefore proceeded to send off emails to the adoption agency, when I received a call from him. This is where we started to go downhill. John had several concerns about the agreement and asked if I had checked up on the company itself. I had been so caught up in the emotional aspect of this decision, I had neglected the practical aspect. Thank goodness he is so careful. I mean, we have never, ever, even thought of investing a fraction of that amount of money before without checking and double checking the source or company involved.

You will learn about us as you live with us—but there is nothing left to chance in this family! John is good at squeezing every penny out of a deal that he can. For example, when we go to buy cars, he has a whole system. He researches the car he wants, decides what he wants to pay (which is blue book price plus $1000 to the dealership to make a modest profit) and then waits until the last day of a quarter. Then he starts calling around dealerships and talking directly to the sales manager and starts the conversation with a question, "Have you made your quota of sales this quarter?" If the answer is no (which it almost always is) he then proceeds to offer a cash deal at his prearranged price. After he waits a decent interval for the poor manager to pick himself up off the floor or stop choking, he reiterates the offer. He will continue to do this with dealership after dealership in ever widening concentric circles from where we live until he finds a yes answer. And believe it or not—we have always gotten our cars at ridiculously low prices!

I know that I am getting off topic here, but I can't stop myself. But enough fun at his expense—I am to be implicated in this as well. I am frugal as well, after all pinching pennies has become a habit from our early days out of grad school when we had no money. So sorry for the aside, but I think it really shows our personality—frugal to the core.

Bearing this in mind, we start checking out this company and come to find out that it is not licensed, bonded, or insured. This freaks out Daddy John and so he fusses at me to start to research the company and see what I can find out. I of course am happy to do so, horrified at my lapse in judgement, but also hopping up and down thinking it has to be okay because we need to be able to get you.

So, to make a long story short, it takes us a week to research this company in particular and adoption agencies in general. We came to find out that most adoption companies are not licensed, bonded, or insured, and this goes double for agencies that specialize in international adoption. We found out through research on the internet, calling Better Business Bureaus, and calling state agencies that find out there have been no complaints about the company, that they have a good track record in Ukraine with the American embassy, and to annoy the employees of the company with endless questions and issues that we needed answered. We had numerous conversations with people that had used this agency and others both with good and bad results.

The resolution to this matter—this is one area where John and I will have to go on faith and accept all the risks. As you can imagine, a hard pill to swallow from a family who has never made an impulsive decision in our whole life!

So, now I think everything is settled, at least for now, and we are moving forward. We have come to peace with the situation and have decided to focus on the outcome not the process.

Gotta go for now. And as always, thinking of you Dema!

Love,
Bethany

7: What's that? I can't understand you

Dearest Dema,

We are just finishing a road trip (we left the week after you left to go back to Ukraine) and will be going home soon. G4 starts his fall semester next week and we want to be settled before he has classes.

I got an email today on how to contact you through letters and phone calls. I can't wait to talk to you, but I am nervous that I won't be able to communicate, so I have been trying to start to learn Russian. I have not had good luck learning languages in the past—even after four years of Spanish in school, my communication is rudimentary at best. So I started researching different methods of learning languages. There is the grammatical way, learning verb conjugations and noun declensions focusing on accuracy, and the conversational way which focuses on communication and being understood more than accuracy. Neither way has worked for me so I was trying to find a program that blended both types together.

I know that you are bilingual already, speaking both Ukrainian and Russian, so you already have a major one up on me. Now I know I am focusing on Russian and you will say, "What about Ukranian?" and I get that—but since most people in Ukraine are already bilingual and speak both Russian and Ukrainian, and since Russian is spoken in a few more places in the world and Russian books are more widely available, we will stick with that! I am convinced that there is no greater gift in this global world than to be bilingual. There actually is a lot of research on the subject of the best way to learn languages as I found looking for language programs on the internet. I got way off track from my learning Russian and ended up by getting into the area of ESL instruction for you learning English, but I allowed myself to get distracted since this will be a subject of great interest to me when you finally get here.

So, back to my initial point here, that I want to learn Russian. After all this research, I am more convinced than ever it is necessary, not only to help ease the transition, but also to make sure that your ability to speak your native tongue is preserved. But now remember my ability level here! The first thought was Rosetta Stone, but I had already tried Rosetta Stone with Amanda when I tried to teach her Spanish, and she really didn't like it. I have also looked at purely grammatical texts and have finally come to realize that there is no magic way to learn—the conversational method vs. the grammatical method. They both have to be done in order to have true fluency, not just conversationally but also to be literate in a foreign language. Guess what—back to the computer for more research. I soon realized that I would just have to look at a lot of books and pick and chose which one looked good to me.

On our trip, with every city we went to, I would go into a local bookstore and would look in their textbook section for their introductory Russian textbooks. Finally, I found the one I wanted, Golosa. It is a great textbook and workbook that also has internet links. It is a good blend of conversational and grammatical techniques, with a lot of listening.

Of course, I couldn't jump right in, because Russian has a different alphabet! I feel so stupid—having to start with the alphabet again! The worst part of it is those letters of the Russian alphabet that look like some letters of our alphabet but have completely different sounds. For example an H is pronounced N. I think I have just about gotten letter recognition mastered, but pronunciation is a completely different thing. I am going to keep doing about a lesson a day when I can and hope that by the time you are ready for us, I can at least speak a little and understand you.

I have been proud of the little I have done so far. On our trip, we were walking around Pike Place Market in Seattle and came across a little Russian bakery. It was called Piroshky, Piroshky and had all kind of delectable goodies. We picked out an assortment, because what better way to study a language than to eat local food, right? Maybe ingestion is the one way of learning that I haven't tried yet! There was an article in their window that was written in Russian and I was able to sound out the title. Then I was able to translate a couple of the words! I was so proud of myself.

So look out Dema—I am aiming for complete understanding when you get here—you will be surprised!

Love,
Bethany,

8: Off to a Grand Start — Maybe Not

Dearest Dema,

    Well, we are finally home and starting to get back into a routine. It is hard after being gone so long. We have gotten all the paperwork started for the adoption process and in doing so noticed that our passports were expiring soon.

    It seems hard to believe that the whole process of adoption needs to take place in a foreign country first, but that is due to your citizenship. We will be given custody of you in Ukraine first and then will have to apply to bring you back into America next. The whole process will take a month or so over in Ukraine, so we will be gearing up for a big trip to come and get you, hopefully sooner rather than later. Good thing we noticed the passports as we could have gotten the call to go to Ukraine and then uh-oh, expired passports! So I spent an hour waiting in line to renew the passports (watching a man in front of me get passports for himself, his wife, and their seemingly endless posse of children) only to be told after my paperwork was done that there was another line to wait in to mail them off — even though this was all at the post office, the part that did the processing of passports would not do the mailing. This is my first experience in needing patience as I navigate through bureaucracy.

    So I left the office of the passports to walk five feet to the next line where I could mail them. Except as I took the first step to the next line, I swear a bus arrived with at least fifty people that had been saving up their mail needs for the past six years. And they all were accompanied by screaming babies. I looked at the line, then looked at the counter where there was one desultory post office employee moving at a snail's pace, and decided that I would come back tomorrow. So, basically I have failed at the first extremely simple task set before me to get you, one that I had complete control over and required no agency help. Ack — I hope this does not portend of events to come.

    Next comes fingerprinting and forms for all the states we have lived in. It seems like such a process to go through for adoption, but yet people are allowed to just give birth to children all the time without any special forms or background checks.

We are also learning that there are reams of paperwork to be completed in a very precise order with seemingly silly requirements (like blue ink only on one form and black only on another), but we will persevere and get through it.

I am nervous about the homestudy though. The homestudy is like an interview of your home and your family. A social worker schedules a time to come to your house and will interview each family member separately and then together, and then walk through your house making sure that you are ready in all respects to welcome a new child into your life. It is very intimidating as you feel as if you are on parade, laying your life down for someone else to judge your fitness as a potential parent.

It seems like the most important part of the process now but everything I have read from people that have gone through one says don't worry. I guess it is like being pregnant. When I was pregnant, all I could think about was the delivery, but once I had my babies I forgot the delivery in a moment, and started to focus on my lifetime ahead with my new baby. So, while I am sure we will be fussing and worrying about the paperwork and homestudy, we will try to keep our hearts focused on the lifetime ahead with you in our family.

We were reading out loud as a family last night and Amanda made a joke and then followed it up with, "Oh, Dema would like that. I miss him and wish he were here!" So don't forget, we are always thinking of you.

Love,
Bethany

9: You can't win — no matter what

Dearest Dema,

Hope you are doing well. As I told you last time, we have started the paperwork chase to get all of the forms filled out and papers signed. I am sure people that have adopted before will laugh and say that we are not even in the thick of things yet, but I feel already like this has been going on forever! I never realized how many documents were needed to adopt. We need criminal background checks, certified copies of our marriage certificate, doctor's notes, copies of passports, etc.

One place that I will not miss after this is the post office. After the marathon session there the other day, I found myself back there today. After running all kinds of errands, here and there, that was the last one. Actually, I shouldn't even have had to go. Usually John can FedEx things from his office cheaply and expediently, so all I have to do is to get papers together and then give them to him. But on this day, he noticed the address I was supposed to send the papers to was a post office box and FedEx won't deliver to one. So back to the post office I went, dreading the experience.

As usual the line was huge, so I settled in for a wait. I made some phone calls and figured I would be able to at least get some business accomplished in my wait. Well, wouldn't you know—the one time I come prepared to spend some time, the line zipped right along, and before I knew it, it was my turn at the front and I was getting dirty looks from everyone as I tried to get off the phone to get the papers mailed. Oh well, you can't win... And as I am writing this, I just remembered one thing I forgot to include in the papers, a copy of John's driver's license. Arghh—back to the post office tomorrow with that!

To clear my mind from all the frustrations with paperwork, I also have started cleaning out closets in preparation for shuffling some things around to make room for you. It's amazing how much stuff you can find hidden back in the recesses of a dark closet. It's also kind of frightening since none of the closets in our house have lights in them, so you never really know exactly what you are going to find. Today, it was the craft and game closet. I was able to clean out bags and bags of bits of fabric, googly eyes, dried out glue sticks, and old, stiff paint brushes. I figure at thirteen, you probably aren't going to want to play with arts and crafts!

The problem with starting a task like this is that it always takes more time than you have allotted to accomplish it. Or even in the unlikely event you have allotted enough time for the task, life will interfere. For you it will be friends, schoolwork, and chores, for me it is kids—like, they need to be fed, they need clean clothes, etc. Either way, I promise you, that you will be pulled away from the task before you are done. Then you face a decision. Either leave all the items out until you can come back and finish later, or do part of the job and come back and finish the other part later. The problem with the second solution is that if things are put away nicely, there is very little impetus to go back and continue the job. You pretty much mentally wipe that task out of your brain with a little imaginary check and then later when you go back to the closet, thinking that it was cleaned out already, you get a nasty shock finding it very different than you were expecting. Then you have an unexpected amount of work to do extra at the last moment, which tends to induce panic attacks.

The first solution, sounds better—doesn't it? But after consideration, you realize that this isn't too much better. It leaves everything in a big mess. And once other people start coming around, inevitably there are two things that will happen. The first is that people will accuse you of doing nothing but making a big mess, and the second is that the system you were using will deteriorate as others come in a pick up things saying, "Where did you find this? I have needed this."

Anyway, I opted for the first method and left everything out. I am sure I will hear about it later. . . .

Love,
Bethany

10: The Doctor Is In

Dearest Dema,

Ok, option one didn't work out so well from last blog. Everything sat out for a day or two, then got stuffed back into the closet. I did manage to clean out two boxes, which is a start. I got together a couple of boxes of craft stuff that is still good but that I won't ever use and loaded it in the back of my car to give away at the next Girl Scout Service Unit Meeting which was conveniently scheduled for the next day. But, alas, it was canceled. So my great closet clean out has netted me two boxes vomiting of craft supplies (to give away heaven knows when) taking up room in the back of my car (spilling contents out every time I go around a corner), and a slightly less stuffed closet. I really can't win!

So, onto the topic for today's letter—the post office again, or I guess to be more accurate, the doctor's office and then the post office. I am guessing the post office will be a prominent figure in this process; maybe I should get a job there. . . .

Anyway, we have gotten most of the forms together for the home study. We have assembled birth certificates, driver's licenses, copies of tax returns, proof of medical insurance, fingerprint cards. You name it and I have copied it and put it in the mail. The last item on the list was the doctor's evaluation of our health. So, knowing that this was going to take a long time (our doctor usually has over a month wait for a physical) I called to make an appointment. I had to leave a message, so in the mean time, I realized that there were two sets of forms that had to be done by the doctor. There is one set from the local authorities for the home study and then there is another set for the Ukrainian government. Well, patting myself on the back for quick thinking and resourcefulness (I was only going to have to go to the doctor once instead of twice), I called to get these forms sent to me, with the addendum, "Don't worry. No rush. Just please send them when convenient."

Thinking I was just the guru of organization, I sat down to congratulate myself when the phone rang. It was the doctor's office letting me know they had an opening for the NEXT DAY! This is unheard of, but probably was cosmically arranged to teach me a lesson about timeliness. So, after scrambling and apologizing, I finally was able to get the forms set to me by email. No problem I thought, I will just print them out and off we go. Well, four hours later I am still sitting in front of the computer trying to reformat the forms as our Mac makes things look different. Then I saw in the email that these need to be on the doctor's letterhead. ACK!! I don't know if they have letterhead, or how to get my form onto it.

So, ever the problem solver, and because I was getting really cranky at this point, I decided to make up letterhead for the doctor myself. And if I do say so myself, it looked really good. So, I stumble off to bed, not looking forward to the next morning as we have to get up early as the appointments that were available of course were the first appointments of the morning — more evidence of cosmic punishment for being me.

At the doctor's office the next morning, still wiping the sleep out of my eyes, I was valiantly trying to sort out the forms, as two were being sent to the state (simple physicals) directly by the doctor after signing and the two for Ukraine (requiring seventeen vials of blood to be drawn and tested for every known disease) need to be signed in front of a notary. And of course after questioning, no, there is not a notary in their office, we will have to arrange for one to come out to the doctor's office and notarize the documents there. It was enough to reduce one to tears, especially when I do not handle blood-draws very well and hadn't had breakfast because it was so early in the morning. But everything was done, and thank goodness, all the tests were normal. And finally, we have been declared physically fit to adopt.

So off to the post office again (fifth time in seven days) to mail more documents off. I am beginning to become known there — embarrassing — and can now help other people in line find appropriate documents, etc. Surprise, surprise, I walk into the post office and there is NOBODY in line. Unbelievable I know, but I was in and out of there in two minutes. I know that this will never happen again.

But, Dema, I did send off your first package to you. Just some pictures and some small gifts. We are anxiously awaiting the next steps.

Love,
Bethany

11: Half way done is as just begun

Dearest Dema,

Well, it has been a while since I last wrote you and a lot has happened. We had our home study and passed! Yea! So, at least from the US standpoint, we are ready for you. We are now busy starting to get together all the documents for the Ukrainian government. But I can't leave you without a blow by blow account of the home study, can I?

We were referred to a social worker who had worked with families of international adoptions before, so she was very familiar with the requirements of the report. As she explained to me on the phone when I contacted her, she was an independent social worker, hired by us and paid for by us, that would interview the family and inspect the house. Once that was finished, she would write up a report that included her findings and make a recommendation. If the recommendation was good, the study could then be submitted to the state or in our case Ukraine, if not, then we would have a chance to remediate the deficiencies and try again.

So, to begin with, we are now having our grass cut by the boy who lives next door. I came home Thursday night with Amanda from Tae Kwon Do to see that the front yard had been half mown! He had run out of daylight and couldn't finish. Yikes, tall was OK, cut was OK, but how was I going to explain a half-done lawn? But it was late at night and the next day was a school day, so I knew that he couldn't fix it in time, so I just devoted myself to cleaning inside. I thought I will dazzle her with the inside cleanliness and maybe she will forget about the state of the lawn!

So we scurried around, cleaning and picking up all Thursday night and Friday morning. The home study lady was due to arrive at nine in the morning so I went outside about ten minutes before to make sure there was no dog poop, etc. that would cause a problem, when I saw our neighbor's mom outside preparing to take her baby for a morning walk. I laughingly told her about the situation of the home study being that morning, and she was so worried about the lawn, she said, "Don't worry, I will just finish the front lawn up right now." She turned and went back into her garage to get the mower, with me chasing after her ineffectually saying, "Really, don't worry about it! She will be here any moment and it's no big deal." Well, I wasn't being listened to and she got her mower and was mowing the lawn when who shows up—you guessed it—the home study lady! ACK! She was a very proper looking, middle-aged lady looking very official with a big briefcase and a lot of papers in her hands.

She gets out of her car and our neighbor's mom looks up and says, "Hi, I am just their neighbor." So the home study lady turns to me and asks, "Your neighbors do your lawn for you?" What could I do but smile sickly and say, "No, no. See her son didn't finish last night…" Seeing her look, I just trailed off and weakly asked her inside. What a way to get started.

Thank goodness, things picked up from there. It was a good session. She asked a lot of questions about our parenting technique (superior of course), personalities (untouchable), and attitude toward adoption (unparalleled). Even G4 and Amanda were well-behaved and well-spoken. She spent about two hours with us, interviewing John and myself separately and then G4 and Amanda. Only a small portion of time was devoted to looking over the house, but as we were interested in a teenager, the house portion was not as important as if we were trying to adopt little ones and needed to be safety proofed.

I was nervous after the social worker left, but about a week later, we got the draft of the home study in the mail and looked it over—it was very complimentary and should be accepted well by the Ukrainian government. So, back to the paperwork drills and probably back to the post office again.

Things are pretty much the same around here. I am still trying to learn Russian. I have mastered the alphabet and have learned a few phrases and words of greeting. I am able to work on it a few nights a week. Not quite the ambitious schedule I had set before, but still better than nothing I guess.

I hope you have received our package by now. The hosting program facilitator sent out the phone number for the orphanage to everyone that hosted children, so I will try to call you in the next few weeks or so. It is expensive to call internationally, so we won't be able to call often, but I want to be able to contact you at least every month or so. We miss you a lot so it would be great to hear your voice again.

Love,
Bethany

12: Just One More Thing

Dearest Dema,

Well, since I last wrote to you I have learned a lesson in humility. After our home study was done and the immigration paperwork sent off, I was feeling very superior. I was thinking, "This adoption paperwork isn't that hard—we are most of the way done and it hasn't been too bad." This was accompanied by many slaps on the back and expressions of job well done!

Well Dema, remember in life there is always just one more thing. And this one more thing was seventeen more documents that needed to be obtained, notarized, and apostilled in the state capitol. I am not joking—seventeen more documents! So I quickly deflated and went back to work. This next set of documents is for Ukraine and was composed of certified marriage licenses, powers of attorney, employment letters, pictures of the house, etc. Oh, and before I forget, MORE fingerprints. The first set was for the homestudy. This set is for a criminal background check and then we will need more for an Interpol background check. We have gotten most of the documents together and are waiting on a few stragglers that will hopefully be tied up before the immigration paperwork comes back.

I am starting to have worries that we will not get to you by your birthday, which is in four months. I really want you to have this next birthday with us. We have been at this process for two months already, but I have to remain positive and realize you will be with us for the rest of your life so a few weeks shouldn't matter—except it does. I hate to be separated from you. I want to start making you part of our family, learning from you and in turn being able to teach you. I am normally pretty patient, but I have to confess that my patience is wearing thin. And I am not the only one—G4 and Amanda talk about you almost every day. They are getting anxious too.

Anyway, we will keep our fingers crossed that everything will work out for the best. I just don't want you to forget us!

Love,
Bethany

13: At last we speak

Dearest Dema,

    I have so much to update you on that I can't even remember what. So, I will start with us trying to get in touch with you. We were given the phone number to the orphanage after you left to go back to Ukraine, and after several failed attempts we were finally able to get a call through. Here is where it started to go downhill. I thought my Russian was better that it actually is—well, I got a comedown pretty fast! Anyway, I think I got from the conversation that someone would be back at ten o'clock that spoke English but then I fell asleep because it was the middle of the night.

    We were getting discouraged and kept trying, but kept getting no answer. So, I got the brilliant idea to ask a neighbor, Victoria, that speaks Russian to call you. So I called Victoria up and begged her to help us and thank goodness that she agreed to help out. So I ran over an international calling card, the phone number to the orphanage and a list a questions to ask you. She is from Moscow and had met you once when you were with us in August. I felt that since we couldn't get a hold of you, at least someone who you knew had a connection with us would be second best to talking to us.

    We didn't hear anything back for several days and I was beginning to get anxious, but lo and behold—she called and left a message this morning that she had heard from you!!!! We were so excited. She said that you were doing well and sent us your love. You didn't want anything specifically but were anxiously awaiting us. I am so happy that you are still looking forward to being a part of our family. I was worried that as a teenager, you would rather be with your friends and not with some strangers! Maybe that is a crazy worry, but trust me, I know that teenagers can be crazy sometimes.

    I will be calling her back later to squeeze every detail out of her about your conversation, but as of now I am basking in the knowledge that you are OK and are still waiting for us.

Love,
Bethany

14: Keeping our cool

Dearest Dema,

I feel like we are going back to the beginning of all the paperwork here. We finally got the appointment with the UCIS office for the immigration paperwork in and were able to go get fingerprints done (for the fourth time!) We had an appointment for November the eighth but everyone told us to go in early. So, John took time off from work and in we drove. We went to the office and had to go through the equivalent of airport security to get to the reception desk. We were questioned about an appointment. When we told them that we had one for next week, we got quite the look as they explained that the office was moving and consolidating and would be at that location next week, but as of that day, was still at their old location about thirty miles away. And, just for the frosting on top, it was added that probably the machines would be turned off in anticipation of the move.

So we jump back into the car and hightailed it to the old office. We screeched to a halt, jumped out and raced into the office. This was very low security compared to their new office. This was just a few middle-aged women in an office in a strip mall! They listened to our sob story and nicely agreed to fingerprint us. So we got accomplished what we needed to that morning and felt vastly superior!

Well, that superior feeling dissipated quickly over the next few days as we tried to get the immigration letter pushed through. This letter is important to have as it allows us to bring you back into America after we adopt you in Ukraine. I called every day for about a week and kept nicely asking but kept getting put off. Then a week before Thanksgiving I finally got through to an officer and now felt absolutely awful! The case had been initially assigned to someone that was now leaving immigration on maternity leave. The new officer that was reassigned to the case put all the other new cases at the bottom of her stack! As she told me, they weren't her cases and she was going to work on her own cases first. And, even though I gave the whole sob story, she was unmoved.

It took me a while to recover from this blow. There is no hope of getting you before your birthday now. We were hoping to get the paperwork off to Ukraine by the end of November to be able to get the first appointment the State Department of Adoptions in Ukraine offers in February. Now, we are looking at not being able to submit the paperwork until February and then maybe not getting an appointment to come get you until April or May. Unfortunately, the State Department of Adoptions closes down over the holiday months (December and January) and doesn't start back up until February. This makes me so furious—I have already decided in my mind that you are my son and as you come to know me, you will realize that I can't let anyone else get in the way of one of my children!

But, neither can I move governmental agencies any faster, so I will just have to relax and hope that nothing else will go bad. I am trying to find the good in all of this and have come up with the fact that it will be warmer in the spring and you will get another year of schooling complete before I come to get you. These are pitiful positives but positives nonetheless.

But, we will persevere and continue until we finally can bring you home!

Love,
Bethany

15: Count to ten

Dearest Dema,

OK, trying to calm down — taking deep breaths and counting to ten! We just got our immigration letter in — so I guess my appeals worked, but two days too late! Why toy with us I ask the Almighty? Either give us the form in time or make it good and late so I can complain, fuss, and generally blame everyone else for my misery in not having you now!

Anyway, in other news, Amanda got her braces off today and is sooo happy. I told the orthodontist to get ready for you Dema. I know you won't be happy to hear this, but you are in for some major dental work. I showed them your photo — so they will be expecting you in the spring!

I keep showing your photo off to everyone — I keep it with me in my purse so that I can whip it out and brag about you. Sorry to embarrass you before you are even ours — but I am a mom and just can't help it.

Love,
Bethany

16: Finally, Eagle Scout!

Dearest Dema,

Getting ready for the holidays is always fun, but our hearts are heavy knowing that you will not be with us this year. I wasn't even really counting on being able to get you by Christmas, but the reality of a holiday season without a family member that should be here is upsetting. There is always so much activity this time of year, with decorating, shopping for presents, and cooking, and I wish that you were here to share it with us. I want to shop for presents for you and make Christmas cookies with you and have you help decorate the tree with us. I want to also learn about some of your traditions and incorporate those into our life as well. But without being able to include you, we have been pouring our energy into G4 and scouting.

We have been busy with G4's court of honor for Eagle Scout. He finished his eagle project this summer before you came, but the paperwork took a long time too. See, it isn't only adoption paperwork that is hard and time-consuming! We ended up by scheduling his court of honor for December. What was I thinking?

However, it was a beautiful court of honor. I am so sorry that you missed it but, in a way, I am glad that it is out of the way now and one more thing I can cross off my list, so that I can concentrate on you when you get here.

I have spent a lot of time thinking about how life will change when you arrive, but the reality is that I really don't have any idea of what it will be like. I wonder what kind of things you will like to do and what kind of things you dislike. I want to plan all kinds of things, but not knowing you as a person makes it really difficult. I can imagine all kinds of problems, all kinds of fun, but I do know that reality is rarely what you think it will be, so all I can do is to imagine and wait.

We hope you are doing well and know in your heart that we are still coming for you.

Love,
Bethany

17: Christmas Wishes

Dearest Dema,

Merry Christmas! We wish you were here to celebrate with us. All day today as we have been opening presents, we have been thinking about what it is going to be like for you next year. Will you understand what we are doing? How good will your English be by then? Will you understand our prank gifts? How will we keep gifts a secret from you?

This year I really feel like I understand the phrase that it is better to give than receive. I just want to give, give, give to you. I want to buy presents for you, see you open them, share our traditions, and generally open up my heart to you. It is so frustrating for me to see all the excess I have in my life with presents and advantages and to know that you are overseas in an orphanage and not able to partake. It also saddens me to think of all the other children that are there but don't have families coming for them.

We have to get back on the paperwork for you. While the last month was going by, Ukraine decided to change the name of the adoption agency, so we get to go redo all the paperwork with new titles on it! You can imagine some grinding of teeth noises and comments under my breath on this information. And to add insult to injury, several other forms were revamped and so we needed to be change ours as well to meet the new forms standards.

So, once I get Christmas stuff put away, I will get to work on the forms. My goal is to get it off by the fifteenth of January. We have an appointment to submit the paperwork to Kiev on February fourteenth—Valentines Day—I thought that was special!

Oh, I heard from the family, the Radzinski's, that hosted your friend Sergei from the same orphanage. They are trying to adopt him and his little brother Max. We were all a little worried when he had not found a family at the end of the hosting program this past summer, but I am sure he will be happy when he hears the news. Anyway, we still miss you and can't wait. Hopefully time will fly by and you will be with us before you know it.

Love,
Bethany

18: Yippee — no more paperwork!

Dearest Dema,

Well, I have great news! We finally got the papers sent off to Ukraine last week. It was a little frustrating at the end with all of the changes to the documents that were needed. We had everything ready to go in November, but the immigration letter was late. And then, since the next appointment date flipped over into a new year, there were a lot of changes that had to occur. The new year meant that half of the documents had to be redone since they needed to have been executed in the same calendar year. Also, we needed the past year's tax return and a new year meant a new year's tax return. Then the medical forms were changed and then there was a new form, and then they needed duplicates of the interpol forms, and yada, yada, yada. It seemed never-ending.

But we persevered through the documents and they were sent off at last. Now everyone says waiting is the hard part, but I think the hard part was actually the documents. The waiting I can fill with getting your room ready, buying you clothes, and figuring out how to teach you. I can also fill it with worry about whether you still want to come home with us, whether you will truly integrate into our family, and how long it will take you to learn English. I can go on and on about the worries I have, but as you can see, I am at no loss to fill my time with things while we wait.

I am still trying to learn Russian but my early enthusiasm has dimmed somewhat with how difficult it is. Granted I am not the most linguistically talented person on the face of the earth, but everyone I talk to agrees that on a scale of hardness, Russian is up there near the top.

We have ten days until we hear about an appointment with the SDA — the State Department of Adoptions. Our neighbor Victoria is going to try to call you again. She had luck that one time, but none since then. She tried around your birthday in January — we desperately wanted to get to you by your birthday — but that didn't work out. But hopefully, she can get in touch with you to let you know about the paperwork being on its way.

Love as always,
Bethany

19: Time to panic

Dearest Dema,

Well, after a few days of basking in the glow of paperwork sent off—I am starting to feel the itch of concern as we wait. We are still waiting on confirmation of the delivery of the documents, the appointment for submission, and then the date to travel. All of course are out of our hands.

So, to ease the strain, I put together a little party of people that hosted some of your friends from the orphanage this past summer so that everyone could get together and commiserate on their progress on adoptions, or lack thereof. It was a great party—you would have recognized everyone there. It was nice to reconnect with everyone and find out where they were in the process of their adoptions. But it had one unintended consequence: I got freaked out! I realized that we were the furthest along of anyone as the next closest family had yet to receive their immigration papers and that really there was not a lot of time before you came. A few months at most. I wasn't any closer on learning Russian, your room was only half set up, and I hadn't continued cleaning out closet space for you.

Many of the other families are still waiting for their children to become available on the adoption registry—it usually takes a year of being listed domestically in the country before a child is available for international adoption. However, it is nice that the parents that are adopting together have bonded together.

This has served to kick me into high gear as I am motivated now to get everything ready. I promise that things will be ready for you. I want to make things as nice as possible for when you arrive. I know that you will want to put your own touches on the room, but I want to feel that you have everything you need to start off with.

So, off to start getting things ready for you!

Love,
Bethany

20: Time to worry

Dearest Dema,

 Well, even though we haven't heard about a travel date yet, I still feel positive about moving forward to get you. We had a long Skype call with Alex yesterday evening and he said that he would try to call you. It might be easier for him to get in touch with you than for us. I told him that I want you to know we think we will be coming in April or May. I am sure that it will be a shock for you—here we have been working so hard and constantly praying for things to move along—so it will not be a surprise for us to finally see you. But I can imagine it might be a nasty shock for us to show up and you to realize that you will be leaving all things familiar.

 This point is especially concerning to me, I actually lay awake thinking about it at night! I worry that you might not want to come with us. You will be leaving friends, a familiar place, your country and your language to come live with virtual strangers. I worry about how to convince you that it will be OK, that we will love you and give you all the benefits of a loving family life. You will find friends and make a future with us as your back up whether here or back in Ukraine, but this is going to be hard for you to understand. And I am sure that it will be hard even when you get here and you are lonely or frustrated.

 I have joined several email groups about adopting older children in an effort to try to understand everything you will be going through or possibly facing while with us. I want to anticipate every possible scenario so that I can help guide you through it, but I sometimes get overwhelmed with this. I don't know you yet, so how can I predict what you will be feeling or how you will react?

 All I do know is that all of us are desperate to have you a part of our family. We talk about you at least once a day and have planned out trips and things to take you to. I am afraid you will be a little frazzled with everything we want to show you! I know that one day, we both will look back on this and laugh, but for now, I am obsessed with making sure you have a smooth as possible transition to our family. I know that you will enrich our family no end. We are all looking forward to the new family you will help us create.

So, here I am counting the hours as they pass too slowly to hear back from the Ukrainian government and passing the time worrying about you. You are now fourteen, we did miss your birthday, no matter how much I wanted to get you by that date. I cried when I woke up that day, but I had to put the sorrow away and focus on a lifetime of birthdays that I hopefully will be there for you.

Love always,
Bethany

21: We don't live in a cardboard box — honest

Dearest Dema,

    In this crazy upside down world that adoption is — I have been in a high high and a low low all in the same day. The day started off promising enough — the first two families from North Carolina that participated in a similar hosting program with our adoption agency heard about a travel date. They submitted their paperwork a week or so before ours. So I was at the calendar in a flash to count out seven days so that I knew exactly when we would be notified of a travel date for you.

    Then came the disappointment. We heard from the adoption facilitator that our dossier had been approved with one minor problem — they wanted a third party (meaning yet another uninvolved person) verification of our lease even though they had the lease contract and a notarized, apostilled statement from the landlord. ARGHHHHHH! And to further complicate things, if we did not back date the document to November (when we had all the other documents done) we were going to have to resubmit the paperwork all over again with updated dates. So — deep breath — then we found out the lady that had notarized all the documents to begin with who worked for John had just left the company several days previously to start a new job. What are the odds of her backdating a piece of paper for us and notarizing it? When her notary fees are paid for by a new job now?

    I had to struggle back tears and for the first time felt a little hopeless. I felt we were so close and then it was snatched away. I truly felt that we would not get to you until you were twenty-two! Then luck shined on us — John was able to get in contact with Melanie (the notary) at her new job. After hearing the story, she agreed to notarize the new paper if we could meet her between 12:45 and 12:50 which was the end of her lunch hour.

    Now to find a third party that would verify the lease contract. Luckily, the family you had stayed with a few days before coming to us stepped in. It just so happens that the mom is a real estate agent and was willing to help out. John faxed a copy of the lease to her and she signed a statement verifying its authenticity. She was willing to meet Melanie at the specified time, and voila! It was done!

So in the end, over the course of three harrowing days, everything worked out. We got the paper done, signed and in the mail. It should be in Ukraine in several days and everything should be back on target. We hope to be traveling by the middle of April!

Can't wait to see you,

Love,
Bethany

22: Sitting on Pins and Needles

Dearest Dema,

We have been up and down again these past few days. We got the paper in that was needed, only to hear from the Ukrainian facilitator a few days later that we again had our paperwork thrown out because the notary had gotten married and her name had changed between the first November date and now. So we were a little worried that everything was going to get thrown out for a while and we would have had to start over. But, we were lucky! The facilitator over in Ukraine is worth his weight in gold—he was able to convince the staff in the State Department of Adoptions that in America it is customary for the woman to change her name and it was the same person. In Ukraine I gather that it is not a custom for women to change their names.

I got an email yesterday from our facilitator saying that the paperwork went through—everything was accepted and we should be hearing within a day or two! Yea! Now I have to go panic again and start getting your room ready. We purchased a bookcase and dresser for your room but haven't really decided what to do about the beds yet. So, much to decide! But we want to wait for you to get here to make a lot of these decisions. IF YOU EVER GET HERE! I guess I am getting a little impatient and want you here already like yesterday!

But we are getting closer—day by day. I am feeling pretty good about it now—I just feel like we will be traveling over there the second or third week of April.

Bye for now, but hopefully not for long!
Bethany

23: 8 Days and counting

Dearest Dema,

OMG!!! We got THE CALL yesterday! Our facilitator stateside called to tell us that everything was approved and we had an appointment in the State Department of Adoptions of Ukraine. I am so excited and can't wait to see you. The only problem, which isn't really a problem, is that it was so soon, we are still in March. We were all expecting the end of April and all of a sudden to find out that we have to leave in 9 days—mindboggling.

Of course, we are excited to get over there as soon as possible and get you. Every day that goes by is another lost opportunity in my mind. Anyway, poor John spent three hours on the phone last night with Delta trying to get all of us first class tickets to travel. We have been saving frequent flier miles and had plenty—we could have flown everyone to the moon and back first class with the amount of miles we have. But (there is always a but) there was no availability to use them in any configuration to get to you. We tried every combination but the best we could do was pretty crappy flights in coach through Minneapolis and Amsterdam. The flight times are not great either. But it is what it is. We will try to upgrade at the airport but don't count on it.

The good news is that the trip is going to coincide perfectly with John's business trips. We are going to try to stay over there while we have the mandatory ten day waiting period for you and accompany John on some trips for business. His company has offices in England, Sweden, and France. He has to go on business and Amanda and I will tag along. Unfortunately G4 will not be able to come—he has classes and finals are the end of April. He is a little upset, but he said he will gladly stay behind and help get things ready for you.

We have gotten the ball rolling with getting ready for the trip. I got out the suitcase I had set aside for you and will go shopping for your clothes soon. I hope I can guess the size—otherwise we will have to shop there. Victoria is going to try to call you also these next few days so you can anticipate us, but if she doesn't get through, you will be in for a big surprise.

Hopefully, all will go smoothly these next few days as we prepare. Another regret I have is not being able to learn more Russian than I have. I have learned a lot, but certainly not enough to really effectively communicate. I will redouble my efforts though—I will spend the plane trip studying! But nothing is dimming our excitement to see you and bring you home!

Love as always,
Bethany

24: Mortician or spy? You decide.

Dearest Dema,

 Well, things are in full swing as we get ready to come and get you. You would not believe what we are going through to make this happen! First, money. Apparently we have to take most of our money in cash and it has to be nice bills — maybe not new, but unmarked and uncreased. At least that is what we are being told by the facilitator. So I went to our bank yesterday and found out that you can't just get new money. They looked at me like I was a little nuts when I told them what I wanted, but then when I explained what it was for and showed your picture to them, they got right down to work finding pretty money. So I sat there for an hour as every teller went through their drawer to find the prettiest bills they had. And then it only amounted to half of what we needed, so back to the bank next week to get the rest of it hopefully.

 Then I had to switch gears and move on to G4 — who still doesn't have his driver's license. We keep fussing at him that he has to get it by the time we leave, because he will be all alone. Grandma doesn't get into town until the eighteenth and we leave the sixth, so count 'em — twelve days alone. There is no way he can ask others to drive him around. He just has to do one more class for his driver's ed certificate that he was scheduled to do tonight but missed it. ARGHHHHHH. Just wait until you have kids. You will understand the maternal angst I am having. I don't want to leave him alone but have no choice. But if I am going to leave him, I don't want him stranded.

 In other news, we went clothes shopping for you today. That was a fun exercise since we have no idea how much you have grown. So it was guess work. And quite by accident, trying to pick out clothes that we thought you would like, we ended up by getting everything in black! You are going to look like a mortician, or as G4 said, a spy. Hopefully you will like them and they will fit. But if not, oh well, we will have to try to find something there. The only positive thing I can say is that the color will hide dirt.

 I am impressed and a little surprised with how many people we are touching with this adoption, from the bank tellers to our friends. This whole process started out just with a mom and dad wanting another child to love, and making a very private decision. Then we brought in the rest of the family, but it didn't stay small for long. There is a whole adoption agency working for us, and all the peripheral people that have helped, from Melanie, our faithful notary, to the policeman who fingerprinted us and told us he was adopted from the Philippines as an infant and was happy to see us adopting, to the post office employees who now recognize me. And we just got a call today from some neighbors who want to throw you a welcome home party. This whole process shows me how people can work together for a common good and really make a difference. And it all started with my love for you! You truly are very loved and very wanted already!

Hugs and kisses,
Bethany

25: 4 DAYS UNTIL FLIGHT

Dearest Dema,

We are getting so excited to see you and can't wait to get the trip started. We had a small party at the house on Sunday for the other families that are adopting and they brought gifts for us to take to their kids. It is a little daunting to be the first family in this group to go over to Ukraine. I feel like we are blazing the trail and don't have anyone really to guide us. I feel a little guilty too, as there are so many families waiting for their children and we are the lucky ones! But then I remind myself of the road to get here and realize that we worked our butts off to be in this position right now.

I have been busy making lists of things to pack and finish buying for you — I finally found a jacket that I think you will like. I have gotten your suitcase packed and am starting in on everyone else's.

John should get his driver's license soon. He is finishing all the requirements tomorrow and hopefully everything will go according to plan. I can't believe that we will have to go through all of this with you in a few years as well. I can't even comprehend a ready made teenager right now.

Anyway, gotta go — more packing to do. Counting the hours until we can see you!

Love you bunches,
Bethany

26: Last night in the USA

Dearest Dema,

    Well, it is eleven o'clock the night before we leave and John and I are still up and trying to pack a few last minute things. We have discovered that we are missing a couple of things and have to make a run out to a twenty-four-hour store to get them (razor blades for me and Amanda—you don't want us going bohemian!)

    I am so excited about the trip. I am a little scared, but mostly I can't wait. I have been racking my brain thinking of things to get you, and today I scored a big hit. I bought you a Nintendo DS and found Call of Duty MW3 for it. That should keep you busy!

    One of the other adopting families is actually from Kiev, Ukraine and is fluent in Russian. I asked Vira, the wife, to come over at some point and help me with some common phrases. So she came over today and helped me learn a couple of phrases today like, "We are vegetarian," and "Where is the toilet?" So hopefully I can at least communicate the basics once we are over there. I am mad—can't find my Rosetta Stone CD that I had in a panic purchased, so I will have to use just the Golosa book instead. But I am determined to continue learning Russian.

    I better go now, too tired to think straight. Can't wait to see you and hug you!

Love,
Bethany

PART THREE:

GETTING CLOSER

Traveling Overseas for an Adoption

As I have mentioned before, we had briefly thought about adoption before we hosted Dema and had looked into domestic adoption as our first option. But when that did not work out, we turned toward international adoption. I have talked about the difficulties with paperwork and dealing with foreign entities, but there is one other huge topic in international adoptions that needs to be covered, and that is international travel. And we are not talking Club Med; usually these adoptions will be taking place in areas that are not typically tourist destinations, rendering it more difficult for the traveling family to do even the most rudimentary types of business without assistance.

My husband and I are lucky as I have lived overseas before and both of us have traveled overseas extensively. We feel comfortable in these situations and enjoy traveling, so this helped immensely. But even if you don't have experience traveling overseas, don't worry. There are steps you can take to make the experience more comfortable and fun, and to allow you to focus on the most important part, your child.

Each foreign country will have different timelines for adoption, but plan on anywhere from one to three months in total. It could even be longer, but those are usually complicated cases. It does sound like a lot of time, but if you break it down into the constituent parts, you can see where the time is spent. When you travel overseas, the adoption isn't a done deal, it is just an invitation from the country in question to come and see about the prospect of adoption. Then once you meet a child, make a selection, and file paperwork, you have to wait for a court date. There could be complicating factors such as sibling separation, family members that turn up, etc. Once you are granted adoption in the foreign courts, then you have to obtain travel documents, and then do the US Embassy paperwork to bring the child back into the US. Each of these steps has a lot of behind the scenes paperwork that a facilitator will handle for you, so you can see where the time goes.

Not all of the time needs to be spent overseas. Many people do travel back and forth or even take sightseeing trips during the waiting periods, but regardless of how you handle it or your specific case, there will be a significant chunk of time away from home.

Extended Absences from Work

A big hurdle to overcome for the working parent is time off from work. This can be accomplished several different ways, but first talk with your boss and coworkers. Is there some way to work remotely? Most places have wifi access and even though time zones are different, you can accomplish some things. I know John was able to get almost a full day's work done most days as he would stay up late to catch his staff in the office and then nap during the day. He used Skype and email to conduct business as normal. Also see if coworkers would be willing to take over some tasks that need to be done in person in exchange for others that can be done remotely.

Also, save up your vacation time. Look at all the time spent on paperwork as time you have been saving vacation to accomplish the adoption. Hopefully, you won't have to use it all, but the more you have available, the better.

But in the end if your work is not very flexible and you aren't able to work anything out, you can always take the Family Medical Leave Act. This federal law will allow time off for family issues such as adoption of a child while your benefits continue. This will guarantee your job if you have to take extended time off, but be sure to find out all the specifics about the act and what you need to do to comply with it.

Sightseeing

Especially for people going to an exotic location they have never been to, you will want to do some sightseeing and exploring of the area. This is natural and expected, but it will be more difficult than you think. First of all, remember that you aren't on vacation, you are there to adopt. I know this seems like an obvious point, but it is easy to forget when you are staring at some awesome sights that you are itching to explore.

Conversely, there will be down times when you are not doing any official business and have time to go sightseeing, but you are frustrated with a slow pace or delays in the adoption process and don't feel like it. So, the trick is to somehow manage your expectations and when the opportunity presents itself, throw yourself into being a tourist complete with taking loads of pictures and buying lots of souvenirs, and then be able to switch into business mode when it is needed.

It will be so hard to turn this on and off, but you will just have to. Take advantage of the time you have and explore what you can, understanding beforehand that it won't be nearly enough when you want and too much when you don't. Remember, this trip is not a vacation, but a life changing journey where you will come back richer and more complete with a new family member.

Different Isn't Good or Bad—Just Different

This is a hard topic to broach as it inevitably leads to misunderstandings and feelings of superiority. We as Americans, living in the richest country in the world, have excess all around us. We are traveling to an underserved area to adopt from an underserved population where there is a dearth of all of life's necessities from the basic, like food to the emotional, like love and care.

You won't have any fun or be starting off on the right foot if you adopt an attitude of superiority and disdain for the country you are in. While I am sure you are reading this thinking, "Oh I could never do that," think again. I thought I was the most amicable, easy-going, accepting person of cultural differences in the world, but when I was confronted with a dirty, smelly hole in the ground instead of a toilet in a bathroom in a government office, I had some less than kind thoughts about Ukraine. They rapidly got worse as I really had to go pee badly and was hopping around trying not to touch anything and wondering how I was going to do this in a pair of pants.

However, in every place, there will be positives that you can focus on. In our case, the people were wonderful and friendly, most of the food was delicious, and the country was beautiful. The cathedrals, parks, and city centers were wonderful and fun to look at and visit. This helped counteract the garbage, smokers, and displays of public drunkenness that were everywhere.

I quickly learned to repeat to myself, "Things are different here. Not better or worse, just different." I would repeat this over and over again and really tried to take it to heart. I found that it really worked and I was able to more easily overlook the parts I didn't like and really fall in love with Ukraine. In fact, I was just in a small European deli the other day and saw some food on the shelf that we had first gotten over there and was hit with a wave of nostalgia and longing to go back.

There is good in every place and you need to focus on that. This is so important to do as you will be taking your child from this country and the fastest way to alienate them is to speak or think negatively of their homeland. After all, this is their home and will always be a part of them. Just think of what you would feel like if someone dissed your country or birthplace.

This doesn't mean however that you need to wear rose-colored glasses and hide the parts that weren't so great. It can be a good exercise for your children to learn the good and bad about their birthplace. Americans are very used to this way of thinking, as we are quick to criticize our country, but other cultures are not this way. They are less prone to criticize. You will want to preserve your child's heritage and culture, but not at the expense of allowing them to repeat the same mistakes their fellow countrymen sometimes make, so making sure they have a realistic view of their homeland is important.

For example, we were shocked with the prevalence of drinking, even in the youth that we saw. We mentioned this to our son, but then followed it up with a discussion of how much we liked the native food. We were shocked at the small apartments and living conditions of so many of the people but made sure that he knew we loved the countryside and the parks we visited. I know this sounds juvenile, but making the effort to find the positive can make a difference when trying to connect with your new child.

They will automatically reject new and long for the familiar, even if it wasn't the best for them. All you need to do is to show them that the familiar has good and bad just like the new has good and bad. They will pick this up on their own as well, if you are open and accepting. Just recently, we were talking to our son and he said, "There is a lot of cruelty in Ukraine and not much in America." He was referring to our help for the homeless, animal shelters, etc. And he is right, there are not social fail-safe networks over there like we have in America. But on the flip side, he hasn't been exposed to some of the cruelty that exists in America. I acknowledged his statement and then told him that he was right in some respects but that we had cruelty here as well, and explained a little bit to him.

This exchange is just what you want with your adopted child: their recognition that all was not perfect in their previous world and that all is not perfect in their current world and it isn't right or wrong, just a realistic world view. They can help change that for future generations, but neither one is better, just different.

Now, I know that there are those reading this that will look at the reality and just state that the standard of living is worse over there and that America is better. While I can't argue that the opportunities for orphaned children are probably better in America, I think this is a dangerous way of thinking that can easily become negative. So, I have adopted the status of always being positive and repeating to my self the mantra that differences are just that not better or worse, just that—different.

Culture Shock

Now that I have convinced you, I hope, that differences are just that, not good or bad, let's talk about some of the differences that you need to be aware of. Of course this will vary from country to country but there are many similarities. The main one is the concept of personal space. Americans think big and they like to have room to spread out. We are comfortable talking to people at far bigger spaces between people in other cultures.

It is usual in other cultures for people to be comfortable with less space between them in just about every activity, from talking, to eating, to living. They will stand closer to you when talking, restaurants are more crowded, living spaces are tinier. If you are at all conscious of your personal space, you will be driven crazy by these tendencies. For the most part, you will just have to accept them. It would seem rude to ask people to back off in social circumstances. But in other cases, usually the facilitators that you will be working with are used to Americans and their idiosyncrasies and will be more accommodating. If for some reason they aren't, it is OK for you to gently say something if it is someone that you will be working with for a long time and will be in frequent contact with.

The next big change you will find deals with lifestyle choices, from everything like the use of cars, to the timing of meals. Americans again are different from much of the rest of the world with their use of cars. We don't think twice about the desire to go directly from point A to point B and find a parking space out front. And we expect it to be the case for just about everywhere we need to go. This is very different from the rest of the world who relies on public transportation and their own two feet. So, take comfortable shoes and expect life to be a little more difficult than what you normally are used to.

Now, the caveat to this is those agencies that hire a car and driver for you to use while you are trying to conduct official business. This was the case for us. There were days when there were so many places to go, back and forth to government offices, the orphanage, and lawyer's offices, that a car and driver were the most efficient way to get around. But that was only for official business (ok, I guess we could have paid for a driver to be at our disposal all the time, but that would have been prohibitively expensive). The rest of the time was on our own, and this got really old when toting groceries back and forth to our apartment.

Apartment? Whoa, where are the amenities of a hotel? How can I cook, shop, and fend for my family overseas where I can't speak the language?

Many times because of the length of stay or the uncertainty of timing, facilitators choose to house their clients in apartments (perhaps even those might even be using those of friends and family who would like to make some extra money). Keeping this in mind, apartments are easier in that you can cook for yourself and usually you will have laundry facilities available to you. These are key when traveling light. As for worries about shopping and so on, your facilitator will help you and if you have questions, feel free to ask. That's what they are there for.

———— ∾ ————

Another cultural difference that we noticed was the lack of people smiling in Ukraine. In my experience, Americans are the most smiley of people in casual settings with strangers. At first, I thought everyone was mad in Ukraine. We never got smiles from cashiers, waitresses, and the like, but once I realized that they don't smile at strangers, only people they know, I started a campaign of friendliness. Whenever we were checking out, I would say hello and smile at the cashier. They would always smile back when they realized I was bumbling the language in my feeble attempts to say hello and speak their language. I learned that the Ukrainians are actually a very warm and affectionate people and I learned not to take the not smiling personally.

The last point I want to point out is that mores are different in different societies. Americans are actually very prudish — maybe our Puritan roots will always show, but other cultures, especially Eastern European, are not as concerned about things like pre-marital or extra-marital sex, displaying body parts, pornography, drinking, or smoking at just about any age. There are R rated movies shown on TV without any modification. There are few or poorly enforced laws on drinking ages and no laws I could see about smoking ages. While these may be shocking to you, more or less, depending on your personal viewpoint, try not to judge the whole society by the presence of these things. This doesn't make the society illicit or more morally degraded, it just pinpoints that there are differences in viewpoints. In some aspects, you might be shocked, but understand that this is the life your children will have come from. To immediately discount and bad mouth their society will cause resentment and frustration. Instead, look upon it as an opportunity for you to learn and experience life in the way your child has experienced it. This doesn't mean you have to accept or even condone these practices in your own home, but you need to be understanding that they do exist without recriminations in other places.

You can also start to develop plans on how to counteract these influences in your own home and think on how to teach your new child your standards and viewpoints, understanding though that it is a transition and continuum and not a point of where a new child will immediately reject their previous life and accept your new worldview.

It will be difficult for you to continue with the mantra that differences are just that, not bad or good, when you see children smoking and drinking, but there are good things too that you need to look for and embrace. Think of the time you have been given overseas as a time to experience another way of life, not one that you want to adopt, or condone, but one that you will need to learn and be familiar with as you look forward to helping your new child transition to life the American way.

Food

Since I have a love affair with food and have never really met a meal I didn't like, I wanted to take a moment and discuss food. I know some of this is country dependent, so bear with me as I know some of this might not be perfectly applicable to the country you are adopting from. But I am sure much is applicable in many situations.

The first piece of advice I have to share is for you to anticipate that food and water might not always be available, whether that is because of travel, meetings with officials, or simply bad timing. So, always, always have a bottle of water and an emergency candy bar or snack with you. The Ukrainians really do not stop to eat or drink! EVER! And if you value food as much as I do, this will save your life.

We get so used to the availability of food and drink in America on every corner and every gas station, that we don't even think about it. However, food is not as readily available everywhere, and there might not be time to search it out as you are trying to accomplish other tasks. I also think that other cultures just look at it as food and drink can be consumed at home, not while they are out and about.

Secondly, a well-timed candy bar can be a present to a child or shared with a friend that you meet, and can be the ice breaker or activity that gives you an edge. When we would visit the orphanage, I can't tell you how many times I brought out a candy bar to help induce a smile on a child's face. And they have the very same Snickers bars that we have, so the taste is familiar.

Next, bring an earth bag with you. I brought a big one that folds up relatively flat that has good big handles. All the stores here charge for bags (which I wish they would do in America to help cut down on plastic bag usage) and the bags are not very good. Having your own helps a lot. Especially one that has good handles and is easy to carry as you might be walking a long distance with a heavy bag. This bag became as important to me as my purse. At first I used it only to carry food back from the market, but then I realized that anytime I went shopping, whether for food or books, I needed it. Also, when going back and forth to the orphanage, we would take food and drinks for all the kids, and needed something to carry it in. I know this sounds like a menial thing to point out, but when you are comfortable and not struggling with heavy, breaking bags, everything else seems easy!

Lastly, a word about eating food that is unfamiliar. I know that there are many of you, me included, that look askance at strange new dishes. But approach shopping and menus as an adventure. Expect that at times you will get something that you do not like and is even downright heinous, but more often than not you will be surprised and find new dishes that you love. We had a big challenge being vegetarian, but still were able to find dishes. I have even tried to duplicate some of them at home with varying levels of success. I would recommend learning the words to a few basic foods that you can eat in the native language. I would also recommend learning a few phrases relating to any foods that you can't eat or have allergies to. But otherwise, experiment and be happy with the results. You might find yourself leaving the table hungry a few times, but might be pleasantly full at others. And as strange as you might find some of the foods, just remember that you are asking a child to experience the same things, with the exception that they don't have the feeling of temporary suffering that you have; theirs will be permanent.

Many people go so far as to pack jars of peanut butter and snack bars to take overseas with them. I recommend against it. They will be heavy and if you can just muster some strength and fortitude, you will be able to find food. The few times that we were baffled as to what to eat, we would ask for some fresh foods at the market and got some bread, cheese, and fruit. It was simple, but tasted great and was pretty familiar tasting.

Also, don't forget to eat regularly and healthily. The doctor in me is coming out. There is a temptation to skip meals and rely on the stash of candy bars, but you really should avoid doing that as much as possible. While it might be unavoidable at times, you need to keep your strength up. You need to make sure that you are taking in the necessary vitamins and minerals to keep your physical health up. You don't want to risk illness, or other manifestations of physical stress while you are going through the adoption. The emotional side of adoption is so taxing that you can't allow yourself to get physically run down. It will just make the trip that much harder and leave less of you available for your new family member.

Packing

Packing is a hard subject to broach, as people have varying ways of approaching it. But I will say, universally, pack light, as light as you can and still appear nicely dressed and put together. Some people swear by packing only in carry-ons; we actually checked luggage, as we knew that that we would be traveling to other countries during our tenure in Ukraine and that we would need different clothes for those climates.

A couple of tips though that I picked up from our many overseas travels. The first is to stay away from cotton as much as you can. The main reason is that it takes so long to dry. You will likely have access to a washing machine at best or the sink at worst, but either way, there probably won't be a dryer.

We discovered that most of Europe considers a spin cycle to be the "dryer." (OK, not really.) But this does leave you with the problem of how to dry clothes, and cotton will drive you crazy. So try to take synthetic fabrics as much as possible. Not only will they dry faster when you wash them, but they will wear better with fewer wrinkles. And you will be surprised how many things are available in synthetic fabrics nowadays for both men and women.

Along those same lines, let's talk underwear. I told you we were going to talk about everything, didn't I? I bet you didn't think that your bloomers would be on the list, but they are. It is totally worth it to go to REI or another specialty store and buy their special travel underwear. They are moisture wicking, anti-microbial, and fast-drying. When we went to Ukraine, I bought three pair for each of us going, one to wear, one to wash out, and one extra just in case of a necessity. The system worked out great and was well worth the expense of the underwear in the first place.

The best way to go about packing for an extended stay with a lot of unknowns is to try to coordinate your wardrobe as best as you can. Women will find the little black dress (or a variation) invaluable. You can accessorize up or down as needed and wear it for multiple occasions. Take things that can be layered if you hit unexpectedly warm or cool weather. And as I mentioned earlier, comfortable walking shoes are a must.

It is important to be comfortable, as you will be facing difficult traveling conditions and emotional upheavals as you work through the adoption process in unfamiliar surroundings. The last thing you want is to be too cold, too hot, pinched in uncomfortable clothes, or with blisters on your feet. These are distractions that you simply don't need and really can't afford as you will possibly be facing difficult decisions such as dealing with siblings that were previously unknown, or bribery fees that deplete your bank account.

However, as important as it is to be comfortable, you must also realize that you are somewhat on parade, and will be judged at almost every step, and need to look nice and professional. Add on top of that the fact that Americans are much more informal than most of Europe and many other places as well. They don't wear sweats and jeans like we do. In a discussion with our facilitator, he mentioned that Americans tend to have more comfortable clothing and the Europeans tend to have fewer items but of higher quality. So how do you reconcile these different competing needs, fashion vs. comfort?

Well, very carefully! You will need to try to find outfits that fit both needs well and that are not in cotton. I know this sounds somewhat insurmountable, and as a mom who spends most of her time in comfy clothes, this was quite a stretch for me. But I found quickly that leggings were comfortable and could be dressed up or down as the occasion needed and were suitable most places. I also took a knit, black, pencil skirt that could be accessorized with a jacket and hose for court, or a t-shirt and tennies for sight-seeing. Overall for the five weeks we spent overseas, we ended up taking about five outfits each that could be mixed or matched together.

Try to resist the temptation to take too much. It is possible to buy what you need if you forget something. There are stores just about anywhere that can fulfill your needs, so try to bring what you think you will need and don't panic, you can always purchase something overseas if you discover a need that you didn't anticipate.

Some things are actually cheaper overseas and you might want to even stock up on these items before coming home. I know that our new son needed some clothes, as all we had for him was what we took over in a small carry-on suitcase. So, we took him out shopping and got some great designer jeans at a fraction of their cost in America. And that now brings me to the subject of buying clothes for you new child or children.

Packing for Your New Family Members

You will have to consider your child when you pack. They will not be allowed to bring anything from the orphanage unless it is a few small personal mementos. This is including even their underwear (ok, I didn't plan this, but underwear seems to be a reoccurring theme here, doesn't it?), so you will have to plan ahead. If you already have met your child, you will have some idea of what to get with sizes and such, but sometimes, you won't have this luxury. You can pack a few items, but it is best to shop for your child overseas once you have met them and know their sizes.

Since we had met our son the summer before, and knew roughly his sizes, we shopped at an outlet mall for some things before we went. We figured that if they didn't fit, we would donate them to the orphanage and buy new there. But regardless of which way you go, you will need a suitcase for them and you will need things to keep your child busy on the trip back.

Electronic devices are a universal hit, no matter what the age of the child you are adopting. Even a very small child will enjoy the games that are on a Nintendo DS or iPad. So make sure you have some sort of charging system that works and some sort of gaming device. This will save you when you are delayed in airports, waiting for papers, or any other various places you will be stuck with your child without help. Remember that for a while, you won't be able to communicate very well, so a solitary activity that distracts them could be a lifesaver for you.

You should also pack other sort of distractions. Again, if you don't know your child first, this will be more difficult, but there are other things that are usually universally appealing, such as drawing paper and pencils, cosmetics for girls, and sports equipment for boys (like a ball for throwing). Many times these items can be found overseas, so don't necessarily feel like you need to take them over, but you might want to consider it.

Extra Things to Pack

I wanted to break up the packing and traveling talk a bit with talk about how to keep yourself busy and sane through this process while you are overseas. You won't have a lot of control over your time while going through the adoption, but at least when you have time off from adoption business, you have an opportunity to be your own master and set your own agenda. In the times that you are just waiting for paperwork to be processed, appointments to be made, or evenings and weekends, you can accomplish work, sightsee, or rest, depending on what you want to do most.

During the rest of the process, there is a fair amount of time you have no idea what is going on but you just have to keep the faith. There is such a large amount of behind the scenes work being done by the facilitator and government officials that we do not know about. It takes time and effort to explain exactly what is happening and we are just an encumbrance to the process. So, just sitting back and letting everyone else work without complaining is the easiest thing to do. And another point, as hard as it is, just staying put will help streamline the process. The facilitator is kind of your babysitter over here, but he doesn't want to babysit you when there is work to do. You might think that they value independence, which up to a point they do, when it does not interfere with anyone else, but try walking off when they are looking for you or ready to move on—oh boy!

You need to be prepared for a lot of down time followed by frantic activity. For example, there were several times when we were taken to a lawyer's office by our facilitator and told to sit in the car and wait. We waited for at least 45 minutes and then he would return and fuss at us to hurry up, go in, show our passports, sign documents, and then whisk us off to a government office to do the same thing all over again. This type of thing happened day after day as we worked through the red tape of the adoption.

The best way to deal with the down time when you are just sitting and waiting places is to bring things to do during this time. Whether it is a lot of books (better yet a Kindle or Nook) or a computer—something to keep yourselves busy and productive. Don't forget to bring a deck of cards or other game that can be played when electronic devices die and can't be recharged. These will save your life and keep you entertained and busy when otherwise you would be dying of boredom.

Also, try to think of things that require very little brain power to accomplish as you will need to be able to disconnect from them fairly quickly. This trip is not the place to bring hard core work you need to catch up on as your emotions will probably get in the way of serious work. If you must bring that kind of work, try to reserve it for the apartment at night and bring something else to keep you busy when out and about during the day. It is hard to disconnect from your life for several weeks—but that is what you have to do. Things just move at a different pace and they take on less meaning when you are away.

So, don't forget to consider your mental state as well when packing. Save some room for devices or things to keep your mind happy as well as the things to make your body happy. It will be worth it in the long run. As you contemplate how to add a new family member to your existing family, you need to have ways to keep your brain occupied in a constructive but light-hearted way. I pointed out earlier that things seem to have less meaning when you are away overseas, so bringing items to work on that remind you of home or need you to be engaged in your home environment could be difficult. Bringing items that can give you a sense of accomplishment without pressure can be rewarding. When you are frustrated, homesick, or just worn out, having a piece of needlework, a favorite book, or a crossword puzzle might be just the recipe to keep you happy. If you are not big on mindless hobbies, start to consider what you might be interested in. One dad I know took up Sudoku and really enjoyed it. Another mom brought her knitting, and yet another took up drawing. There are all kinds of possibilities, so investigate and try some out before you go. You will thank me when these give you some sort of emotional retreat and sanity when you need it most.

Getting To Know Your Child Overseas

The hardest part of adopting internationally is the problem of having to get to know your child in a foreign country, usually in an orphanage, under the supervision of others. It can be a stressful experience for both you and the child. If you have met your child beforehand through a hosting program, than at least you will have some idea of what they are like, but if you chose your child from a dossier that was shown you and will be meeting them for the first time, well, you are going to have to guess what they are like. However, even if you did get to meet your child ahead of time, it was on your turf so to speak and now you will be in their country, on their home ground. Don't be surprised if they act like different children in this different setting.

So how can you get to know your children in this artificial setting? How can you judge the goodness of fit in your family when probably your whole family isn't even there? These are valid questions that need to be answered and considered, but unfortunately ones that don't have decision making rubrics that come along with them. The answers will be different for each one of you. There are some things you can do to make your time easier though and allow you to interact more freely and naturally with the child.

You will probably be given a window of time in which you are allowed to visit with your prospective child. The first time you see them—well there is nothing like that wonderful feeling. You wait (and wait) all day for that precious one to two hours to see them. You get there and if you do not know their language—you just sit there and grin like an idiot. Now the little kids are a bit easier because you can just play with them, but someone like a teenager is a little more complicated. They have to look cool, but still are trying to be on their best behavior, and there is *nothing* cool and keeping in with good behavior to do. For the parents, you want to keep the child happy, but you also feel like you are being judged by the staff as appropriate parental material! This is a no-win situation. As nerve-wracking as this time can be, it still can be fun and interactive. After all, these are the first memories you are lying down permanently with your new child. You can share pictures, play games, and listen to music together. I will cover in later chapters more detail about specific activities that you can use during these awkward times, but always remember that they are your beginning point as a new family and sometimes just peaceful, quiet, camaraderie is OK.

Bonding and Attachment

I want to cover attaching and bonding early, as these are extremely important topics with adopted children. We will cover this topic again, but for now, I just want you to start thinking about it. There are reams written about attachment disorders and problems with attaching and later on we will devote time to discussing attachment disorders and where to find resources and help.

However, at this point don't even worry about attachment disorders and try not to stress about it. Attachment and bonding will proceed at their own pace regardless of what you do about it. You need to be aware of the process, but try not to push it along too fast. And don't worry if your child feels like a stranger at first, after all, they are! They are a new person to you just as you are to them and you need to understand that. However there are a some points that I think are extremely important to make generally about attachment to children before you even really start your life with your new child.

The first is that attachment is a process, not a single point in time. There won't be a moment where all of a sudden you are attached whereas a second before you weren't. Even if the bonding occurs quickly, it is still a process. And even when you are attached and bonded with your child, there is constant refinement and fine tuning that must occur to keep the relationship healthy and well-adjusted. After all both you and your children are people and people change with time, therefore so should relationships. There will be times when you are more hands on, the relationship is more intense, and the bond feels stronger.

Conversely, there will be times when you feel there is a rift between you. But these are normal as you cement your relationship together and as your child moves through different developmental stages and you move through the phases of your life. Many people focus only on the developmental stages of children, but be sure to consider the fact that even though you are an adult and are grown, you are still changing and going through phases in your life as well. People are never static, whether they are children or adults.

I think this point, the fact that parents are also changing constantly, doesn't get enough attention. Most parenting advice is centered around consistency and sameness on your part, but there are many times when you don't feel the ability to be consistent. Your attachment and bonding back to your child will be in constant flux just as theirs will be for a while and to try to deny that will just cause problems. The best tactic is to acknowledge that you are dynamic and that environment and circumstances change constantly. It is OK for these things to change, but what you can do is stress the consistency and sameness in the love you feel for your child or the fact that you will always be there for them. These you can guarantee and feel good about while at the same time understanding the dynamic nature of trying to wrap a new family member into your existing reality.

Also, remember that the process of attachment occurs with biological children as well. This is not just a phenomenon that is limited to adopted children. The difference with biological children is that you have time and natural developmental stages to go through with them that are compressed with adopted children, especially older children.

It might seem like attachment and bonding with biological children is immediate and absolute, but this is not the case. You have all of pregnancy to get used to the idea and have moved through many of the early stages by the time you give birth. You aren't given this advantage in adoption and because of this, it feels different.

Our family is a microcosm of what can happen in the realm of attachment. We have the spectrum of timelines and experiences. Between our new son and myself, the attachment and bonding was as quick as I could ever have imagined. The bond was almost immediate, strong, and very intense. With my husband though, the bond took much longer to develop and grow. Then with Amanda and G4, there is the on again off again relationship of siblings, where the bond is tight at times and then dissipates at other times when they annoy each other.

So while you are overseas, realize that you are on the very beginning of your journey of attaching and bonding to your new child. It will feel awkward and unusual at first, but realize you are just beginning to learn about them. Spend this time getting to know them in a non-threatening way without any expectations. All too soon, they will be yours and you will have to shoulder the burden of attaching to them and caring for them together. While this is not hard, while you are overseas, and they are still in the care of an orphanage or other entity, relax a little and revel in the removal of some responsibility from your shoulders.

Secondly, to some extent the process of attaching is dependent on both the parent and the child. It can't come from all one source or the other. You can pour your heart and soul into a child, but if they aren't ready, then they will not attach to you. It is all a complex interplay between the personality of the parents, the child, their previous life, your previous life, and everyone's expectations. All of these factors intertwine together making it very difficult to predict how bonding and attachment will proceed. This is a hard realization to process as you might at times be ready for more in the relationship than the child is, and vice versa they might want more out of you than you are willing to give at times. Finding the right time when both you and your child are in sync emotionally can be hard, but treasure those times when it does happen and drop everything to maximize them. Alternatively, don't try to push the emotional attachment when you both are not in sync. It will just frustrate one or the other of you. Letting this proceed naturally and not forcing confrontation about it will work in the long run.

Recognizing those times when you both are in sync isn't hard, but you will have to be ready to take advantage of those times. You will feel like you and your child are both comfortable with each other and are comfortable with expressing emotions. These could be both good and bad emotions, but you will notice there is no withdrawing from them. You will see your child receptive to your overtures and you will feel more like making them. You will feel a degree of comfort with your child and will want to become closer.

When these times occur, don't immediately try to implement every device you have reserved for drawing them closer to you. Try one or two, maybe even just starting with eye contact as a first. Don't overwhelm yourself or them. When I started this with my new son, the first time I felt we were at a good point together was during a conversation. I wanted to say I love you as I had many times before but wanted it to be different and representative of the feeling of the moment, so this time I moved closer to him and placed one of my hands over his heart and the other over my heart as I said it. He accepted it and for the next several days every time I said I love you, I would repeat the hand gesture. After about a week or so I stopped, but now anytime I think he is hurting all I do is put my hand on his heart and he looks and me and I can see that he understands my love for him and feels supported. This might seem like a simple gesture, but even small things like this can promote bonding together.

You and your child can move closer and farther away from each other over time and in different situations. It is more of a continuum than a point in time. It is normal to feel like you have moved backwards a time or two, but this is an important part of the process as well. There could be places where your relationship wasn't as cemented as it should have been and moving backwards will allow you to revisit that place. There could also be times when your child or yourself will need more affirmation than others. So while the backwards movement is irritating, rest assured that it is part of the whole process. There is no right and wrong timeline, so no need to feel like your individual situation is flawed in some way. There is nothing farther from the truth. Your individual situation is just that, your situation, and can't be judged by anyone else's yardstick. If your process is moving slower, it could be that either you or your child is not ready for the intense emotional burden quite yet.

Thirdly, and this is the most important in my mind, is to get rid of any preconceived notions of what the relationship is going to be like. You can imagine and hope, and you might end up with something very close to that dream, but many times, the relationship you end up with is far different from what you ever could have imagined. Again, this parallels biological children; there are times when they don't turn out the way you expected. But the difference again is that you have more time to adjust to that reality as you see it developing. In adoption, the results are sometimes just plopped in your lap and you have to accept them more quickly than you might be ready to.

There will be a grieving process that you must go through to let go of the old ideas and get used to the new. Now the new reality is not always worse, and in many ways, can be better that you ever imagined. It is important that you look at it this way and count yourself lucky that these changes you never even imagined have come your way. But it does take time to accept differences. Letting go of expectations can be a difficult task and one that takes patience and time. However, look at your time overseas as a golden opportunity to be accomplishing this task of letting go of expectations. You are probably going to find yourself in situations you never could have even imagined, in countries you probably never even intended to visit, so what better place to start. You can observe your child and see how they are reacting to situations. They will feel more familiar and at ease than you are, so take advantage of that. They are comfortable with the language and customs, so they will be more at home. You can simply sit back and let their behavior flow more naturally than directing it. This early time with your child will be invaluable later when you are trying to be more directive. The more you know about them, then the more accurate your expectations will be. There will still be lots of surprises, though.

If you feel that you are harboring feelings of regret or frustration, again, don't feel guilty. This is normal as you let go of your previous life and settle into a "new normal." It might be that you want to seek a support group or other venues in which to share your feelings and listen to others, but always acknowledge these feelings. Not acknowledging them can lead to future problems. And while you work through these feelings yourself, you can focus on others aspects of your relationship with your new child so that you can still feel some positive forward momentum.

NO PANIC!

I have tried to bond with my adopted teenager, but they are reluctant and recalcitrant and I honestly am not feeling any love right now! Help me!

This is normal, expected and understandable. You are trying to love a stranger with different values, customs, and beliefs from yours. Bonding will happen but there are a lot of other steps that need to be taken first while the bonding is happening. Sometimes just stepping back and looking at the situation will help you find your balance.

What Kind of Bonder Are You and Your Adoptive Child?

There are so many different paths that bonding can take in adoption and I want to highlight several of them. While this is not exhaustive, it does cover the most common paths. Look for yourself and your child in these descriptions but don't be disappointed when you find yourself described by more than one. Just like everything else with adoption, things change with time and you will find yourself identifying with one way at one moment and another way just a few moments later.

I liken bonding to building a path to a complete family and walking on it at the same time. As you encounter different terrains (problems), you will need different materials to build with and these represent the different ways to bond. So, let's go through them one by one and help you become familiar with them. And remember, these apply to both you and your adoptive child; after all they are bonding to you at the same time you are bonding to them.

The Obsessive Bonder

Much like overprotective first time moms, obsessive bonders are just that—obsessive. They nitpick, over-analyze, and helicopter their way around the adoptive relationship. While the description is unflattering, this isn't as bad as it sounds. It actually is rooted in some excellent early advice to closely observe your child. There is no single better way to get to know your child than to observe them, and really no better way to observe them than to be in close contact at all times.

The obsessive bonder parent rarely misses important clues that your adopted child might be giving off that will lead to a greater understanding of their nature. You won't miss the fact that your child shrinks away from a certain type of interaction but welcomes another kind. You will be able to find those moments of emotional harmony because you are closely monitoring for them.

The obsessive bonder child will follow you around, rarely giving you a moment of peace. They will resist your attempts to separate and are joined at the hip to you or a particular family member. While the obsessive bonder parent will over-analyze the child, the obsessive bonder child will do the same back to the parent to the extent of their abilities.

This type of bonding has good and bad points. The good points of this type of bonding are the attention that the parent and child are paying to each other. This is a great start to bonding and early on can lead to a greater understanding of each other. This is good in the early stages of getting to know each other. Unfortunately, this can also be an exhaustive type of bonding that will easily become overwhelming. Too much can be counterproductive as you won't understand everything about the other person and might become frustrated. This is especially true when you might rub up against cultural and language differences that aren't understood.

If both you and your child are in the obsessive bonding phase at the same time, it can be a great time together with a lot of sharing and growing closer. However, when one is obsessive and the other isn't, it can become a hilarious but trying cat and mouse game with a pursuer and an escapee. This can be difficult as the child who is obsessive will wonder why the parent isn't engaging with them, and the parent that is obsessive will be concerned their child doesn't love them.

In these instances, it's important to understand the dynamics of what is exactly going on and try to meet the needs of the child. If you are finding yourself obsessive and your child is receptive to your attentions, great. But if they aren't, you will have to back off as much as you can and find other outlets for your obsessive bonding. Maybe doing it from afar and contenting yourself with watching them interact with friends, or such, will help satisfy you while giving them their freedom. You will need to figure out how to meet the needs of both you and your child, but just understanding the obsessive nature will help you from freaking out when you try to take two minutes to go to the bathroom alone and they are knocking at the door wondering where you are. Also, it will help you when your child is freaking out under your attentions but you aren't in a position to let up on them.

The Fake it Until You Feel It Bonder

This is a very common phase to be in, especially for a long while after the initial honeymoon period. Although it's equally common in kids and parent's, parents are more likely to admit to it. Often times, parents will find themselves in possession of a teenager that maybe is recalcitrant, snotty, poorly communicative, or really any other common adjective that you can throw at teenagers, and really won't feel love toward them.

It is hard to feel love and attachment towards a person that pushes you away, but as a parent, you need to show it. So the old fake it til you feel it comes in here. As you get to know your new family member and get to understand their moods, needs, and motivations, you will naturally become closer to them. However, this will take time, and before you ultimately make peace with the person they are, you will need to supplement along the way, thus the faking.

This is also a great coping mechanism that can be explained to teens to help them in their bonding journey. If you are worried that your child isn't bonding, you can confront them. Understand that this won't be the type of clear and introspective conversation you might want to have. You have to take into account maturity, language and communication problems. But it can be a powerful tool. Explaining to your teen that it can be hard to bond with a new family and voicing your understanding of their difficulties will be a great start to true bonding. Especially if your adopted child had some family left to them, it can be hard for them to bond with you without feeling like they are abandoning the others.

When you give your child the option of fake it til you feel it, you will be showing them that it is OK not to feel love right away. It takes the burden off of their shoulders and gives them permission to not feel anything right away or over a period of time. It also however shows them how they are supposed to act. This can in itself be a powerful tool as sometimes these children have not been properly socialized into a loving family relationship and might not even know what a bonded parent-child pair acts like. There is nothing like practice makes perfect.

For the parent, there is very little down side with this strategy as long as your child does not find out. They need to be convinced of your love and devotion. Same goes for your teen, this is great strategy but at some point needs to be moved beyond to true bonding.

The ultimate test of this strategy is that some day you will look at each other and realize that there is no more faking it — real love and bonding have replaced the faking and you are a true bonded pair.

The Anxious Bonder

This type of bonder is based upon the anxiety of losing a new found parent or child. This is very common as well at certain stages in the process of assimilating a new family member. When a child who has been longing for a family finally finds one, they can be so scared that it won't last. This will bring on anxiety and concerns that will manifest itself in certain behaviors. Much like the obsessive bonders, the anxious bonder will want to be close to their child or parent at all times.

Unlike the obsessive bonder though who is more observant, the anxious bonder is more concerned with some harm befalling the object of their attention. The parent will be insisting on excessive safety precautions, not allowing freedoms because of perceived dangers, and even inventing wildly fantastic scenarios to have their children avoid certain situations in which they feel a lack of control.

The anxious bonder child will be concerned about any separation from the parent. They will express concerns when a parent is late to an arranged appointment that they were murdered, in a car accident, or a victim of a crime. They will check door locks in the house, worry about wrong numbers, and insist that safety precautions be followed at all times. In public places, they will come back and forth to check on the parent and make sure they are OK.

In parents, being an anxious bonder is understandable as you have been wanting and hoping for a child, and finally you have them. You want to make sure that nothing happens to them and no harm befalls them. This is especially helpful when you don't know your child yet and are not comfortable with their abilities or limits. It pays to be ready and watchful when at playgrounds, swimming pools, beaches, and other places where you don't have a wealth of experience with your new child's capabilities. This however, can be detrimental once you are confident of your child's abilities. This can lead to exhaustion on your part and an inability to be objective.

For a child, being an anxious bonder can be a safety mechanism to help them adjust and feel safe in a new environment. This however can quickly become detrimental to the child as they can be consumed with worry. They can feel like they have to be caretakers, patrolling the house and ensuring the safety of the family. They will take too much responsibility on their shoulders and become exhausted and worn out.

The Slow and Steady Bonder

This is the ideal type of bonder to be in the long run, but hard in the beginning. These other types of bonding I have discussed above will help fill the void, before the slow and steady bonding sinks in.

This follows the normal process of bonding that occurs biologically, as it is a slow and steady process that starts in pregnancy and really never ends. Of course, in adoptions, there is not the time for the process to take place in this way, but the course starting from nothing and continuing up is the same. This mimics the course of learning about your child and them learning about you, becoming comfortable with each other, and finally internalizing each other into each other's respective hearts.

This process though can be the slowest on earth to you as you are anxiously awaiting a fully integrated family. But patience here is a virtue. Pushing bonding with a child will likely push them further away. This type of bonder is one that you probably will only notice years later as you look back on the process of adoption.

A Final Word on Bonding

In adoption, the attachment and bonding process can be exhausting and intense, as it feels like life is happening in fast forward. There is not the natural and organic process that has time to develop in biological children. There will be high highs and low lows, but the ride is unforgettable. But wait, what if you truly feel there is no bonding at all happening? What if you are resisting it or you have a resisting child?

Try first to figure out why you are feeling this way. Ask others for their input of what they see going on. It could be again that the problem of expectations. You might have set expectations about what bonding would have been like with your child and it isn't living up to your expectations. It could be language problems. It could be something simple or it could be a sign of something more serious like a reactive attachment disorder. But for now, put your worries behind you and learn more about your child and yourself. Explore your relationship first, and if you still are having troubles, then look at the last chapter of this book, but I want to invite you to not worry too much in the beginning.

Treasure all of the moments together with your new child as they are the beginning of making memories and building a new life together. Ultimately the journey of bonding and attaching to your new child is a journey that you will take together, leading to new places of emotional depth and love.

Let's Talk

The excitement of adopting will rapidly be replaced with reality—especially if it is an international adoption. There are many barriers between you and your new family member, but let's start with the biggest one, language.

As you picked up in the early blog entries, I was consumed by the need to learn Russian. I wanted there to be as few barriers to communication as there possibly could be. I knew that teenagers were dicey on communicating anyway, but that the language barrier would give Alex a great reason not to talk to me. So I tried several different methods, including textbooks and Rosetta Stone, and basically came away from it with a sense of failure. I am not a linguistically talented person and wasn't able to master more than a little vocabulary and a few simple sentences.

So I turned my attention to teaching our new son English. I did a lot of research on language acquisition and ESL materials and found that there is some controversy surrounding ESL in public education. ESL in public schools has been simplified and downsized so that now, there is just one ESL track in schools and all children that are non-native speakers are lumped into it together, regardless of their situations. The problem is that there is a wide divergence in the home environment of these children.

When children are living with an immigrant family, they are exposed to their native language at home and therefore need the conversational instruction at school. When you have children that are being exposed to solely English at home, like most international adoptees, they will excel in their conversational status, so much so that they will be indistinguishable from other children within a year or so, but their academic language will not be so lucky. Their ESL instruction will stop after conversational fluency has been reached, accounting for the major discrepancy that is seen in many cases of academic performance.

So, back to the original issue, how to teach your child English in a way that is engaging and quick so that you can focus on other aspects of their life with you? There are a number of considerations, so we will break them down and cover them one by one.

Previous Educational Experience
It's important to take into account the mastery that exists in the native language before you even consider the teaching of a new language. Children that have a good mastery and solid foundation in their native language will have a much easier time learning a new language. If their native language skills are shaky, then they don't have a solid foundation with which to build upon with a new language. The process of decoding language and learning to be an effective communicator is basically the same in any language.

I recently attended a talk at a convention by Andrew Pudewa, the creator of the Institute for Excellence in Education. He made some very compelling and interesting points about teaching language arts. Language arts is a catch-all phrase to encompass both spoken and written communication skills. If you ask a teacher what are the fundamental parts of language arts are the answers would be something like phonics, spelling, grammar, etc. However, there are more fundamental parts to language arts that need to be considered. The first is listening, then speaking, then reading, then writing. And if you really sit back to consider this, you will see how true this is.

Children first listen to others and their language patterns before they start to mimic them and speak back. The same goes for writing, you have to be able to read first to bring in information before you can mimic it and spit it back out. And this applies to any language, not just English.

So, if your child had adequate chance to listen to adults and others as a child and learn how to speak properly, then have educational instruction on how to read so that they could learn to write, you will just mimic these steps in English. But, if you discover that your child is lacking in their native language, then you will have to accept the fact that the

English acquisition will be slower and more cumbersome. You will have to adjust the pace of instruction and cover many basics of language, like parts of speech and grammar, along with the language study to make a complete curriculum.

If your child has even had some instruction in English, be thankful as your job will be that much easier. But don't ignore the basics either. Later, I will lay out a plan for helping adoptees get started with their acquisition of English that will be adaptable for both children that already have language mastery and for those that are more of a blank slate.

How Not to Lose Native Language

Another phenomenon that occurs widely in adoptive families is that the acquisition of English will become replacement instead of additive on top of the kid's native language, as they have no one reinforcing their native tongue at home. Children from immigrant families will be able to keep their native language as they have someone to help them and practice on. This is an important point as additive learning helps to expand the brain and make new neural connections. Replacement simply overwrites old material with new and doesn't stimulate the brain.

I know that there are many families who want to limit their new child's exposure to their native language in the beginning to help force the acquisition of English, but I don't feel this is the right way to proceed, for several reasons. The first is that it will create a time where the child has no adequate way to express themselves, when their grasp on the new language is too tenuous. This will cause them to retreat within and will set up a pattern of behavior that will become engrained and will be hard to break later even when the English language skills are proficient. Secondly, it can breed resentment as the child will think you are rejecting them. It is hard for even a teenager to separate things in their mind, and a rejection of their language will be interpreted as an overall rejection of the person.

The building of the relationship between you and your adopted child will be so important, and there is no need to litter the path with obstacles. It is worth a slight delay as things settle down and the language skills develop to tolerate a bit of time where you allow your child to express themselves with you and others in their native language. It will help feelings and ease the transition. Encourage them to talk in the beginning in their native language. They can express ideas and you can pick up a lot with tome of voice and body language. Even if you don't understand what they are saying sometimes letting them get it out and then a hug afterwards is worth more than total comprehension.

Therefore it is preferable to strive for a nice mix of the two languages. This can be a hard balance to achieve, but it can be done. A mix allows for the acquisition to be additive and not replacing the native language. It might mean that English might come along a little more slowly, but that will allow the child to keep as much as possible of their native language, while acquiring their new language.

Now in the case of smaller children, it might not always be possible to keep their native language. They just simply might not be good enough in their native tongue yet to hold on to it. However, in this case, you have the luxury of time that older adoptees don't have, so the language issue won't be as important.

As far as keeping their native language skills good, you will have to search out other people that speak that same language, and hopefully other children that do. The internet is a great source and many times libraries have movies, audiobooks, and books in foreign languages. This will help with the retention of grammatical skills as well.

I also feel that keeping native language skills are important for future employability and schooling. Being bilingual is a prized skill in certain job markets and can lead to opportunities and experiences that are not available to others.

How to Teach English

I don't profess to be an expert in teaching language, but there are some tips and tricks I have picked up that will start the process off. The first one is to start teaching English yourself to your new child. It is a great bonding experience and can provide for many shared moments and memories. I know that many families have a lot of trepidation about teaching English and want to hire a tutor or get the kids in school right away, but I really think it is important to resist the temptation in the beginning.

In the very beginning, making it fun and engaging is the best way to go. If you force English, it will feel onerous and difficult. If you allow it to develop naturally, then it will happen almost effortlessly. Your child will want to communicate with you as much as you want to communicate with them so you have a natural impetus built in. Play upon this and teach words that they really want to know first before you worry too much about parts of speech and an academic vocabulary.

Learning as much of the child's native language as you can is helpful. Then you will be in the position to give them the native word and then the English word for something, to help the process along a little. This will provide endless opportunities for giggles and laughs as you mangle the words in trying to pronounce them, but it will be that start of the bonding process. You will be sharing an experience with the child that no one else has been able to, even if they have had some English instruction in school. This will be unique to you and will be the start, however small, of the process of becoming a family.

I also think that by learning at least some of their language and asking for their help, the children will appreciate your willingness to embrace their life and culture. You will be showing them that adoption is not a one way street and that they are an important part of it as well. This can be empowering for children who have never felt wanted or needed. By giving them a place and a job, you will earn their respect and allegiance even if in just a tiny way. You will have started the path to rebuilding their sense of self-esteem and self-worth that has probably been badly compromised by life's circumstances. You will find yourself learning as much from the child as they learn from you. This give and take over language is one of the best ways to promote bonding early on when you don't share many other things in common.

Teaching Listening

As I outlined earlier, listening is the first step in language acquisition. You need to speak constantly to your child. For the most part, whenever they are around you, there needs to be constant narrative of what you are doing and what they are doing. Repetition is important; even if it bores you, it will give them a chance to adjust their ears to the lyrical quality of English and begin to decode subtle differences in the language. Even if your child is not paying attention to you, talk anyway. The unconscious brain will still be processing language in the background.

When you are not available, there is nothing wrong with the TV, audiobooks, radio, really any source of language that you can find. Obviously, the better quality, the better for the child, but in the early stages, this is not as important. Also, having a variety of speakers will help the child learn with different accents and intonations.

However, I want to give a cautionary note to my enthusiasm here. You need to give your child some time every day where they get a break from language. They need some quiet time to process what they have taken in and mentally chill out. The constant exposure to a language they don't understand is exhausting and mentally taxing. So, also make sure you have some quiet time where your child is not expected to listen or communicate back. However, the tendency with this is to then leave the child alone while you get tasks done or take time for yourself, and unfortunately, as nice as this sounds, it is not in the child's best interest either. Many times in the middle of the processing time, they will experience a leap forward with language and understanding and want to share it, and if you are not there, you could miss a bonding moment. So, even just giving them a toy or puzzle or some other activity, and you sitting down near them and reading or doing computer work, or any other quiet activity can accomplish this goal. You should probably strive for a couple of hours of processing time every day where you are near but not communicating with them.

Teaching Speaking

The next step in the process of language acquisition is speaking. Now all of these are not separate entities and you don't finish one and then start another. They will all be happening at once; you will not stop talking to your child when you expect them to start speaking back, but you will see that the main focus of your time will be on different things.

The most important part of speaking, however, is not to criticize or correct your child's diction unless they ask. Any correction, even a small one, can shut down expression in children, and this can hamper the language acquisition process. Sometimes you can get away with it, but some children are more sensitive than others and even pretty tough kids can have sensitive times, so it is best to just stay away from that practice.

They will make mistakes in pronunciation, word usage, and grammatical context and it is OK. Let them talk away and for the most part just listen. If you don't understand something, ask for clarification, but only if it doesn't interrupt the flow of conversation.

Now I know that some of you are rolling your eyes and saying, "But we have *teenagers*. They never talk, at least to me." and while that is true for some, not all. There are some kids that are just more naturally talkative than others. If yours is a talkative one, rejoice and be happy. If not, then there are some tricks you can use to get them talking, but the most important thing to remember is that you need to listen to them when they talk. This is my cardinal rule of parenting a teenager, just listen to them when they talk and don't talk back. Even if they say something that you need to address, save it for another time: you are interested in them talking for the primary reason of practicing English, and also for shared time together.

NO PANIC!

My teen seems to only want to talk when I am tired, l or am otherwise engaged. Help!

This is probably when they need you most, when you have withdrawn from them because you are busy, tired, etc. Children can sense when you are not engaged one hundred percent with them and they want to remediate that and bring you back to focus on them, especially emotionally needy children. As best you can, swallow your irritation and tiredness and go with the flow. They need you and you will be paid back in spades by being patient and listening to them. You will gain knowledge and insight into their character and a bonding moment.

So, how to draw out a teenager? The easiest way is to give them a time of day when they have to talk. If you homeschool, this is very easy as you can incorporate it into your daily lessons. There could be poetry memorization, narration of a lesson just done, verbal exercises, really the list of things you can do is infinite. If you send your child to a traditional brick and mortar school, then you won't have as much control, but you could still ask for an accounting of their day and don't accept them saying "fine."

There are other more subtle ways to encourage speaking as well. You can give your child messages to go tell other family members. You can ask them to dictate a list of things you need to buy at the supermarket, or even ask their siblings to offer help with asking them questions that require more than a simple yes/no answer.

In fact, no question should have a yes/no answer, and don't let them get away with it. They will hem and haw and do just about anything but you can just smile right back and not react until you get a full answer.

Once they realize that you aren't going to critique their every word, children will usually loosen up. There will be some personality types that are more reticent than others but overall, patience and time should cure just about everyone.

Teaching Reading and Writing

I don't want to digress from the topic of adoption and make this into a how-to guide for ESL instruction, but there are a couple of tips and tricks that I picked up along the way and saw used with other international adoptees with success that I would like to pass on.

The steps of reading and writing are going to be dependent on a number of factors, including the previous fluency of your child and educational level in their native language. Because this is so variable, it is hard to generalize, and you might feel bewildered with where to start.

For starters, think back to the previous time with your child and assess how well they did with their listening and speaking skills. Then asses their overall maturity and developmental level. Once you have done this, you can back off a little bit and figure out where to start.

Honestly, there is no harm in starting at a lower level than what you think your child can handle as having some easy lessons will boost their self-confidence and give them an easy win. However, this must be balanced with the ego of your child when they realize that they are working at a level far below their age level.

For a beginner learner, just learning the English alphabet, the series *Explode the Code* is wonderful. It combines short, easily understandable phonics lessons, either online or in workbooks, with reinforcement and reading comprehension at the same time. It is comprised of eight levels with no correlation, between level and age, freeing your child of worrying about which level they "should" be in.

For students that already have mid-level mastery and know the alphabet and sound out words, there is a wonderful website called www.englishforeveryone.org, that has worksheets and other activities for English learners. It is pretty comprehensive and is divided into levels, not grades, so there is no embarrassment.

For those of you that send your children to school, the way in which they are taught will be dictated for you, but you can still supplement at home. I do however want to raise a hand in caution here. It is tempting to push children along fast. It makes everyone's life easier when you can communicate so it is hard not to want full fluency fast. But, there is a lot that these kids are processing and it takes time. Rushing the natural process along can lead to gaps and frustrations that you don't need to add on top of your already full plate.

The best way to proceed is pretty much the same way you have done everything else: do your homework, be prepared, and then have patience and flexibility as things play out in a natural and organic fashion. In the next set of letters you can see first-hand how John and I dealt with the language barrier and navigated our way around the issues that presented themselves.

PART FOUR:

WORLDS COLLIDE

27: Day 1 — Kiev

Dearest Dema,

Well, we are finally here. The flight was pretty good actually. I had been dreading it after the last trip we made to Ukraine, but this went relatively easy. Our last trip was about six years ago to visit Alex's family (our former exchange student). We spent three weeks with him and his family, but found it to be a hard trip. We didn't know the language at all and were at the mercy of another family. While they were the nicest people, it was a whirlwind of sightseeing complemented by Amanda and myself catching the flu. I had enjoyed the previous trip overall, but I was apprehensive about going back.

We left Utah in the middle of a snowstorm and flew to Detroit. From there it was only an hour layover to get on the flight to Amsterdam. We gave Amanda the one first class seat we had and boy did she have fun. She was well fed and enjoyed at least four hours sleep in the comfy chairs. John and I did not fare so well — we really didn't sleep at all. We were lucky to have booked two aisle seats without anyone in the middle — so we were able to stretch out — but I guess excitement and nerves prevented me from sleeping and he was complaining he was hot.

Anyway, we made all our connections easily. The only problem was the smell of B.O. on the last connection from Amsterdam to Kiev. I forgot how much Americans are phobic about smells and how much the rest of the world doesn't seem to care.

The plane to Kiev landed right on time and we filed out of the plane, down the stairs and took a bus to the terminal. We got in the non-visa line, which was the slowest moving line of all, and slowly inched our way closer to Ukrainian soil. When we got up to the passport control officer, he asked us what the purpose of our visit was. We were told not to give the answer of adoption since many people were not favorable towards international adoption, so we answered, "To visit a friend — Sasha." who was actually the Ukrainian facilitator. He wanted to know where, so thankfully I had the email that our American facilitator sent to me of Sasha's address pulled up and ready to show on my phone. He actually copied it down! We were then ushered through without any problems and then went to get our bags.

After we got the bags, we went to a little kiosk in the middle of baggage claim that had customs declarations forms on it. One side had English forms and we were preparing to fill them out declaring our cash and so on when an airport employee came over and asked us why we were filling them out. (It was odd that we were the only ones!) He told us that unless we were each carrying over the equivalent of 10,000 euros in cash (I think around $13,000 USD) that we did not have to fill them out. Since we were only carrying the equivalent of $8,000 each—we skipped the forms. The rest of the money for the adoption we had paid stateside, but the whole amount to be paid to the Ukrainian team had to be taken in cash. We took the bags over to an X-ray machine where they were x-rayed (without anyone actually looking to see what was in them) and then waltzed right out of there. Easiest customs I have ever gone through!

When we went out of the customs area, we saw immediately two men holding a sign with our name on it. One of them introduced himself as Sasha and the other was Sergei our driver. Sasha was our facilitator in Ukraine, who was there to guide us through the entire process from landing to taking off. He will accompany us to all official appointments and help us with all the paperwork. He would also be present in court where we would officially petition for you to be adopted by us. So I was very anxious to meet him and make sure we got along; after all, we would be relying on him a lot and spending a lot of time with him.

He seemed very nice and personable and understanding that we were tired and cranky from a long trip. I breathed a sigh of relief. They helped us with our bags and into a van and soon we were driving away from the airport. I remembered from our last trip that the drive from the airport into the city was depressing. It seems that it takes you through the worst areas of town! But after fighting traffic for forty-five minutes, we were driven around the city to a nice suburb where Sasha lives. We did some grocery shopping and exchanged money and were off again, this time to the apartment.

All of our accommodations were arranged by our facilitator in Ukraine. This was very nice as we didn't have to worry about it at all. For the most part, they try to put families up in apartments so that you have a little more home-like experience with washers, cooking facilities, and a little more space. This does make the travel a little easier as you don't have to worry about laundry and such on a long trip.

Another thing I had forgotten was how small the apartments are! This two bedroom apartment is smaller than a good sized hotel room, but that is just the way things are done here. I have gotten too used to spreading out more and more in my big American home. However, sometimes things can be too small! When we come back to Kiev with you, Dema, we will have to look for someplace bigger—I honestly don't think four of us would fit in here together.

But all in all, it is nice to be back in Ukraine again. We are so anxious to see you Dema—hopefully Wednesday will be the magic day! I've got to go now before I fall off my seat in tiredness.

Can't wait!!!
Bethany

28: Reflections in the dawn

So, it is 6:45 on Easter morning. I am awake now, all messed up on time zones. Amanda was up in the middle of the night for a couple of hours but was able to get back asleep. I see the wisdom of arriving a few days early to get acclimated to the times.

But as I sit here in this tiny apartment, I can't help but wonder exactly what we are doing. At home, everything seemed very clear. We fell in love with you, Dema, and wanted you to join our family. Our kids approved, our family approved, everything was easy — but now over in Ukraine — everything is not so clear. There is such a different way of life here and it seems so hard to wrap my head around it. And I have even traveled here before! If there is one thing that I hate, it is being out of my element — pushing the envelope so to speak. I am a little control freaky and not feeling in control of my own destiny is hard. But what are we expecting out of you? That same thing in spades. This is only a trip for us but for you it will be a lifetime. And you are younger and more alone. You will have our support, but for a while I am sure that you will not feel it, even though I assure you it will be there. I know you are strong and smart, but I hope you will come through this OK. You will be such a blessing to our family and I only hope that we will be able to be the same for you.

But on the other hand some things never change no matter where you are. I have already done three loads of laundry. It seems that laundry followed me halfway around the world!

I know that your Easter isn't until next week — but Happy Easter early!

Hugs and kisses,
Bethany

29: Day 2 — Kiev

Dearest Dema,

We had one fantastic day despite the yucky weather. It started raining about two pm here and hasn't stopped. Thank goodness John had me pack some travel umbrellas. It was a smart move.

We started out the day pretty slowly, still a little jet lagged from our plane trip. Sasha came over with the accountant at eleven o'clock and we got to hand over the money. The most money I have ever seen in one place before! But it was nice to get that off our shoulders. Then Sergei, our driver, arrived and took us downtown to the Kiev Opera House. I know that opera is probably not your thing, but this is what we like to do when we go somewhere new, experience the best of the area has to offer. The Kiev Opera House is world famous and highly recommended, so we thought we would take in an opera tonight if we could. We managed to get seats on the third row for only about fifty dollars total. What a steal.

We then decided to do some other sightseeing and went to a large WWII statue and museum. The statue was cool—huge in fact. There was an observation deck part way up that we went to and got some pretty pictures. I am not sure how much of Kiev you have been able to see, but once we get you, I would like to show you some things you haven't had a chance to see.

Then we went to the WWII museum which is underneath the statue and learned a lot. We had no idea that Ukraine was occupied during WWII and had death camps in it. We were reading an English flyer posted by one of the exhibits and found the following sentence very funny: "It is worthwhile noting that while the majority of the Great Patriotic War was fought on the Eastern Front, there were some small contributions by the English and Americans on the Western Front." Of course the same bias exists on our end—I never even learned about the Russian involvement other that they met us in Berlin pressing in from the east. I got a little frustrated with historians—why does it always have to be so biased? It is important to learn the facts and make your own conclusions, and history really doesn't change depending on where you learn it! But practically, I guess it does. I feel that it is important to get all the facts for you and all the history and culture that I can since I feel you needs both sides.

Anyway, back to our day. After the museum, we walked up the hill to an authentic if touristy Ukranian restaurant. We are somewhat hampered by eating since we are all vegetarian. We gave up veganism for the trip—no way we could exist without eggs and cheese! But still no meat or fish. So we ended up with vireniky with cheese, stuffed cabbage rolls, wild rice pilaf, and borscht. It was delicious—but expensive. We then walked around a little waiting for our driver. Once he came, we asked him to take us to a market to get some bottled water and a few other essentials. We are now feeling very at home in the supermarkets over here!

Then off to the the opera house. We got there early but it was OK. It turned out to be a three-and-a-half-hour spectacular opera—Don Carlos. The inside of the opera house was beautiful. We really enjoyed it. The costuming and sets were wonderful and of course the voices—world class. But it did last a long time and we are tired now!

We are so excited about the SDA (State Department of Adoptions) appointment tomorrow. It will feel nice to get the ball rolling over here. It does seem ridiculous that we are here in Ukraine, but still so far from seeing you. We can't go to the orphanage yet until we get official permission from the SDA and that is what we hope to get tomorrow. We are going to get to see Alex, our old exchange student tomorrow—we can't wait to see him either. So I better get to bed—big day tomorrow.

Love and kisses,
Bethany

30: Day 3 — Kiev — rain, rain, go away

Dearest Dema,

Great day today — again despite the weather. The rain ushered in a fantastically yucky cold front. It was windy and rainy today with some mist. The wind is wicked here!

It has been a great day on a number of fronts but first let's start with adoption news.

We started out this morning by going to the SDA for our appointment — it went great and we will go back tomorrow for our referral letter. It was very quick and professional. They asked John and myself a few questions about ourselves like how long we'd been married and how we met you. I was nervous at first but quickly realized that it was just a formality. We did discover that you have a half-sister (same father, different mother), and we will make sure that we enable you to keep in touch. We were surprised to find this out but will hopefully get more information at the orphanage. I was thinking we could visit her but Sasha recommended against it, saying that we don't want to do anything that could jeopardize the adoption. As he pointed out, you might not even know her, or there might not even be a substantive relationship. He recommended that after everything is done that we can contact her. Sasha was great as usual, helping us out through every step of the morning.

We will be going back to the SDA for our referral letter tomorrow and then will be taking a train to Mariupol overnight. We will hopefully be able to see you Wednesday — we can't wait to see you. We did get to see a picture of you that was in your file — you looked so small! It made me so anxious to get to see you and hold you again! (I know, just what a fourteen-year-old boy does not want to hear!).

Now on to the next part of the good news — we saw Alex today! He got back in town from his flight to Vietnam this morning. So after he dropped his stuff off at his apartment, he came and met us for lunch. We had a great time visiting and talking (and a great lunch too!) He came back to the apartment with us and visited for a couple more hours, but he had been on the flight for eleven hours, so he was tired. We said goodbye with promises to meet again tomorrow. It was so wonderful seeing him—it has been too long—three years since we last saw him. He just fell back in with the family without any trouble!

I have just been spending some time repacking our suitcases—it seems everything has gotten messy and disorganized in the space of just a few days. I am also doing more laundry so we can leave for Mariupol with all clean things. I am going to go cook some dinner in a little while. I was trying to finish up everything in the fridge we bought at the market before we go tomorrow but I think I was a little too good at doing it—we might have not much to eat for breakfast tomorrow! By the way—the food here is fantastic! You can just look at us and know that we know and love food! But truly, we have had some great food—and we are pretty picky being vegetarian. I made sure I knew a few key phrases to use at restaurants and it has been pretty easy to find good food at reasonable prices.

Anyway, I better go and finish preparing for leaving tomorrow! Time is just flying by here—already Day 3 and it seems like we just got here.

Sending love your way!
Bethany

31: Day 4 — Kiev to Donetsk

Dearest Dema,

We are going to see you tomorrow! YEAH!!!! We are so excited. Everyone has recommended that we do not act as if we know you when we first see you as Ukraine does not allow pre-selected adoptions to take place, so we are going to just have to stifle our excitement. I don't quite understand how this works, as there is a letter in the file stating that we met you when you came to America, but that is just one of the many inconsistent things you will find here. So we will have to be a little stoic. Don't think that it is for a lack of love — if it was up to us we would rush across the room and squeeze you until you couldn't breathe!

In most cases, when families go to adopt in Ukraine, they are shown a dossier filled with pictures of children that are available to adopt. They have to select one, and then are given permission to travel to that orphanage to meet with the child. After a few days, they have to make the decision as to whether this is the child for them. If so, the adoption can proceed, if not, the family has to return to the state department of adoptions and request another appointment and then look at the dossier of children's pictures again.

I would think that process would be very difficult, and I felt so fortunate that we had the chance to meet you before looking at your file in the State Department of Adoptions office. There was no way that the full depth of your personality could be portrayed through a little file that seemed to have far too few documents in it to accurately portray who you are. However, on with the story.

Today has been another great day. We had a quiet morning doing school work with Amanda and John getting some work done. Poor Amanda slept in late because her online physics class was at 3:15 in the morning because of time zone troubles. I had to get her up and stay up with her for a while to make sure she wouldn't fall back asleep, but she got through class OK and was able to go back to sleep.

We were picked up around three thirty and were taken back to the SDA for our letter of referral, which is basically permission to visit your orphanage and meet you. There were several other families there unlike the day before when we had our appointment. Quite an international assortment, with one family from Spain, one from Italy, and two from America. The process went quite quickly; we just had to sign our names and then we got the letter. It was here we really realized how good our facilitator was — he was the only one greeted by name and was obviously respected by the SDA staff.

After getting the referral letter, we then went to a cellular store to get a wifi card. We really need internet access for both my and John's work and Amanda's school work. It was a lengthy process and quite expensive. We had to spend $150 for the wifi card, but it only costs about a dollar per day to use for unlimited data. We didn't have time to set up the card or worry about installing drivers, so let's cross our fingers that it works.

We have skyped G4 at home several times and he seems to be doing well. He says he misses us but I think that is only lip service! He is managing so well—I am really proud of him for being on his own. We got the cellular phone unlocked for international calls so John and I were able to call home and talk to our moms. It was nice to hear their voices — my mom is flying in to help G4 out next week.

Anyway, we then went to the train station to go to Donetsk. We wanted to take the train directly to Mariupol, but it left earlier in the day and therefore we had to take the train to Donetsk and then get a driver to Mariupol. It was five o'clock so we went to a nearby restaurant to get dinner. Our facilitator tried to take us to McDonald's—yuck! I told him they need to ban them from Ukraine (and the rest of the world for that matter). The food here is so good — there is no need to resort to pink slime filled processed burgers! But there is nothing there we can eat anyway. So we talked him into going to another restaurant and had wonderful vireniky filled with potatoes and cheese. Even he had to admit that it was better than McDonald's.

I do feel bad about G4 though! We are living a scene out of a dream for him on this train! The train has been a great experience. It is something right out of an Agatha Christie book—I feel like any moment there will be a bell announcing dinner in the dining compartment. I feel this urge to dress up and go the lounge. Of course there is no such thing—but we have two first class compartments right next to each other — one for

Amanda and myself and one for the facilitator and John. There is a cute little table and two bunks and the restroom is at the end of the hall.

It was cute and very cool for about fifteen minutes! Then reality set in. The biggest problem I have encountered so far has been that it is very stuffy in the compartment and very hot. There does not seem to be any mechanism for air flow or a/c. I feel sorry for families that travel this way in the summertime. Maybe there is air and it was turned off because it is still cold out. The second issue was the swaying back and forth and the jerking along over uneven tracks. It was noisy and uncomfortable, and by the way, did I mention I felt a little like a roasted chicken in the oven? So, it is worth looking at flying back and forth. I know John stated emphatically that we would be flying exclusively back and forth from now on!

So, we are going to go to bed now—don't know how good we will sleep with the train moving back and forth. But we will try because we want to be well rested to see you tomorrow!

Counting the hours,
Bethany

32: Day 5 — Donetsk to Mariupol

Dearest Dema,

Ok, we have concluded that train travel is not all that it is advertised — I think combined we three got one hour of sleep. It was way hot and stuffy and for some reason the moment my body knew that there was not a private bath readily available, it decided I needed to remove all available fluid on a very regular basis. So I was running up and down the corridor all night to the bathroom.

So after an *awful* night, we cleaned ourselves up as best we could without a shower in time for the train to arrive at seven am. We were met by two cars and drivers because there were more than two of us and lots of luggage, two big suitcases, three computer bags, three carry-ons, and purses, camera bags, etc. (We tried to pack light — we really did — but to no avail — however so far I can conclude that I have packed just right — nothing yet seems superfluous.) We then drove to Mariupol but thankfully stopped for some breakfast — ok a snack really at a minimarket in a gas station — but at least it was something to eat and drink.

We arrived in Mariupol and waited in the car outside a government building while our coordinator received a letter of referral from the local authorities. This took a little while so we all took the chance to grab a few Z's in the car. Once we got the letter, we were off to the orphanage. When we pulled up, I was struck by such fear and doubt — here we are crumpled, smelly without a shower, tired, and certainly not at our best. And I was paralyzed with the thought that maybe you (Dema) wouldn't want us or maybe you wanted some other family! What if you just thought it was a fun visit and that was that? Ack. I realized that I was so full of doubts. You never really said yes to us that you wanted to be adopted. We had had very little communication with you once you left and now, here we were, trying to take you home with us and not even knowing if you really wanted to go. I had so many doubts about taking you away from your country, your family, and your language. But balancing all of that was my love for you and the certain knowledge that you really were my child and that we had to be together.

I was worried about the lack of communication we had with you after you had left America. We hadn't been able to speak with you at all, and our neighbor, Victoria, had only gotten through twice. I had no idea what you knew about the adoption process, or if you even knew that we were coming that day. The three of us had been preparing to see you since the day we got the phone call to come to Ukraine, but I worried about the shock to you, especially if we were not what you really wanted in a family. I knew that generically you wanted to leave the orphanage, but specifically is a different matter. You were used to freedom and a lack of parental oversight that I am sure would feel smothering when it is suddenly imposed and not grown into. But despite all these feelings, I still couldn't wait to see you. I was so hopeful that you really wanted us as badly as we wanted you.

We were taken into a room and left there while official things were taking place — what official things, I don't know. Our facilitator, Sasha, seemed to have it all under control and was talking away a mile a minute to the orphanage staff, so we just sat still and minded our P's and Q's. Overall, we could not ask for a better, more protective person to work with than our facilitator. He is absolutely wonderful and dedicated to this task.

So, enough digression, and back to the story. We waited for about thirty minutes and then were ushered into the office of the orphanage director. She sat at a desk and then at a table in front of the desk were the orphanage vice-director that we all met at the hosting program and the orphanage doctor. The meeting started with the orphanage director talking about you and telling us all about your background. I will summarize it here, but someday I am sure you will correct us and fill in the blanks.

Your mom was not around after birth and your dad gave you to Grandma to be raised. You lived with her until the age of twelve when she became ill and could not care for you. When that happened you were placed in the orphanage (much to your dislike we heard) and an effort was made to contact your dad. Unfortunately he had passed away in 2007. Your Grandma has been to the orphanage to visit you a couple of times but we heard that it was very difficult for her to travel and that it was hard for her to visit you. She has written a letter to the orphanage saying that it was OK for you to be adopted. So this is good news that there are not any legal issues standing in our way.

We heard that when you first came to the orphanage you really didn't want to be there and kept asking why your mom couldn't come. Apparently they looked for your mother but had to declare her missing after she could not be located. You then came over to America and stayed with us, and according to the orphanage director when you came back were asking all the time when could we adopt you and when could you leave to go back with us. She said that your school work got much better and that you were very open about expressing that you wanted us as a family. She said that you had even speculated when told that we were coming yesterday that you thought it would be Mama, Papa, and sister—and you were right! Apparently the orphanage staff was not worried about the pre-selected adoption stuff, only the government officials. Usually there is one present at these meetings, but for some reason, he was off today, so we didn't have to worry about showing that we knew you.

At this point, I was struggling to hold back tears. I knew that we were expected to be stoic, but this so deeply affected me that you really wanted us and were looking forward to being a part of our family. I felt like all the worries were just lifted off my shoulders! I didn't have to worry that you didn't want us. We felt so blessed that you have expressed a desire to be with us—we feel very lucky to have the opportunity to add you to our family.

The orphanage director went on to say that your schooling had been hit or miss before the orphanage and that many times you had not attended school while with your Grandma. So, now I have a whole new set of challenges on how to teach you. So, mister, get ready, I am up to this challenge! I would like to visit your school before we go and talk to your teachers and figure out where you are and then hit the ground running.

Then the doctor went on to tell us about what little is known about your medical history (which is almost nothing) and then they brought you in. I thought I was going to die—I was so happy to see you standing there. You looked great and I just couldn't help myself from rushing over to give you a hug. I almost killed myself tripping over a chair but I wasn't going to let anything stand in my way from getting to you. I know you were surprised but after we all three got finished crushing you in hugs—you finally smiled!

Then they led us to another room so that we could visit with you and our facilitator had to go do more official business. We just sat there and stupidly grinned at you for a while. I am sure you were wondering about this crazy family that just sits and stares. I was so tongue-tied, I couldn't even get out some of the Russian phrases I had so dutifully been practicing. You know very little English, so we basically just used hand signals and smiles. And of course lots of hugs. Visiting with you was great—it is so hard just to visit and know that it will still be the better part of a month before you can come permanently with us. I feel bad that we did not have any of the gifts that we had brought for you but we hadn't even been to where we were staying in Mariupol yet. So we promised you to bring some the next day.

After we left you (very hard to do by the way!) we were absolutely starving. We had not eaten since the snack at the minimart on the way to Mariupol and it was now about two in the afternoon. We went to a restaurant and had a delicious lunch and then were taken to start the paperwork. We had to go to a lawyers office to sign some more papers and fill out the local petition to adopt. So we felt glad that we were able to start the process today—let's hope everything continues this smoothly.

We were taken to the apartment after that, which is very nice and a little bigger than the one in Kiev. We were so tired and, after a really good lunch, it was time for a great big power nap. All three of us sacked out for about three hours. Then John walked across the street to a little mart to get some food and after doing that we have just vegged out working and catching up on email.

Anyway, this was a great day—emotionally. Exhausting—physically. Can't wait to see you tomorrow and continue to work on getting you home!

We love you so much!
Bethany

33: Day 6 — Mariupol

Dearest Dema,

Day 6 and going well! We are so happy to be here and to be able to see you every day. We really like Mariupol. It is a pretty city and much lass hectic than Kiev. We slept in this morning and just lazed around for a while. It looks like John is catching a cold so we want to be careful that it doesn't get any worse. We ventured out around lunch time and went to a really good restaurant across the street. We got some mushrooms, tomatoes, and potatoes baked in cheese in a little pot—delicious. We also had a greek salad and some borscht that were also good. Unfortunately, Amanda is drinking way too many sodas here, but sometimes that is the only choice other than beer. Not everywhere has inexpensive bottled water, and we get really tired of paying premium prices for water when beer or soda is cheaper.

I can see why our facilitator stated that this is the boring part—he has a lot of work to do, but we don't have much to do. We are just sitting around a lot and visiting the orphanage every day for a few hours. But I look at it as a chance to explore the city, learn more Russian and work on my book. Amanda is getting a lot of school work done and John is able to work—so all in all—not too bad or boring.

We went back to the little market across the street and picked up a few more essential supplies so that we could do some cooking in the apartment. It is a cute little market with several different areas. One counter has meat and cheeses, another fruits and veggies, and still a third with drinks and snacks. It feels funny to shop a little at one counter and then have to pay and move on to the next counter and do the same in a space that is the size of a gas station minimart, but there you go.

Around three o'clock we were picked up and taken to the orphanage. We met with the doctor again and received your medical records and then met with the psychologist who basically told us that you were fine, but needed a firm hand! They really believe in discipline here. She also mentioned that because you were so good-looking that they had trouble with the girls hanging on and around you. (We had figured that out long ago when we hosted you in America and saw how girls hung all over you!—both that you are cute and that girls will be a problem!).

Then we got to see you again. It was so great to see you. You are really coming along with your English—I am really proud of you. You have been practicing your greetings in English and your numbers. We had a lot of fun talking to you. Okay—mostly charades—but I think we communicated pretty well. The most hilarious part of the day—John was using his iPhone and Google Translate to communicate. He was using Siri to allow you talk into the phone to then translate it into English. It had been working pretty good but on this particular situation—not so well. You spoke really fast into the phone and it translated it, "My penis is lonely." When we looked at it, we started laughing and I know that bothered you. After we showed you the words, you turned soooo red! We couldn't stop giggling.

All too soon our time together ended and we had to leave. We gave you a watch and some gum and candy and promised to be back tomorrow. We wanted to give you something tangible to keep even though we were leaving. We know how hard it can be for you to be promised a family, have them finally appear and then have to wait some more. We feel the hardship too. So, we figured giving you a few tangible reminders of us would help the process along. Selfishly, we also figured that if you were really happy and focused on other things, it wouldn't be so hard to leave Ukraine. And while mentioning presents, we gave you all the presents for the kids that were waiting to be adopted by families that we knew. They had brought them to our house before we left and we had carefully carried them to Mariupol. You promised to give them out and when the orphanage staff saw all that you had, they helped out distributing them.

After leaving, we then went to a big supermarket where we stocked up on some more staples (like pasta, cereal, etc.) and then came back to the apartment. Our facilitator went to add more money on our phone and wifi card and we settled in to do more work. Sasha has been great.

We are also starting to make some plans to go to Europe before the court date. Amanda's birthday is coming up in a week and we are trying to get her to Paris for it. But if it doesn't work out it is because we are here doing things with you—so we really can't lose!

Until tomorrow!
Bethany

34: Day 7—Mariupol—paperwork
moving along nicely

Dearest Dema,

    Well, John is officially sick! He was coughing, sneezing, and sniffling all night long. Hopefully it is just a head cold and Amanda and I will not get it. I don't think I could face it right now. I am currently bemoaning the fact that I feel like a pretzel after sleeping on that bed for a few nights. Maybe it is the effort of sleeping on the edge as far away from John as possible to escape the germs, but I woke up this morning sore and stiff with the discomfort mostly in my lower back. We are a fine family looking to adopt—sick and crippled!

    But here is where the quiet days are very welcome. We don't have anything to do until this afternoon when we visited you. So, we spent the morning soaking John in the tub to drain everything out of his head, soaking me in the tub to loosen up twisted and hurting muscles, and kept Amanda busy with school work and games.

    Amanda and I then walked around a little in downtown Mariupol, drifting in and out of a few stores having fun. We bought a few items (restocked our emergency Snickers bars) and then went into a learning center we saw advertised—Oxford English Center. We talked to the director there and looked at some of the workbooks they have to teach English. They were OK—but nothing great. I haven't found the perfect piece of curriculum yet. As you will learn with me, being a homeschooling mom, I am very picky about the learning resources I choose. They have to be just right, and so far nothing has struck me as being just right yet. Never fear though, I will persevere.

    We went to the orphanage again today and saw you again. One order of business that we had to go through when filing your paperwork is deciding what name you would have after the adoption. I was glad that I had the thought to discuss it with you today. We found out that you were okay with keeping your name and just adding Gardiner as a surname. That relieved me as I wanted you to keep your name. If you decide to change it someday, that is up to you. But for now, it is who you are.

When we first met you, we had no idea that Dima, your name, was a common nickname for Dymtro. We spelled it phonetically and came up with Dema. Well, when we were talking to Alex earlier this week he mentioned that we had spelled it wrong. I checked with our facilitator here and found out that indeed—the spelling is Dima. So now I have half of a blog and a blog title that is misspelled. So from now on, I will spell it correctly. I was going to back through the blog to correct every misspelling, but then I thought better of it. It will be a good story for us to tell someday.

So, when we got to the orphanage we had to wait a few minutes while the staff went and got you. Tanya, another child that is slated for adoption later this year, came in when she recognized us and visited for a while and then you came in. I had prepared a few things for you to do while we were together. I had made a small family history chart on my computer and put names and ages in it just to familiarize yourself with your new family. I worried that your family was not on it—I don't want you to think we are replacing your family—we are merely adding to it—making it bigger and better. We practiced both the Russian and English words for family members. I am determined to learn Russian—as determined as you are to learn English. As John said, the race is on—I will learn more Russian than you learn English. (I am pretty sure that youth will triumph in this case but I also figured that it is a good motivator).

We got to stay about two hours with you—that seems to be a standard visit give or take. Sasha then gave us an update on the paperwork and its progress. He said that he got all the paperwork from the orphanage this morning and then went to track down your paperwork from the district of Mariupol that you were born in. He said that it wasn't easy, and the gentleman in the government office was a little snippy, but that he managed to get everything done. He was then able to turn everything into the local office to get the recommendation for adoption that has to be taken to Kiev next week. We are on schedule and even a little ahead of schedule so we are very happy. Once the paperwork goes to Kiev, we can start to look at court dates and make some decisions about whether we can go to Paris for a week or so.

Afterwards we went out to dinner at a local hotel across the street from our apartment building. It was an excellent meal—we are getting spoiled by the good food here—also by the great beer. We have missed Stella Artois in Utah, but it is on tap everywhere here.

    Amanda and I finished up the night with a little more schoolwork and a couple of card games. John went to bed early to try to shake this cold that he has. Tomorrow we are privileged to be able to take you out of the orphanage for a few hours—you said you wanted pizza and a movie, so that is what we will do!

Till tomorrow,
Bethany

35: Day 8 — Mariupol — relaxing and visiting

Dearest Dima,

Daddy John is officially on the mend. He feels much better and has had a couple of good nights' rest and is not coughing or sneezing as much. Thank goodness — we have too much at stake here not to be at our best.

We picked you up at eleven o'clock this morning to spend the afternoon together. Sasha said that we were very lucky to be able to do this as he was having to take personal responsibility for you. I guess because usually he has other families to take care of and work to do, he is not available for things like this. And because you are not officially ours yet, the orphanage doesn't like to see you away from their care. But since this is the Orthodox Easter weekend here and not much is going on and also because we are the only family here right now, we got lucky! Thank goodness, we are desperate to spend more time with you.

There wasn't enough time to do both lunch and a movie, so we decided to do a movie (since you wanted to). There was a little extra time before the movie, so we went to a local park that overlooked the sea and took some pictures and walked around a little. Then we went to the movie theatre. You wanted to see Wrath of the Titans in 3D — so we did. It had been dubbed in Ukrainian but it was an action movie so we pretty much were able to follow the story line anyway. We shared popcorn and drinks so we sent you back to the orphanage well fed and entertained. I figured that once you get to America you will have to spend a lot of time watching things that you don't understand so it is only fair that we do the same over here.

After we said goodbye to you (which gets harder and harder to do by the way) we asked Sasha to take us to a bookstore. He was rolling his eyes wondering about these weird Americans, but you know us homeschoolers! A bookstore is heaven no matter what language the books are in. I was looking for some fun books for you to read in Russian and also some books to help teach you English.

I figure that we are going to get a couple of hours with you everyday and there is only so much smiling and hugging we can do. And I might as well start teaching you now. So, I found the Hobbit in Russian, which I am very excited to have, and then found a picture dictionary with words in English and Russian and pictures, and a workbook with some easy exercises. Then as I was walking around I found some flashcard sets that looked great. I know they are a little babyish, but I think having pictures will help you in the beginning.

Sasha thinks we are crazy, I think, but this is just the homeschooler in me coming out! I can't stand to have time not spent in education (at least in the afternoons). In the mornings—nothing functions much before ten am so . . . (We told you that you get to sleep in as late as you wants at home and you seemed very happy about that fact.) I am really excited about the books I got though, and plan to pull them out later and begin looking at them deciding where to start.

After that we came back to the apartment and Amanda and I did school work together for a while. She is going to get behind in some subjects that I didn't want to bring books for, but in others, she will be ahead, so it will all even out. Then she had to watch several lectures for her online physics class, so John and I ventured out to do some shopping. I wanted to get you something for Easter. As Ukraine is an Eastern Orthodox country, your Easter is a week after ours. Easter is just as big here as it is in America, but it definitely has more religious overtones. Everywhere we go, they are selling Easter bread which is supposed to eaten on Easter day. The Easter bread is decorated with special frosting and I found some packets the mix in the supermarket that you can just mix with water to make. I figured these would keep, so I bought several of them to use next Easter when you are home with us.

The weather here is nice today—it has been overcast and rainy most of the time we have been in Ukraine so far, but today we finally got to see some blue sky (okay—a little blue sky looking through the smog). The air pollution is really bad here. It makes LA look pretty clean!

John and I got turned around and wandered farther than we had anticipated, but it was fun just watching people and looking in stores. We found some Agatha Christie books in Russian, so we got those for you. We ended up at a supermarket and got some chocolate to give you for Easter tomorrow and a few other snack items as well. We were laughing as the truth hit us—even the most mundane things like a package of crackers looks more interesting when it has a foreign label on it!

Well, I am off to cook dinner. So far it has just been simple things to eat like cheese and crackers and potatoes in the apartments, but tonight I am going to be brave and try a pasta pomodoro with salad. We will see how I do without my normal accoutrements.

We are going to get to see you tomorrow again and spend the afternoon together. We can't wait!

Love always,
Bethany

36: Day 9 — Mariupol — happy orthodox Easter

Dearest Dima,

Dinner last night was great. The salad and pasta were wonderful. It was nice to have a little familiar comfort food. But in a small kitchen — clean up needs to happen as you go along! Which makes clean up quick after the meal.

This morning we were up and ready for you. We met Sasha and went to get you at the orphanage. It is Easter morning here — we heard that you were up and out to church at seven o'clock this morning (while I was still resting comfy in bed!).

I'm glad that we are Catholic — pretty close to your Eastern Orthodox, but I guess it really doesn't matter. You can believe what you want, I'm not here to change it. I guess now that I am thinking about it, what religion you are or even if you aren't anything doesn't really matter to me much.

We were so happy to see you. We brought you a little Easter present — not much I am afraid, but the best we could do over here. Ludmila, the orphanage director, gave us a small Easter bread that we will enjoy.

We went to the seaside and walked around a little and took some pictures. Then we went to a great restaurant where they had little touch screens at every booth to order from. They had a variety of cuisine, Italian (pizzas and pastas), German (lots of sausages), and other foods. As with any other teenage boy, you ate a lot!

It was funny, while we were eating at the restaurant, there were several men who were obviously basketball players that came in to eat — they were from America. Apparently basketball is big over here and they import a lot of players. It was nice to hear English spoken again! We can't get used to the fact that we get so many stares speaking English here. In Kiev, not so many, but I guess not a lot of English speaking tourists come here, so the stares are quite common.

After eating, we went to a park and walked around a little. Then we found a few benches and sat down while I taught you some English. I see no reason to wait — take advantage of every opportunity I say. The flash cards are great. I worried that you would think they were too babyish, but for gaining vocabulary, it is really the best way, and you seemed to take to them OK. I am hoping that you will learn most of the words by the time we leave, because then I will be able to leave the cards behind.

All too soon, it was time to go and take you back to the orphanage. As usual when we stepped in, we noticed the best smells from the kitchen. It always smells like mealtime in there. We said good-bye and then came back to the apartment. Need to catch up working on my next book—it has kind of been forgotten about with all the stuff that is going on. We figured it would be a good day to hunker down and get work done since it is Easter and not much else is going on.

We have asked Sasha what we can do to buy gifts for the kids in the orphanage or otherwise help out. We have a lot of downtime here, so I thought I could help with the infants. I would love to cuddle, feed, or even change diapers if necessary. But he said that I would not be allowed to since I am not an employee. I understand, but it would be nice to help out. I thought and thought about it and finally came up with a good idea. The orphanage director we found out keeps a store of toys and gifts that she gives out to children for various reasons. I thought that we could go to a toy store and stock up her supply, so that when a child has a rough day, maybe goes into the orphanage, or any other reason, she could ease their disappointment with a gift. I did tell Sasha though to make sure that she understood that this was a separate gift from us—not to be expected from any other family. (I have empathy for those that come after us!).

Tomorrow, we have some shopping to do—and I want to get you some jeans to wear. All the clothes you have been wearing are community property of the orphanage and you can't take any with you when you leave. I just want to make sure you have enough when you finally leave the orphanage. And tomorrow another family arrives so it will be nice to see some familiar faces. Also looking forward to this coming week where we can get back on track after the Easter holidays with getting paperwork done.

Love you bunches,
Bethany

37: Beautiful spring day

Dearest Dima,

Another awesome day today! When we woke, it was clear with a beautiful blue sky. We realized that just down the street from us is the sea (we had not seen it before because of the smog!) It is a holiday here because of Easter yesterday. There was no school so we got to take you from eleven to two. Not nearly long enough, but I guess better than nothing!

When we got to the orphanage, I was dismayed to see you limping pretty badly. The orphanage doctor had told us when we met with her that you had broken your foot twice before in soccer games, but I somehow lost something in the translation and thought this was in the distant past. However, upon talking this morning, we found out that it was just in February playing soccer. You hit a goal post with your foot and fractured several metatarsal bones. They didn't heal right and had to be reset—hence the twice broken that we heard. Apparently you were playing this morning and re-injured the foot. I hope it is nothing serious but I will be taking you to a sports medicine doctor to get it looked at—and we have plenty of experience with sports medicine doctors, believe you me!

Looking online this morning, John found one geocache in Mariupol—it had been placed several years ago and had only been found once. So, we decided to take the GPS and introduce you to geocaching, since it is one of our favorite pastimes. This one was a fun multi-stage cache that walked us all around a pretty park in the middle of Mariupol. Sasha had never been geocaching either, so it was a great introduction for both of you!

We started out, and discovered that there were dead batteries in the GPS—ack! But there was a convience store close by that had batteries, so after a short detour, we were back on track. The cache took us by a mosque, a church, and pretty grove of birch trees, until we found the cache beside the path under a pile of rocks. It was a great cache, with a small log book and some Ukrainian stickers. We left two American dollar bills figuring that is pretty unusual in a cache here.

This took about an hour. Then you told Sasha that you wanted an outfit to wear to a soccer game on Wednesday night. I couldn't figure out if it was to wear during playing a game or to go to a game, but you were pretty sure of what you wanted—so off we went to a store. It turned out that you wanted an athletic suit (Adidas) so we found a nice one that was black and yellow. I am secretly thrilled because in your suitcase that we brought over here, you will find a pair of black Adidas sweat pants that I know now you will like. I was unsure when I got them if you would like them. And I picked the size right! Woo-hoo! We will be giving you all of these things on your last day at the orphanage—you will have to change into our clothes to be taken away! It will be a red-letter day.

We only had about a half-hour left at that point so you had asked for McDonald's—yuck! I should never say never because it always gets you. Whenever I read other people's blogs and saw that they went to McDonald's—I always sneered and said never me—I mean we don't go to them in America, primarily because we can't eat anything there, but also because they represent the very things that are wrong with our food supply in America—hormones and pink slime in beef, high fat, high salt, high sugar, etc. . . . So why would I ever go to one here? Well, obviously because we love you! We watched you snarf down a cheeseburger and fries with a smile on your face.

Too soon, it was time to take you back. Parting gets harder each time we drop you off. Before we said goodbye, Sasha talked to you for a while and I understood that you mentioned documents. I asked him afterwards as we were walking away what it was about and he said that you had asked if everything was okay and was just checking we still wanted you and hadn't changed our minds. I wish there was a way to make you understand that absolutely nothing, and I mean nothing, could change our minds. Even if they stopped the adoption, we would still be part of your life. There is no way that you can get rid of us. You are one of us now and all that that entails, good and bad! Hopefully more good than bad! We will love and cherish you forever. You are adding to the circle around you with four people that really feel blessed to be able to call you ours! I know that this concept is hard for you to understand, but hopefully through time and many demonstrations, you will learn this.

Hugs and kisses,
Bethany

38: More day 10

Dearest Dima,

    I felt that it was a good place to end the previous letter—but I had more to say. (If you ask John, he would say that I always have more to say!) I wanted to share some of our impressions about Mariupol in particular and Ukraine in general. We have really enjoyed Mariupol. It is a very nice city without the hustle and bustle of Kiev. The only problem that I can see (and it is a big one) is the horrible pollution! The steel mills pump out soot and smoke at an unbelievable pace. It is probably better to live with a smoker than to breathe this air.

    The apartment we are in is about five minutes from your orphanage. Across the street is a little market that has a few items in it. Honest to goodness, one of the the ladies behind the counter uses an abacus to count up the purchases. Amanda had never seen one so we took her in just to point this out.

    When we leave you every day, I always wonder about what you will be doing. For us, tonight we were lucky to meet another family who are from our area in the states for dinner. It is nice to share the experiences with others. They are here only for a few days because of a paperwork snafu but will be coming on a second trip soon to finalize their adoption. We had a wonderful time and were thankful to connect with a little piece of home.

    Tomorrow we will get to go in the afternoon to the orphanage again to see you and then also to fill out paperwork to take to Kiev. Once this is done, the paperwork has to be approved in Kiev to come back here to have a court date set. Things are moving along well, not as fast we want of course (we want you yesterday) but as fast as could reasonably be expected.

    I am enjoying writing to you. I can't wait to hear your side of the story some day. Hope you will enjoy reading this someday!

Till tomorrow,
Bethany

39: Day 11 — Mariupol — What's in a name?

Dearest Dima,

Another beautiful spring day here in Mariupol. The trees and flowers are just starting to bloom. We had a restful morning not venturing out till noon. We went back to a restaurant we had been to before for lunch and then relaxed at a cafe for a while before being picked up to go to the orphanage.

Before heading to the orphanage today we went to an office to sign the official application to adopt from the local region. All of our paperwork was processed and is currently in the hands of a courier on its way back to Kiev. We have been very thankful that everything has gone so smoothly. It has been about as quick as it could be. Tomorrow we should be able to request a court date — hopefully before the end of April.

Then we were able to go to see you for a good long visit. It is always great to see you and spend time with you but it is hard to see you at the orphanage. The first time — well there was nothing like that wonderful feeling, seeing you for the first time again after so long a wait. But soon after that it gets a little more complicated. We wait (and wait) all day for that precious one to two hours to see you. Then when we get there, we just sit and grin like an idiot since we don't know your language. If you were five it would be easier, we could just play games with you, but as a teenager, it is a bit more complicated. You have to look cool, but still are trying to be on your best behavior, and there is NOTHING to do. For the parents, you want to keep your child happy, but you also feel like you are being judged by the staff as appropriate parental material! This is a no-win situation.

So, I decided, why not start schooling now. It fills the time and makes us look productive. And in an instance where there really aren't any other good activities — this is the best I could find. Definitely, bring pictures on a computer or iPad to show. I also made a little family tree to show of our family. Games would be okay, but not for teens! They want music — so bring something that can play music like an ipod or iphone. We also have gone outside to take pictures, the lighting is just better. But after exhausting the above activities — it boils down to simply sitting and grinning at each other. We even pulled out the phone and called my mom (who just talked and talked like you could understand) and Alex (who probably lectured you — he wouldn't say) and G4 (who had just awakened and had to go quickly to get ready for class).

We had three hours of this today and were really getting desperate when Sasha came back and said that it was time to go. But he dropped one little bomb on us — that we needed to pick your name by tomorrow! Your name that I had thought would be is Dimitri Suprunchyck Gardiner. We had asked you before and you had said OK, but then we started to doubt ourselves. After careful consideration and the input of Sasha, we all have decided that that name is a mouthful and would be too difficult. So, that leaves us with Dimitri (since you will still be called Dima) but that could be your first or middle name. So you could be Dimitri fill in the blank Gardiner or fill in the blank Dimitri Gardiner. Yikes!

So of course we all have our favorites. Mine is Dimitri Alexander Gardiner, Daddy John likes Carlton Dimitri Gardiner and you said the name Jason or Artoom. That leaves us exactly nowhere. I have been searching online for names but they all seem wrong for you. This isn't like naming a baby that has no personality to begin with. You are you and we have to pick a name that perfectly embodies all that you currently are and will be.

So, the visit was three hours of boredom on your part (and yes, I could tell that like any other teen-aged boy — sitting with parents is boring) and ten minutes of sheer panic — and then it was time to go!

However, I must share something you said to me yesterday and again today. When we said goodbye yesterday, you said, "Bye, Mom." I was surprised and felt it was a precious thing to keep to myself for a while. But today — you said it again loud enough for others to hear — I must tell you — I had a hard time not crying in front of you. I know that would probably embarrass you to no end so I didn't. I kept my tears to myself — but it really affected me. Sniffle, sniffle — I am in love!

I can't tell you how happy I am to have you refer to me as Mom. It is something I hoped and prayed for, but I had set my internal expectations that it might never happen.

Love always,
Mom

40: Day 12 — Last day in Mariupol for now

Dearest Dima,

My heart is heavy today as I know that this is the last time we will see you until the court date. Our paperwork went in to Kiev without incident and we also filled out the application to petition the court as well. So everything is moving along. There are a number of holidays coming up in May and it is our plan to be done with court before the holidays so they can pass during the ten-day waiting period. Because of holidays, if we do not get court done on the twenty-eighth of April, we will be moved all the way to the seventh of May. Then the ten-day waiting period will kick in. I was worried before that you would be twenty-two before we got over here—now I am worried that I will be seventy-two before I get home! But, Sasha said he was eighty percent sure that we would get court on the twenty-eighth. So, let's hope!

The other problem facing us is the fact that the State Department of Adoptions has moved offices in the government—not physically, but in terms of hierarchy. They used to allow five days to get the court permission back, but now with the change, they have ten business days. Sasha is hoping that it won't be that long, but again, we really can't be sure.

So, back to our day. We have decided to travel to London tomorrow as John needs to go into his London office. We wanted to go to the Paris office, but things changed and he needs now to be in London. He had saved up work overseas to do for a while, and we are closer here than at home. I know it makes good sense, but I don't want to leave you. I have grown accustomed to our daily visits and will miss them terribly. I know that soon this all will be a distant dream, and in no time once we are home it will seem like you have always been there, but for now, all I have are these small visits to sustain our relationship. It doesn't seem like enough. I also worry that you will fear that we are not coming back, but I promise you that we *are* coming back. I will be counting the days until we return.

Anyway, enough maudlin meanderings! This was the first day that we arrived at the orphanage without Sasha, so we weren't quite sure what to do, but there is a nice security guard that is always on duty that took us under his wing and got us to the visiting room and signed in appropriately. Today we were excited to hear that your soccer game went well, your team won 1-0. It seems like your foot is better. You weren't limping as much today.

We worked on flash cards again today and I am so proud of how good you are getting with your English. I can tell that you are really motivated (and we sweetened the pot by promising you a computer once you know English pretty well). We met one of your friends today, a lovely young lady, who gave us a picture and seemed very nice. Several people came in to see you as we were working with you and they all seemed very nice. It is hard not to get jealous of these interruptions, as we get so little time with you, but on the other hand, everyone seems to want to check us out and make sure we are appropriate parent material for you!

As for the name problem. We had brainstormed and asked all our friends to brainstorm and had come up with a list of about twenty possibilities. None of them were really clear winners, but we all agreed upon Dimitri Alexander Gardiner, Nicholas Dimitri Gardiner, and Alexei Dimitri Gardiner. Those were the current frontrunners in our book. So when we saw you, that of course was the first thing we asked, "Have you thought about a name?" Without any hesitation you answered, "Alexei Dimitri Gardiner." So, that turned out fine.

And now what are we going to do with Alex? He is going to be ticked off! Especially if we call him Old Alex! He still feels sixteen! So maybe Alex 1 and Alex 2? And I wonder how hard it is going to be to break the habit of calling you Dima? Well, when we get back, we will have to see what your preference is and try our best to do it.

So, after all too short a time, Sasha arrived and announced that since we had a name we had to hurry and make our petition for a court date. We were bummed — not wanting to leave you of course! We said goodbye and made sure Sasha told you that we were coming back for court. I hope you understood that and don't harbor any misgivings! In our hearts, you are ours — even if we need a piece of paper to make it official. I think you are recognizing it too. You now regularly call me Mom, but every time I hear it, I turn into a little pile of goo. Pretty soon I will be a shapeless mass of maternal sentimental feelings!

After doing the court paperwork, we came back to the apartment to visit with Sasha a little before parting ways the next day. He is on his way to Lugansk to look into some paperwork for another family, while we are driving to Donetsk to catch the first leg of our trip to London. We peppered him with questions about all kinds of things—the court date, the ten day waiting period, the visit to your grandmother, etc. Poor guy—but he rallied and we made some tentative plans, everything hinging of course on the court date.

 I finished up the night by doing some laundry, packing your bags (which we will leave here), and packing our bags for the trip. I must admit that even though it has only been not even two weeks—it feels like it has been a much longer trip. Maybe the emotional component makes it so trying? But it has been very tiring so far. And I have probably a month more to go!

Counting the days until we get back,
Bethany

41: Day 13 — Mariupol to Kiev

Dearest Alex,

I am wondering whether I should start calling you Alex now. I guess I will try to think of you as such until I can ask you again. But you said that is what you wanted the last time we asked you — so that is what I will go with.

Today was very hard emotionally, having to leave you behind. I know that Daddy John has to do work, and I know that we had planned ahead of time to travel some, but now that we have been here and spent time with you, it doesn't seem right to leave without you! We did stop by the orphanage to try to see you one more time before we went but you were not out of school yet. Bummer.

We spent the morning packing up and getting ready. We had taken a bag filled with clothes for you, but we really don't need to be taking it all over Europe, so our driver, Sasha, was nice enough to take it and another bag we don't need and store it for us while we are gone. We packed up the rest of our stuff and I did the last load of laundry since we will be in a hotel for a week in London. No laundry facilities there.

Sasha (driver Sasha) picked us up and took us to Donetsk to catch our flight. It is about a one and a half hour drive and we were making excellent time until — boom. The car started swerving all over the road and we heard a flapping in the rear of the car. We had blown a tire! We were in a five- or six-year old Chevy Aveo that had been converted to run on natural gas. (My environmentally conscious self liked this fact.) So half of the trunk was taken up by the other gas tank, and all of our luggage was thrown in around it. So we pulled over to the side of the road (highway?) and got out hoping that he had a spare. Which he did — yay! Boy, he must be used to this as he whipped the luggage out of the trunk, got out the spare and in less than ten minutes we were back on the road. We got a look at the old tire before he put it back and saw that it was just plain worn out — almost bald. We gave him some money for a new tire since we felt responsible for it — probably it blew as a result of the four tons of luggage we were toting around.

So no delays! We were lucky, getting to the airport at four thirty pm for a five forty pm flight. We managed to get checked in and on the plane in record time and made it to Kiev just on time. We met Alex at the airport. He had worked a morning flight but had gotten back at three pm and was able to change and relax before meeting us. The hotel (Hotel Korona) had a shuttle service that wasn't too expensive, about seventy hrivnas (about nine dollars) so we were able to just hop in and go right to the hotel. We were tired, so Alex joined us for dinner right in the hotel restaurant, before heading back to his apartment.

We have to get up early tomorrow for our flight to London, so I will end it here.

We love you,
Mom

42: Day 14—Kiev to London

Dearest Alex,

    We left Kiev this morning and flew to London. When we got to there, we had booked a bus service to get into London since the airport we flew into (Gatwick) was so far out. Here the problems began. The bus left us off in West London, nowhere near Central London like we thought. There were no taxis around and we were still a ways from the hotel. Then it started to rain!

    We walked a few blocks to a tube station and bought tickets for the tube, but then it was a workout muscling all of our suitcases up and down the stairs and onto the train—in the rain—since it was an outside station. We were able to figure out where we were going, dismayed to find out there was a change of line—so more muscling bags up and down stairs and escalators, finally to arrive at our stop. Now it turns out the hotel was actually an apartment service that rented out apartments. We didn't realize this and spent an hour walking around (in the rain and wind now) trying to find it. We finally found the reception desk only to be told that the apartment was not in the vicinity—about a fifteen-minute walk away. So, at this point (with continued rain and wind) we decided to catch a taxi. The taxi driver spent fifteen minutes driving around and finally said, "Here it is—it is down this walkway." So we got out only to discover that indeed the taxi driver did NOT know where the apartment was and had dropped us off near it but without knowing exactly. The rain had stopped during the ride thank goodness, but we spent the next thirty minutes wandering around (of course there was no one else around) trying to find the apartment building. We finally found it, just in time, as John had a business meeting that he had to get to.

    Amanda and I relaxed and when there was a break in the rain, we ran out to a local market to get some food. Of course the moment we stepped out of the apartment building, it started raining—hard! But we got back OK and then flipped on BBC only to find G4's favorite show, *Top Gear*, on.

    We are anxious to start sightseeing tomorrow!

Love,
Mom

43: Day 15 — London — happy birthday Amanda

Dearest Alex,

Happy thirteenth birthday to Amanda!

We gave her the few presents we were able to pack and then it was off to see the sights. We started with the Portobello Market (where Paddington Bear used to shop) and then on to Regents Park and the London Zoo. It rained on and off all day, alternating between sun and warmth and then freezing winds and rain. Weird weather.

Then we rode a double decker bus and got off at Trafalgar Square. I have never seen such a mass of people in my life. If this is the way the city is now, I would hate to see it during the Olympics! We walked around and stumbled upon a vegetarian Indian restaurant that was delicious. We have never had Indian food that good.

Then we walked to Piccadilly Circus and on a whim decided to check out one of the theaters. The Crittendon Theatre was playing a comedy, *The 39 Steps*, which looked good, so ten minutes before the show, we walked up to the box office and got tickets! It was a great play, and we got great seats — front row of the balcony. But after the show, we were all tired out. We have been spoiled in Ukraine with a car and driver. Our feet hurt from all the walking here. So back to the apartment to collapse.

Love,
Mom

44: Day 16 — London — shop til you drop

Dearest Alex,

Another rainy day in London! I swear, someone should have warned me that we were traveling to Europe in monsoon season. Rain has followed us everywhere! Good thing I packed those travel umbrellas.

This morning Amanda and I took the tube into Kensington to go shopping at Harrods. Six floors of fun. We have never had so much fun going through a department store. There was a pet area that shames anything in America. There were more outfits for dogs alone than a whole Nordstrom's. Then their food area! Oh my! The only problem was the prices. We saw a scarf for 1099 pounds (about $1600) which would be about 13,000 hrivnas. Really? For a scarf? We did find some fun things in the toy area — some Doctor Who items that G4 will love.

Afterwards, we found ourselves near the Baden-Powell house. Lord Baden-Powell was the founder of Boy Scouts and holds a prominent place in boy scout lore. Since G4 Eagled last year, we thought that we should go and look at the museum and take a tour of his house. Wrong! Several years ago, it was turned into a youth hostel. There is still a conference center there and a small exhibit — but no museum. We were a little disappointed.

Then on to a traditional English tea with the most sublime lemongrass teas and delicious scones and clotted creme at a teahouse called Bumpkins. And then back to the apartment for Amanda to get in her physics class. She has opted to go to another section that meets in the evening European time (rather than getting up in the middle of the night).

We really miss you Alex (or Dima). We go back and forth calling you both names! We want to show you all of these sights and feel bad that you are not here with us. I was just reflecting how much you are a part of our life now even though you are not physically here. We got word today that the court date has been set for the twenty-eighth. This is great news — now we just have to hope that the SDA gets the paperwork back in time.

I have taken some of this time that we have been separated from you to think more about how we will teach you and integrate you into our family. Emotions are not running as rampant as when I am near you and just want to baby and cuddle you (Probably much to your disgust!) It is easier for me to be more objective away from you right now! I know that you have been in survival mode in the orphanage since you have been there and have become somewhat hardened to life. It shows when we are with you—you tend to act very much more like an adult than we expect. However, at times you are very much a little boy—almost like on one level your maturing stopped at twelve when you went in the orphanage. I want to give those years back to you—where you are just carefree and loving life, knowing that you are loved, rather than just surviving. But I know it will be a delicate balance as you are used to hard core video games, smoking, explicit music, and other things that are foreign to us. You will think I am babying you for a while and taking away fun things, but I promise I will replace them with other things like a family, travel, movies and sports, etc. Hopefully this will not be too traumatic to you! But know that we are doing it for your own good—not to be mean or restrictive. We will show you that fun and games can be had in other ways.

I was also thinking more about the time in Mariupol. I treasured those days—that were pretty lazy days really. It was fun doing things with Amanda, school work and games. John spent most of the time working on his computer but Amanda and I lazed about. It was great time for us—I think it will prove to be very useful in the future to have spent this time bonding with her as I am sure there will be times when I am super busy with you. Hopefully there will not be too much sibling rivalry, but I am sure that there will be some jealousy!

I am feeling a little disconnected from reality here. The things that seemed so important at home are just a distant memory here. Weird, but true. I am looking forward to getting back home to a normal life at some point—but I will always treasure the time when the most important thing in my day was to go visit with you for a few hours!

Love,
Mom

45: Day 17 — London

Dearest Alex,

Well, the rain wasn't too bad today. It was on and off all day but more of a drizzle really. Amanda and I went first to Buckingham Palace to see the changing of the guard, then to the Queen's Gallery, and then to tour the Royal Mews (stables). The Mews were fascinating—we got to see the Gold State Coach that is used to take monarchs to their coronation. It was beautiful.

We then went to Oxford street and did some more shopping! We went to the official store for the Olympics at the John Lewis department store. So much fun! Then onto the London Eye at sunset for a truly spectacular view of London.

As we sightsee here, I am just so excited to think of showing you these sights someday. I know you haven't gotten to travel very much and I want to be with you when you experience some of these sights first hand. There is something magical about the first time you get to see certain places. And even though you might go back, the first time is truly special. I am glad that we will get the chance to do some of these things with you first. We have missed a lot of things in your life that I can't recover, like the tooth fairy coming when you lost your first baby tooth, your first day of school, your first birthday, or your first date. But it does warm my heart a little to know that I will get some firsts with you.

It's all about building a life together, and experiencing things together will help us all bond as a family. Sharing common memories will also help to bring you into the fold. That's part of what I want to do here by getting all my thoughts and impressions down on paper. I know after a few years, these intense feelings of uncertainty and fascination will fade away, but the fact we experienced them together and have the shared memories of them will mark the point of the beginning of our new family with you in it.

Anyway, back to our trip. Let's hope the rain goes away tomorrow! Miss you terribly and wish you were here with us.

Love,
Bethany

46: Day 18 — London — rain again!

Dearest Alex,

We are *not* having fun in London. It rained like we were in a hurricane today. *All day*! And the wind was awful—the rain was practically horizontal at times with the force of the wind. Amanda and I stayed inside in the morning, catching up on schoolwork and doing laundry. I lucked out here, as there is a washing machine in the apartment we are staying in. Or maybe not lucked out, laundry does get a little trying at times.

Finally, when we decided that the rain was just not going to stop, we ventured out determined to stay as dry as possible. We went to Canary Wharf and explored there and then went to the Tower of London. It was amazing, but hard to really experience when you are darting about from covered spot to covered spot trying to avoid being blown into the Thames by the wind. The Crown Jewels were very impressive, you really would have been dazzled by them.

Finally got to Skype with G4 tonight. It has been hard to get in touch with him because he has been studying for finals. But they are finally over! We are going to work on bringing him over to Europe to stay with me while I am waiting for your ten-day waiting period to be up. Let's hope we can work out flights. He asked about you several times. I think he is anxious to have a baby brother he can order around!

Can't wait to leave London day after tomorrow and get back to Ukraine. Let's keep our fingers crossed that there will be good news from the SDA about the paperwork! We miss you terribly and can't wait to see you. I hope that this period of time hasn't been too hard on you. Here you are, waiting nine months for us to come and then once we get there, you see us a few hours a day and then we leave again. I know we told you through the translator that it was just a quick trip and that we were coming back to get you for real, but I wonder if your really believe that?

Love,
Mom

47: Day 19 — Just tripping along

Dearest Alex,

Well, today just solidified it — I really don't like London. Excessive rain again this morning so Amanda and I just stayed in and caught up on school work. Then we ventured out to Foyles, the biggest book store in the world. We loved every minute, and even stretched out the visit to stay in their cafe.

I didn't want to leave, but finally had no choice — it was getting too expensive to stay. Then Amanda and I walked around and decided that since it was such a nice day with a little blue sky finally showing — we would walk instead of taking the tube. Famous last decisions!

I have noticed that people here are always rushing and running about. Well, as we were walking (Amanda, with her long legs, was ahead of me and I was rushing to catch up) I tripped over an uneven segment of pavement. And I must add, there seems to be uneven segments of pavement everywhere. Anyway, I was tripping along and thought I could right myself, when a gentleman came running by to catch his bus and knocked me off balance. Well, that was the end! I went sprawling on the pavement, knocking my knee hard on the pavement. Several passersby helped me up and I brushed aside their offers of help, as I was really more embarrassed than anything else. Well, that was until I took the first step — agony coursed through me and my right knee and once I realized I was hurt, I could just feel it swelling by the minute. So, after a half an hour where I tried to talk myself out of it, Amanda prevailed and off in a taxi we went to the nearest emergency room.

In short order Amanda and I found a hospital and I was seen. No fracture but extensive ligament damage to the knee. They gave me crutches and sent me on my way. Now, a word about the crutches. They are not regular crutches — they are the 1950s polio-patient kind of arm crutches! I look like I am permanently disabled. But they are actually more comfortable than the kind you put under your arms. So, I hobbled out of the ER in a lot of pain and not being able to bear any weight on the leg.

I am furious wondering how this whole thing is going to look in court, if we ever get there but then — great news. I get a phone call from Sasha saying that everything is a go for court on Saturday! The SDA turned our papers around fast and they are ready for court. YAY! I am super excited about going back to Ukraine and getting moving with this adoption. It has been far to long away from you at this point.

See you Saturday,
Mom

48: Day 20 — London to Mariupol

Dearest Alex,

Tomorrow is court day! We are really excited. I can't believe after all this work and time and effort, it all comes down to one man's decision (the judge). I feel like our whole future lies in his hands. All I can do is to cross my fingers and hope that things go well.

Today we left London, and guess what? It was raining again! We had to take a cab to the train station as I am incapacitated. I had a difficult time walking the distance but was able to hop along with the crutches. Anyway, we managed to get on the train to Gatwick OK and made it into the terminal without incident. I was starting to hurt more, so we asked for and received the nicest assistance. There was a special security line and a little tram to take me to the gate.

The flight to Kiev was uneventful, but the flight to Donetsk was a nightmare. There was some issue with baggage that prevented us from taking off on time but they had already loaded the plane. So we sat there for almost an hour in a small, confined space without any airflow. It was sweltering. And I will just leave the smell to your imagination — remember not everyone shares American abhorrence of body odor.

We finally got to Donetsk and realized that we had missed lunch and dinner. Remember how I said that I would never go to another McDonald's? Well, never say never — we ended up in the drive-thru for McDonald's because there was nothing else open at that time of night. So, we had a very healthy dinner of fries and a strawberry shake. Yum, yum (Not).

Anyway, we finally checked into the hotel in Mariupol. We were not in the apartment because no one knows the outcome of tomorrow. We are trying to ask that the ten-day waiting period be waived but we don't know if it can be. We will find out tomorrow. If it is waived, then we can leave quickly, but if not then we will move to an apartment again and settle in.

That's all for now — I am tired and need to sleep before court tomorrow!

Looking forward to seeing you,
Mom

49: Day 21 — Our day in court

Dearest Alex,

We woke early and made sure everyone was spic and span. John had his best suit, I was in a nice outfit, and Amanda had a skirt on (unbelievable for her)! We went to breakfast and decided there that Amanda should stay at the hotel. No one had said she had to, but she on her own volunteered. I think we were all worried that she would be bored sitting in court just waiting for all the official business to be conducted and I think that she respected that it was all about you today. I think it worked out for the best as you will see, but I also wanted this to be your special moment.

We were eating breakfast at the hotel restaurant, although frankly, I was too nervous to eat, when in walks Sasha. He said that he had talked to the judge and he would be amenable to waiving the ten-day waiting period, for a small fee of course. We were so happy as we had heard this hardly ever happens. But I guess there were some extenuating circumstances. There are several days of holidays coming up and and the weekend, so even though the waiting period can be waived, it still can't take effect until a workday. Then there is my lovely knee which obviously needs medical attention soon (if you could see the black and blue colors today!).

So we go to the court building, feeling very good about the process. Sasha is telling us there is nothing to worry about. He says the judge doesn't even need you to come to court and that it will be a short process in the judge's chambers. Then about ten minutes later he comes up and says, "Well, the judge wants to see Alex, but no big deal." Then about ten minutes later, "Well it is in the main hall, but still no big deal." John and I were a little concerned but we were still calm and collected.

Then you arrived with the orphanage staff. This was the first time we had seen you and wanted to jump up and hug you, but you looked so somber and quiet. You really didn't even bat an eye at my crutches. I was suddenly stricken with fear that you didn't want the adoption after all.

After a little wait, we were ushered into the main courtroom, vintage 1950s. There was even a little caged area with bars in which criminals sit during their trial. Here is where it started to go downhill. The prosecutor was a young woman, who was obviously having a bad day and decided to take it out on us! She started talking very loudly and waving papers at Sasha. At first, he was calm, but started to get more and more agitated as time went on. Then he turned to me and asked, "Do you have anything that shows your income?" I was floored. I basically am a housewife—I know I have written a book and that it is selling pretty well, but this by no means is a windfall. I don't even make enough to pay for gas!

So, we replied, no there isn't anything I can show. Besides, in the dossier there was no mention of anything about my income—it was just ensuring that the family had enough money for another child—not who made it. And we didn't even include my earnings in the dossier as the book wasn't even published until March. Then the prosecutor starts waving a manual at Sasha and in his face and pointing to it. They were escalating this whole conversation going back and forth with Sasha asking questions every few minutes of us trying to see if we had documentation that proved my income—and we kept saying no. I couldn't understand what the problem was, as John makes more than enough.

But this whole conversation was cut short as the judge came in. He started the proceedings with Sasha translating everything along the way as best as he could. We were read our rights, and then asked to stand while we were introduced. Then the orphanage representative gave a history of you and why you were available for us to adopt. The social worker gave an account and I was feeling a little better. I thought maybe this whole thing would go away. Ha!

Then John was asked to stand and give an introduction to himself and why we wanted you. He was asked a few questions (you probably understood this all better that we did) and then it was my turn. I was asked a few of the same questions and then the prosecutor started in on me. She attacked me with the same questions that she had started in on Sasha with. And a side comment—she never looked at us when she talked to us, she looked at Sasha. I didn't like her before but this solidified the whole thing. The questions were never-ending and kept coming. I couldn't figure out what this was for. John makes plenty and I would have thought they would be interested in me having time with the kids at home—not out working!

I was getting worked up, and I could tell that Sasha was too—he was sweating like crazy. But he kept saying in a very soothing voice, "Don't worry, it is OK. Everything is fine." He was fibbing, but he probably knew that I was ready to beat the prosecutor over the head with my crutches. Finally with a flounce and a big sigh, she sat down and said no further questions. I was really left with a feeling that nobody really knew what was going on.

Then you got a chance to speak, and it was so heart wrenching. I am not sure exactly what you said. Maybe someday you will tell us, but as it was translated, it came through as something like you wanted to be part of our family and you wanted to be our son. However you said it though just brought tears to my eyes, and not just me. One of the jurors was crying as well—it was so heart felt. I think everyone in the courtroom except that nasty prosecutor felt it!

Then the psychologist for the orphanage got up and stated that after you met us the first time at the orphanage, you were so happy that we had come for you and that you were worried that something would stop us from taking you home. She really laid it on! She mentioned how hopeful you were to be adopted by us.

Then the time came for everyone to make any statements. I think everyone except the social worker got up and stated that they felt that there was more than enough money for us to adopt and that they were in support, the orphanage representative said that as well. Then the prosecutor got on her high horse again and was fussing about my book income. Finally, the judge rolled his eyes and stated there was going to be a ten-minute technical break. I think he was frustrated with the prosecutor and felt that we had given adequate documentation as to our financial security. He was staring daggers at her and addressed her in a very clipped tone. However, he just as easily could have been irritated that this was taking too long and she was dragging out what in his book was an easy denial of an adoption.

At this point, I was freaking out (and so was Sasha) even though he kept saying it is OK. He asked us to get my computer from our hotel room and bring it over. Thank goodness we had left Amanda at the hotel. Vladimir (our driver) went over and got her. I was worried that she wouldn't answer the door, but she heard him say Sasha and court so she opened it up and quickly got the computer and wifi card. Meanwhile at court, the prosecutor was stalking around and I was freaking out but no one was really doing anything. Finally the juror that was crying, came down and talked to us. (It turned out she spoke perfect English—assume everyone can understand you in a courtroom.)

Anyway, she explained that they needed some documents that showed I had some source of income in case John and I divorced, so that I could care for the children. And that my book was real—not made up! They even wanted a copy of it—but of course with all the remonstrations to pack light, why would I take a copy of my own book? But apparently they needed something. So John was able to pull up the website with my sale numbers from my publishers on it and then was able to show them the Barnes and Noble and Amazon websites where it was for sale. We showed these to the prosecutor and the juror was talking to her and finally she just huffed away. There was no indication given about what was going to happen.

When the judge came back in, I was still not entirely sure of what was going on. There was a last discussion from all interested parties. Amanda was there sitting next to you by this time and even the orphanage director pointed out how well she and you got along. Everyone was making a very strong case about supporting the adoption, but when the prosecutor got a chance to speak again—she had to bring up the book! Argh! She did however say that she would accept the virtual representation of the websites that were shown but she said it in such a begrudging voice you could tell she really didn't want to. Then the judge stated they would recess to conference for the decision.

We did not know at this point how things would go. I was a nervous wreck. I was worried that the adoption would be denied, that we would never get you, etc. The time seemed to go by slowly, but I think it was only about ten minutes before the judge came back in. He read a lot of things and then stated that the court approved the adoption and that the ten-day waiting period was waived! Yay! You were officially ours. I couldn't believe it. The decision will not take affect until the third of May, the first working day after the holidays, but it was done!

I was in shock I think. I had been so worried, that I still didn't think it was done. I was still waiting for someone to come out and say—psych! just joking—you can't have him! Then before I knew it, you were shuffled off back to the orphanage and we were left standing there on the sidewalk feeling a little pathetic and let down. We felt like something momentous had happened and there we were—slightly beaten and bruised after the proceedings and now you were gone again!

 We went back to the hotel and had a quick lunch, then our driver came to pick us up to go see you. We were so excited to see you—really for the first time as officially part of our family. We got to the orphanage and ran into the Radzinski family, another family that hosted last summer and decided to adopt as well. They were in Ukraine adopting your friend Sergei, who is also fourteen, and his little brother Max, aged six. We were able to talk for a little bit but then they were ushered into the orphanage director's office. John remarked to me that it seems like a lifetime has passed—it seems like we have come so far! Anyway, we sat there for a long while and then finally saw you come around the corner. There was a whole stampede of kids, then you popped your head in the door and said, "Hi Mom, hi Papa, bye!" and then ran off down the hallway with the other kids. John and I just stared at each other in wonderment. His came partly because it was the first time you referred to him as Papa. But partly in amazement—you certainly fit in our family. John was joking, whoa, we just adopted you, spent all this time and money, and all we got was a lousy Hi Mom and Hi Papa. We laughed, don't worry, we aren't mad. We are happy that you are so easy with us! But this was just the weirdest end to the saga!

We are so happy and excited to have a new son!
We love you more than you will ever know!
Mom

50: Day 21 — Addendum

Dearest Alex,

    This is just an addendum to the previous letter but I have enough to say that I could make it into another letter to you. The day just got weirder and weirder, but in a good way.

    We didn't want to leave you but we had to. We went back to the hotel and rested a while, then called the Radzinskis to meet for dinner. My knee was feeling pretty good so we walked a few blocks to a restaurant that we had frequented a few times before, Mamma Mia's Pizza Restaurant. The servers even recognized us! We were sitting eating, when in walked several American basketball players. We had seen some before at another restaurant in town and Sasha had told us that many come over to play in Europe if they are not drafted into the NBA. We struck up a conversation with them and ended up procuring a promise for some tickets to an upcoming basketball game.

    John figured that the kids at the orphanage would be excited to be able to go to a game and maybe they could be persuaded to come visit the kids at the orphanage. So hopefully we will be able to get something worked out.

    Then the most embarrassing thing (ok maybe not the most embarrassing thing—that was me falling splat on the sidewalk in London) happened. We tried to pay for dinner and then discovered that the credit card machine was not working. Then when we went to get cash—we discovered that most of our money was back in the hotel in my purse, which I did not bring because of my knee. So, here we had tried to buy dinner for Becky and Kevin to congratulate them on meeting their kids the first time that day, and ended up by mooching dinner money off of them.

    After finishing dinner, we were walking back to the hotel when we heard some loud bangs. Resisting the urge to fall flat to the pavement and take cover, we looked around and discovered the most spectacular fireworks display. It only lasted a few minutes, but was pretty and a most deserving end to a special day!

Lots of love,
Mom

51: Day 22 — Mariupol

Dearest Alex,

 We are still so excited about yesterday. I think we are just really getting to appreciate how great it all went. Yesterday I think we were still so traumatized about the problems that arose that we were almost scared to be happy. Having survived such a near miss, it still felt like we were waiting for the other shoe to fall so to speak. But the emotional trauma must have taken its toll because we all slept like the dead and awoke feeling happy and refreshed.

 John and I are so excited about having you as our son. We think you will fit in perfectly and that you will be happy. Even though there might be times when you wish "evil homeschooling mom" wouldn't make you do so much work, overall I think everything is going to work out great.

 We checked out of the hotel this morning and went to another apartment. Sasha (our driver — not the facilitator) had his wife's car this morning and it is a great deal smaller than his car. So we had to take two trips to the apartment, one for the bags and one for us. Then we remembered that you had asked for some paper, so we stopped and got you some. You had asked for some paper the first week we were with you but I misunderstood and thought you wanted lined paper for writing. Then we got caught up in paperwork and adoption things, and then off to London. My first failure to you as a parent I guess Alex. Get used to it — I am only human after all.

 But in an attempt to redeem myself, I remembered the paper and we stopped and got some today. John also got some snacks for everyone to share and extras so you could give them to friends. But by the time we got to the orphanage it was about twelve fifteen. Sasha called us and said it was too late to visit and we wouldn't have long to stay. He didn't elaborate, so maybe there was some official function that the kids were going to later on, but we were a little disappointed. We wanted to spend more time with you. We wished we could have gotten things done with the hotel and apartment quicker, but we could only do it so fast.

 So, we only got about an hour and a half at the orphanage and in an exciting change for most of that time, the Radzinskis were there with their kids, Sergei and Max. Since Sergei and you are friends and wanted to be together, Amanda, John and I joined in the fun with everyone else and watched you all hang out together. We understand that it must be hard for you to be contemplating giving up all that is familiar. Even though you want to, it still must be slightly scary. As we watched you though, you seemed so happy and unaffected by all the turmoil and emotions that have been swirling around you. But also you seemed lighter today—as if a huge weight had been lifted off your shoulders. I think John and I felt like that too.

I know you were always worried that we would change our minds or that something would interfere with the adoption. (Ok—not that we would change our minds—we knew we wanted you too much—but that some paperwork issue would prevent it.) But now that you are officially ours, nobody can take you away. It is a done deal and no need to worry! I think we all felt like a weight was lifted because of that.

While we were visiting with everyone, little Max was called to go to sleep. Becky was sad as it seemed like there was too little time to visit with him and we all were a little down that he had to leave us. But then I remembered a deck of Uno cards that I had in my purse. I brought them out and we all played Uno together. It seems like Uno is a game that most kids over here know. I got the idea from reading adoption blogs, and it was a big hit. Beware, these kids are cheaters. See Alex, we were on to you. You and Sergei were hiding cards, trading them between yourselves, and generally trying to win by any means. We caught on pretty fast and tried to put an end to it with general hilarity. We had a lot of fun with Becky and Kevin and you and Sergei.

All too soon we had to go. It seems like we shouldn't have to say goodbye anymore. And it doesn't seem fair that you can't be with us. I really want you with us—you are ours now and we need to start the process of integrating you into our family. What better way to do it than here in your country where you are familiar with your surroundings. The apartment we are in is plenty big, there is room for you. And even if it is just boring time here together, at least it is a start. We have missed out on fourteen years together and we don't have that much time before you are an adult and want your own life. Watching you today made me a little sad when I realized that I am going to have to compress all of the childhood experiences I want you to have into about five years. But don't think that just because I am moaning about this that you get rid of us at eighteen or nineteen. You are part of this family forever—we will stick to you like fly paper. I want to be by your side for everything you do. G4 and Amanda can tell you John and I stick like crazy glue!

As you can tell, I am so anxious to start bonding with you. I am so proud of how you are doing with your English. You are really applying yourself and it shows. I was so surprised today with how you were doing. You were understanding us really well and even answered back with a few short sentences. I think you will be speaking English in no time. Every day you seem to pick up at least five or ten new words.

Anyway, we left you and came back to our apartment. We had some problems with the wifi card so John walked over to an MTC store to get it straightened out. He also got some food and we spent the rest of the night resting and talking about you and how much we love you and can't wait to finally be with you all the time!

Love always,
Mom

52: Day 23 — Sad news from home

Dearest Alex,

We got some terrible news late last night. A good friend lost her husband and brother in a boating accident during a yacht race. It is so tragic; they were such a wonderful family and had done so much for the homeschooling community. And the most tragic thing is the kids that are left now without a dad. We are stunned and saddened. She had helped me so much with my book among other things and my heart goes out to her. I wish there was something I could do, but being halfway around the world and half a day ahead makes it difficult.

I think this really brought home to me how isolating it is here to be apart from my life for so long. It seems so weird a situation. On one hand, there is nothing more important to me than you right now and getting everything done here, but on the other hand there is everything that is left behind. Now that we have gotten through court and are starting to talk about going home, I see that these two worlds are going to have to mesh together and soon. It sometimes seems insurmountable and at others no big deal. But either way, there is not much that can be done over here about it.

I want to be back on my turf again, with my familiar church, homeschooling books, and friends. But it is hard for me as I feel guilty knowing that every step I take closer to that life, is one step further away from the life you know. It seems cruel to me that we can't have the best of both worlds at the same time.

I fear every little difference could be a battle and I don't know how to ask you to accept us any better than I know how to accept you. I hope that you will accept our Catholic faith, my homeschooling of you, and our family life. However, I am realistic that there might be facets of our life which you don't want to accept. How we will deal with these, heaven only knows, but I am prepared to love you through all of it. I know you are a person with your own feelings, hopes, and desires. I won't pass judgment on those, but when they come into direct conflict with our feelings, hopes, and desires, I pray that we will be able to reconcile them together in a way that satisfies everyone.

I finally was able to get through to my mom last night and find out about things at the house. G4 is wonderful but it seems a little like getting information out of a stone at times. She was able to update me on everything going on and how your room is coming along. I had thought that we had a little more time than we did, so hadn't spent as much time in your room as I had wanted before we came to get you. We had the furniture, but no bedding, decorations, or extra clothes. I had shopped for you and brought those clothes with me, but I know that they will all be dirty when we finally get back and that I won't be up to laundry for at least a few days. So thank goodness, Grandma was able to step in and help out. Once I can make some determinations as to what sizes you are, I will call Grandma at home so she can start stocking up your closet. I don't mind laundry, but I want you to have enough to get through a week or two so I don't have to worry about it all the time.

I know I talk about clothes a lot, but realistically, it takes time to build a wardrobe from nothing. Every time we shop, it adds one or two things, so it takes more than a few trips to amass some volume.

My next task is to deal with the clothes we brought over here for you. We bought a few things that I brought with me to get you home, but that is about all I have. I am going to take those into the orphanage today when we see you to see if they fit. As I mentioned before, all the clothes in the orphanage are communal and children are not allowed to take any out with them. So adoptive parents have to provide everything for their new kids.

Well, I am just laying in bed right now typing on my computer—time to get up and face the day, even if it is with a heavy heart. Hearing the bad news just makes everything I have seem more precious right now, especially you. I just want you to know how much we love you and can't wait for the day when we don't have to say goodbye anymore and know that you will always be with us!

Love,
Mom

53: The rest of day 23

Dearest Alex,

    As usual just seeing you brightened our spirits immensely. You are so happy and fun to be around. We got to see you about ten o'clock this morning. We got your suitcase back from storage yesterday so we were able to take it in this morning and show you the clothes and see if they fit. I was especially concerned about the shoes fitting. You wore a size ten when you came last summer, but on intuition I bought size eleven. They seemed to fit just fine — maybe a little big but not too much. Everything else seemed just fine and I think you liked everything.

    We finally also had been able to charge the Nintendo DS that we had bought for you. Boy was that a big hit. Sergei rushed in and then the two of you were gone, swept away on a tide of video game surf. The Radzinskis came and again I can't tell you how nice it is to have another set of parents here going through the same things that we are. But unfortunately you and Sergei were so excited about the Nintendo that everyone forgot about little Max, as he was still with the little kids in a separate part of the orphanage. Finally Sergei was able to be pulled away from the game long enough to get little Max.

    We let everyone play for a while but then I decided to be evil homeschooling mom and pull you away from the electronics just for a half hour or so to do some English work. You didn't want to come but good-naturedly agreed and let me drill you with flash cards. Again I have to say how proud of your English I am. I am wondering whether or not you will even need a tutor, but I will wait to make that decision when we get home.

    Little Max was all over the place, so we ended up outside visiting with a bunch of kids. It was nice to see everyone that had come over last summer. I know that they are anxiously awaiting their parents soon. We have met one young lady named Yana that seems to be about fourteen or fifteen. She likes you (we can tell) but she is so sweet and polite. She gave us a picture that she had drawn that was on display. We felt so honored. We have it safely packed away in one of our suitcases and we are going to take it home and get it framed so that you have a little piece of a happy memory to look upon. She was doing a beautiful cross-stitch today as the kids were outside, so I sat next to her and talked as best we could for a while.

Everyone had a great time visiting and all too soon Sasha (our driver) was calling telling us it was time to go. Boy, today it was hard to leave you. I still don't see why we have to—I am counting the days until we don't have to say good-bye any more. I am really tired of saying it. But I have to console myself with the knowledge that we are on the downhill side of everything. I should be home in no more than two weeks. That makes me happy, because not only do I miss everyone at home but knowing that you are coming with us is comforting.

We rested a little in the afternoon while Amanda caught up on some school work and then walked over to a nearby department store. It is the same one we went to a couple of weeks ago to get your track suit. We are looking for gifts to take home to everyone. We also got lost in the book department again! I swear, homeschoolers can't stay away from books. We found some great workbooks and I had to restrain myself from buying several more. Space is at a premium and more books would be too heavy to take home.

I have to interrupt myself here for a minute. As we were sitting around this afternoon, our conversation turned to Sasha (our facilitator). We have been so impressed with how great he has been. Reflecting back on our court date (still a traumatic memory) and everything else—he has just been wonderful. We feel so lucky to have his help and support over here.

We met the Radzinskis for dinner. It was lovely. We were recommended a steak house by one of the basketball players we met. There was an outdoor patio with beautiful lighting and trees all around. The food was fabulous and the company great. It was picture perfect. But the curse struck again—we tried to pay for dinner (and this time were able to) but then when it came time to leave a tip—we didn't have the small bills to do it!

So, tomorrow, the routine will be the same—two hours to visit you at the orphanage (which is in my mind twenty-two too little)—and then the afternoon to stew about how much we want to be with you! You certainly are getting a lot of love sent your way from us!

See you tomorrow.
Mom

54: Day 24 — Taxi troubles

Dearest Alex,

Well, this was the penultimate day of visiting you. Only one more day of visits and then we will get to take you away with us. The funniest thing happened this morning. We were heading out the door to meet our driver, Sasha, when Sasha the facilitator called from Kiev and said that his car was broken down and a taxi would be pulling up outside at ten in the morning. He gave very specific instructions—it was black with the number 76 on it. So we dutifully waited. Within about two minutes, right on time, a grey taxi pulled up and stopped. It had a bunch of numbers on the side with a 76 in there, maybe a phone number or address (I couldn't tell which) but John and I looked at each other and just hopped in. We assumed that the colors had gotten mixed up, but how many taxis were there that would pull up outside our building at ten in the morning on a holiday here with the number 76 on it? The driver looked at us and started speaking in a language I didn't recognize (couldn't even tell if it was Russian or not), so John pulled out his phone and started to type on Google Translate.

Now, Google Translate is usually pretty good for communicating the basics if you use short sentences. We haven't had much trouble with people understanding it. But this was a first—I don't know if he was not able to read or maybe didn't understand Russian, only Ukrainian. But regardless of the reason, we were stuck without a way to communicate. So we had no choice but to call Sasha in Kiev on the phone and let him speak to the driver. We felt so bad and stupid of course. Poor Sasha has been so wonderful and he was just trying to have a quiet weekend holiday with his family, and here we are—unable to follow the simplest of explicit instructions!

After a minute of talking to the taxi driver, he handed the phone back and Sasha confirmed what we were now fearing, this was not the right taxi. And right as we got out, a couple walked out of the apartment door right next to ours and waved at the taxi. I am sure they were wondering what these people were doing stealing their taxi!

We were so embarrassed. But as we turned around, there was a black taxi pulling in with the number 76 in its license plate. We very quietly slunk in and went to the orphanage. There was no more discussion of transportation, and when the driver left us, it was obvious he did not speak English, so we just assumed Sasha would call us when it was time to go. We did not want to call him back and be even more pesky that we already are.

We had a wonderful visit with everyone. You and Sergei, the Radzinski's, and us, have all fallen into a routine of sorts, hanging out together. The only hard part is Max, who is so little that he keeps getting taken away to sleep by the orphanage staff, so he isn't having the chance to interact with the other boys and families as much. It is hard because I think if he could see the other boys and how comfortable they are, he would be more at ease as well.

Anyway, we had a great time. The boys played video games for a long time on a variety of gaming devices from Nintendos to iphones to iPads. They were having a great time but every hour or so, we would pull you away and make you do some English study. I found a great workbook at the bookstore a couple of weeks ago and worked with you on it for a while. I was so pleased to see how well you read English. It was far advanced from what I thought you could read and what you can speak. But I guess thinking about it, that is the way I am in Russian and Spanish. I can read far faster and understand more reading than listening to native speakers and speaking it myself.

We drilled with some of the flash cards too and roped Sergei in to school work as well. It was fun doing it together. Then everyone filed outside for fun with sidewalk chalk. We had found some at a store near the apartment for about fifty cents a pack. It was a big hit, with even the older girls joining in. John drew a big hopscotch and everyone was having a great time. It was such a fun day with beautiful weather. The trees were starting to bud when we left to go to London, but now they are fully green and beautiful. There was a slight breeze blowing and clear blue sky. With the holiday and the weekend, the steel mills are not spewing out their usual pollution. You can really tell, and Mariupol is such a beautiful place without the pollution.

By now it was one o'clock and we were wondering about when to leave the orphanage. We hadn't heard anything and as I mentioned earlier, we didn't want to bother Sasha again. So we just waited. We played some card games with the boys, more video games, and more school work of course. At about two thirty he called and asked if we were still there. We said yes and I think we have upset the apple cart a little because he told us it was too late to be there and we had to go. We felt really bad, we don't want to upset anyone, but there was no one around, the orphanage staff didn't seem to care, and we just figured when it was time to go, we would get called.

It was hard saying goodbye again, but I know that there will only be one more time of saying goodbye. Then, it will be lifetime of hellos!

Love you bunches,
Mom

55: Day 25 — Tomorrow never comes

Dearest Alex,

I can't believe it. Today is the last visit to the orphanage! Tomorrow when we go it will be to pick you up. This whole thing has my stomach tied in knots. I am so excited and nervous and scared and happy all rolled into one ball of nerves. I bet you feel the same way. I can't imagine what it would feel like to leave not only the residence with which you are familiar, but your friends, your country, and your language. I have some of the same trepidations of bringing a child into my home that I can't fully communicate with and trying to meet all of your needs.

I hope that I can communicate to you that we love you so much and that any problems or transition you face will not have to be faced alone. You have a whole family that will be with you every step of the way. We can't take away some of these trials, but we can help you with them.

So today, we were back with our driver Sasha and his poor car. It obviously has not gotten all of its problems fixed and we were worried that we would not make it to the orphanage. It had been making some funny noises before, but now it was making really funny noises and the clutch was slipping. There was also some funny lurching back and forth as we were driving down the streets.

Anyway, we finally made it to the orphanage and saw your smiling face. As usual, every time I get to see you, I am overcome with how lucky we are to be able to adopt you. You are such a wonderful kid.

We started with more school work (I know, dull, huh?) but it has to be done! After about a half hour, I let you off the hook to visit with Sergei and Max. Max today seemed more comfortable around Becky and Kevin. He also was feeling very left out as the big boys were playing with their electronics. He kept coming in to watch what you and Sergei were doing and the last time had such a hang-dog expression on his face, it was pitiful. So, I stepped in and fussed at you older boys and I am so proud that you all put down your games and went outside with Max. A soccer ball was procured and fun and games were had by all for about an hour. It was warm out but there was a pleasant breeze blowing. The only bad thing was that the steel mills have started up again so there is more pollution in the air.

But all too soon, Sasha pulled up and we had to go. But this time, I know it is the last good-bye I will have to say. Thank goodness. We are going to be able to come back to the orphanage in the morning to get you. As an added bonus, your Grandma is going to come as well to say good-bye. I am excited about meeting her. John and I went out today and got her some flowers and we will give her some money too. I know she needed medication for her heart, but I think it is easier to give her money so that she can get exactly what she needs.

There was supposed to be a party at the orphanage, but Sasha has asked if we could skip it. I think in a way, that is OK. You have had these last few days of vacation and the weekend with your friends, and a big to do over the whole thing might be overwhelming. Just remember, if you want to come back (and I hope you will to see your Grandma) just ask, and we will bring you. You have special roots here that are precious and unique that I want to nurture and keep. You live in a global world—no one stays in one place anyway.

This afternoon has been a flurry of activity as we prepare to leave tomorrow. Sasha has prepared us that it may not happen, but we are ever hopeful. I know it sounds funny to hear us say that, in America, you would of course know the plan, but here, well everything is different! It all depended on picking up the paperwork from the social minister's office and while it was supposed to be done, these offices have been known to have random closures on occasion. So we are hoping but not counting on it.

We went shopping at the department store nearby again and bought some more clothes for you. It is a little warmer here now than we anticipated and many of the clothes we brought for you will be too heavy. This way, you will have a variety to choose from.

We also went to several small boutiques to get presents to bring home to everyone. Look out, our suitcases are packed to the brim. We bought out the rest of the sidewalk chalk for the kids at the orphanage as well since that was such a big hit.

This evening we went out for our last dinner with the Radzinski's. We have now shown them all around the place and given them our favorite haunts to eat at. They will be carrying the torch from here on out!

Can't wait for tomorrow—my stomach is tied in knots just thinking about it. It's kind of like the night I spent before my last c-section. You know something stupendous is going to happen the next day and make you happier than your wildest dreams, but you still have some feelings that there could be some bumps in the road and know that there will be some painful recovery afterwards! Weird but true.

Anyway, love you bunches dear Alex. We are counting the minutes until we can hold you and never have to let go.

Love,
Mom

56: A very humbling day

Dearest Alex,

What a day! I am so dehydrated that I am a prune I have cried so much! It started early this morning with Amanda's physics class from Stanford. She usually has to get up at three fifteen in the morning am over here to catch the live discussion. I was being a clock watcher waking up every hour or so to make sure the alarm went off so that she did not miss class. Then every time I woke up, I would remember what was happening today and start thinking and worrying, and couldn't go back to sleep.

Finally at two I got up to get the laundry out of the machine and hang it up so that it would dry. I got Amanda up at three, made sure she was in class and then was finally able to go back to sleep. Poor Amanda was left to keep herself awake on her own.

When we woke up at seven, we hit the ground running. We were almost all packed already. I just finished up packing the last few things that I had washed and then we ventured out to go to the orphanage. We discovered on the way out that the lift was broken, so that would mean heartache later when moving the suitcases down eight flights of stairs, but for now, we were just focused on getting to you and seeing your Grandma.

When we pulled up to the orphanage, we saw you sitting on a bench with an older lady, obviously dressed in her Sunday best with a cute straw hat on. She immediately started crying and that started me off. She was talking, talking, talking, and you were trying to translate as best you could. We got some of the ideas of what was being said, but lost a lot of it in translation.

We gave her some flowers and then when she started talking about how much she pays in rent each month and how much heart medicine she needs, we gave her some money. We then all went into the orphanage to sit down. Finally Sasha turned up and was able to translate for us. I know your English is getting better, but you were in no way able to deal with the torrent of words that she was pouring out.

We videoed her talking so that we can listen to it later and so that you can have it someday to look at. We did find out a lot of information though. Your dad was twenty when you were born, so that explains why your grandma was so involved in raising you. She told us that she basically raised you. You will find out when you have children of your own some day that a twenty year old is still a child themselves and is in no shape to raise one of their own. Then he moved away with another lady and in 2007, when she was pregnant with your half-sister, he got appendicitis. He died of complications from an infection from surgery. I am so sorry. It is a shame that his life was cut short by that.

In 2010 you came into the orphanage because your grandma thought that she couldn't care for you anymore. She told us that when you were little, you would cry every night and pray for a real mommy and daddy. Then she said when you came into the orphanage, you cried as well, wondering why you didn't have a family. That just set me off again! I cried and cried until I think everyone was ready to put me in a home! At this point I think you had had enough because you asked for an iPad and disappeared with Amanda into another room. I saw your face get very somber as your grandmother was describing your past and I just wanted to reach out and hug you again. I couldn't though because she was crying too and I was hugging her and crying right along with her. Then finally I stopped crying and was able to visit like a normal person. Primarily it was because Sasha left for a while and I didn't understand what she was saying.

Then we showed her some pictures of our home and John and miscellaneous other things, which caused her to cry again and therefore I was crying again. We couldn't understand her so we had to call you in to translate. You are doing well—I know I have said this a hundred times—but I am so proud of how much English you have learned. However, it has been mostly limited to the vocabulary we have taught you on the flashcards and common things like food and clothing. It was hard for you to translate the feelings and emotions that she was clearly expressing.

All of a sudden Sasha came in and said, "Time to go." We didn't want to leave but we had to do paperwork. We went to a lawyer's office (which if you transliterate is called a notarees—funny enough) and signed papers and then went to get you a new birth certificate with your new name. We were able to get it without any difficulty so then back to the apartment (dragging the luggage down eight flights of stairs) and then to orphanage to finally pick you up.

When we got there, we gave you the clothes we had brought for you and you went to change. Now everyone reading—get your hankies ready. This is where it really got rough for me. You walk out with a few photos, the camera we gave you to take pictures of your last day, a book, and the track suit we bought you two weeks ago. That was it. I was so humbled that this was all you had to represent fourteen years of life. I mean, sometimes I fuss that I don't have things and that life is hard—I will stop doing that now. You have taught me the meaning of humbleness today.

I had to walk away I was crying so hard at this point. Thank goodness you didn't see me. You were off snapping more last minute pictures. I felt such an awesome responsibility handed to me. I felt like I had the weight of making up for fourteen years. Then I realized what a great gift you were to me. I realized that you were such a blessing to us and that making up for this time will be such fun. It will help us bond and become a closer family.

I was finally able to stop crying just in time, as we were called into the director's office and basically given our marching orders! It was her final blessing to take you away from the orphanage. She told us to take care of you and keep in touch with them at the orphanage. She also admonished you to do well in school and to behave for us. She really rules that orphanage with an iron hand but she does love the kids. She was admonishing you to study hard and do well and to take care of your family. She then admonished us to take care of you and discipline you! Don't worry—I am not that much into discipline—I think you will like unschooling! Not too much structure.

After we left, we all squeezed into the car and off to Donetsk. This is quite a feat if you knew the amount of luggage that we had!. We were being driven by Vladimir who had driven us several times to and from Donetsk. I think he actually lives in Donetsk. Nobody uses air conditioning here—so the ride was a little uncomfortable with being squashed into the car for so long. Once we got to Donetsk, we stopped to get passport photos made and then sped off to the passport office. We knew that it would take greasing the wheels to get it done quickly and sure enough $600 made it happen this afternoon!

Unfortunately bribes are a way of doing business here and we knew our time was coming. If we had not paid, the passport could have taken up to a week as it got buried in paperwork on people's desks. However, it seemed a small price to pay to shave a week off our stay in Ukraine.

Vladimir parked the car across from a government building, asked for our passports and the bribe money and took the photos of you that we had just had made. He then made the sign of the cross and off he went indicating that we should wait. Of course, remember that he spoke no English, and we only had you to help us out understanding things.

He was gone a really long time and we were starting to get really uncomfortable. We got out of the car and stretched our legs for a while, but didn't want to stray too far away. Finally after about forty-five minutes he came out smiling and waving a brand new Ukrainian passport in his hand! We had done it—a passport in one day.

Vladimir then took us to the hotel which is a riot. It is called the Liverpool Hotel and is totally Beatles themed. It has only Beatles music playing! There is so much more to tell. I want to type more now but am just exhausted. I need to sleep as we are leaving for Kiev early in the morning.

I am just so overwhelmed and excited that you are finally ours. You are the best kid in the world! We are so lucky to have found you and I can't wait to get home and get you started on your new life.

Today is the first day of the rest of your life!

We love you so much,
Mom

57: Get ready to need more hankies

Dearest Alex,

So, it is now four thirty in the morning and I am even more tired than yesterday I think. The hotel had air conditioning but it was not sufficient let's say. Neither was it cold enough outside when we opened the window! So we are not all that rested and really lethargic. I told John I had to finish yesterday's account just to give me an excuse to stay in bed a few more minutes.

When we got to the hotel, we had to get two rooms, one for you and Amanda and one for us. They only had rooms with two twin beds available. I was beat so I just put you and Amanda in the other room and said let's rest a while before going out to eat. All of a sudden there was a knock at our door. You came rushing in and this went on for about a half hour or so with you running back and forth. Amanda told us that you were like a kid at Christmas. You opened up the suitcase we got you and went through it item by item. I had put some miscellaneous things in it like a bottle of hand sanitizer, a packet of tic-tacs, etc. Everything that you could, you rushed over to share. You wanted us to clean our hands, take a tic-tac, etc. I was humbled all over again. Here is someone who had almost nothing, then gets a little something, and the first thing you want to do is share it! Wow!

Then I was crying again! You brought over a picture of your dad holding you when you were two or three years old. You wanted to share it with us! You are the spitting image of your dad—and that started me off all over again. I think I was exasperating you a little because you looked at me like—what is your problem? Then later Amanda told us you came back to the room and wanted to shower and change again! You was anxious to try out the deodorant and body spray we had packed in your suitcase.

Once you were done, (she said you primped like a girl), we stepped out to go to dinner. We walked about two blocks to a restaurant and once we sat down, you took over. You were helping us with the menu, ordering for us (I didn't have the heart to tell you we had English menus) and generally taking over! It was so cute. We had given you an old iPhone that we had because we don't have a home phone—everyone has cell phones. It is not connected to service yet so it really is just an iPod touch until we get home. But you had it out and were connected to the wireless in the restaurant and every other minute was saying, Dad, or Mom, and showing us something.

It was so rewarding seeing you have a good time. I think we were all holding our breath that you would regret coming with us and giving up the familiar. You were so excited about everything though that it put us at ease. I know everything will not be this easy, but this little glimpse into your personality has been great. I am convinced that we have adopted the best kid in the whole world.

Anyway, gotta go, Daddy John is guilting me into getting up. More later.

I love you always and forever,
Mom

58: Day 27 — American embassy part 1

Dearest Alex,

Another great day. We were up bright and early. You looked so tired this morning. Daddy John asked you if you slept and you said, "No, I was too busy playing games." We are going to have to address the sleeping issues when you get home! I don't really care too much but I will draw the line at midnightish. And while I don't want you up early — I am not even functional before nine in the morning — I would like you up by ten or so to be able to get some work done. But these are issues that will have to be ironed out later.

We made it to the airport and onto the plane. Poor John was so tired he immediately sacked out, Amanda was reading a book, and you were listening to music, so I just snuggled up and put my head on your shoulder and slept for a while too. Hope you didn't mind but I was just so tired.

Once we got to Kiev, our old driver, Sergei, met us and took us right to the American embassy. Apparently we are a family of firsts. Sasha told us that the embassy had just moved and that we would be the first family to have an adoption processed there. When we pulled up, it was another humbling experience. We saw a huge line of people (over 100) waiting outside the embassy. Our driver parked and walked up with us and said something to the guard that sounded like, "Americanski" and we were ushered right in. It was so sad to see all these people who were dreaming of coming to America and here just by winning the ovarian lottery, we were waltzing right in. We had to go through security and then walked over to the visa and immigration area. We were struck by the number of people that were waiting to be helped and again were ushered to the head of the line. We had tried to fill out some of the paperwork ahead of time, but it was impossible without help, so most of it was blank. We have heard stories in the past about people having bad times at the embassy, and even Sasha told us to be aware and fill out the forms completely because they did not like to be held up. I was worried going in there but it turned out that they could not have been any nicer. When I pointed out the blank spots on the form, the gentleman behind the counter just smiled and said, "That's OK, that is why we are here, to help you." And this pretty much was the attitude of every staff member we met. They were so nice and helpful, explaining things to you in Russian as well as to us in English, and congratulating us on you joining our family. It was not a quick experience though—we were there about an hour and were ready to die of hunger. Where was my emergency candy bar? Eaten the day before and not replaced I tell you! But overall very painless and easy.

So we had Sergei take us to a restaurant before we all fainted with hunger. We had been to a nice restaurant near the apartment in Kiev before called Mafia (I know—funny huh?) so we went back there and stuffed ourselves. I know you were getting really hungry but after a two Pepsis and a smoothie and a huge pizza, I think we fixed your hunger.

We had to get a few food items, so then we had Sergei take us to a supermarket. Poor Sergei, we kept trying to get him to come with us, we offered him lunch, but he just sat in the car and waited for us the whole time. As we were in the market, waiting to get some cheese sliced, I had another hankie moment. You looked at me and said, "Mom, I love you. You love me?" I melted and replied, "Of course I love you." But I know that did not even begin to convey the depth of feelings I have for you. I know you need a lot of affirmation of our love for you, and don't worry, we will never tire of giving it to you, but you don't have to worry. You are ours forever!

After we left the market, it was back to the apartment in Kiev. We have so many suitcases now with your two added that I am surprised there was even any room to fit us in! Since we were all so tired, John took a nap, I worked a little on my writing and you and Amanda sacked out on the couch playing on iPads. It was so cute, you all look like twins. I wanted to talk with you, but I also want to be cognizant of the issue that you might find all of us overwhelming, so right now, I will not pester you. I will pick my moments!

A note about the weather is in order here. When we first landed, it was coats all the time. Not heavy coats, be we definitely needed another layer. Now it is so hot, you just want to peel your skin off. And there is no A/C in the apartment here. There are fans, but somehow Ukraine skipped spring and went right to summer. I have noticed there are two kinds of clothes here—bundled up maximally and very skimpy—nothing in between.

I also have to tell you a funny story about your new dad. If I put this in before, I am sorry. He is very frugal—to the core. He will spend money on things that are justified, but he hates service fees, transaction fees, etc. He views those as a waste of money. So, knowing that if we used our regular credit cards overseas there would be a fee—he investigated credit cards without fees. He found an American Express card that had no foreign transaction fees, entrance to all the sky clubs at airports and multiple other benefits. So he paid the annual fee for the card (no small fee I might add) and off we went. The first thing we discovered was that while it promised entrance into sky clubs, you had to send in a form and wait two or three weeks for it to be processed and another card sent to you. So that didn't work out.

That was OK with him as he decided the lack of foreign transaction fees would still pay for the card several times over. Then we get here and he is trying to use that card everywhere and no can do. Nobody takes it. Sasha was always laughing at him saying, "Give it up man." But if you all know my husband, you know he is determined. He kept trying and finally, found one restaurant, in Mariupol that took it. We went there once and it was a stinky restaurant, but he was pacified that he got to use his Amex card. Then he found he could make all the airline reservations online using it so that made him happy. But today was his final triumph. We were at the embassy and after we filled out the forms, we were told that everyone else had to sit down and one person should go over to the cashier's window and pay. So Alex, Amanda, and I sat down while John saunters over to the cashiers window. It was then that I had a flash of oh no! I had left my purse in the car because there are no cell phones, electronics, or basically anything allowed in the embassy, so it just seemed easier to carry our passports in my hand and leave the purse in the car. I realized as John walked over to the window that all of the nice crisp bills we had set aside in American dollars were safely in the car and not in the building to pay the fee. I rushed over to him and he said in his typical laid back way, "Don't worry, I bet they take credit cards." Of course I had little belief that this was the case and sat back down thinking that all of a sudden an official was going to come out of the back office and take you by the arm and march you off saying, "If your parents can't pay, you can't stay with them."

In an interesting aside here, I have to note that as you might have been worried in the beginning that this is not forever and we might change our minds, I have become more and more paranoid that someone will take you away from me! Interesting how this is working.

Anyway, back to the story. As I am watching John, all of a sudden he starts strutting around and looking like a very satisfied cat that ate a canary. When he arrives back to us, he smugly says, "They took American Express." Oh boy, he is going to be impossible to live with after this! Then to further add to his joy — the whole thing at the embassy with fees for the immigrant visa and everything is going to cost only $230. We have to pay for the medical exam of course, but the embassy fees for the immigration visa are much lower than anticipated.

We came back to the apartment and A1 (the other Alex) showed up to spend the afternoon with us. If there is any sibling rivalry going on it will be between you two I think. But at least you finally got to meet him in person and it does help to have a translator around. I know you are kind of bored listening to us in English visit with him, but we haven't seen him much in the past two years and it is so great to catch up with him. And I hate to see you struggle, but I think the best way to win the English language battle is to jump in feet first and immerse you as much as possible.

Anyway, I have gone on far too long here. I just want you to know that in every way our love for you grows and grows. You are a great kid and we consider ourselves very lucky!

Love,
Mom

59: Day 27 — Part 2

Dearest Alex,

    I got tired last night so I didn't finish typing about yesterday. Once we were at the apartment for a while, A1 came over to visit. At first you were a little quiet, and we didn't help matters chattering away in English, but then A1 let you use his phone to call back to Mariupol and after a fifteen-minute talk — you were like a clam that had opened up. You were laughing and smiling and seemingly very comfortable.

    Then I don't know why we didn't think of it before, but we had purchased some Skype credits to call back to America (which is incredibly cheap — like two cents a minute) we let you use those to call your friends in the evening. It is slightly more expensive but well worth the mental effects for everyone. By the way, you chatter like a teenage girl on the phone with hardly taking a breath — it is non-stop!

    Last night after Daddy John and A1 made a lovely dinner, you wanted to go for a walk. A1 said that the river was nearby (note to self — always quantify "nearby" in the future) and we all decided to walk to it. It had rained earlier and instead of cooling off, it made things more humid. We set off, got lost, had to use A1's cell phone to figure out where we were and thirty minutes later, found the river. But it wasn't the river, it was a dank little tributary where there was a boat junkyard and lots of mosquitos. Then on the way back we ended up in an alleyway with lots of garbage cans that were ripe in the heat. And to top it all off the rain had lefts bogs of black mud everywhere. All in all it was a lovely outing.

    I was so tired and cranky and I think you realized it. I took a cold shower and when I came in to check on you, you said, "Mom, you go to bed now." So I took your advice and sacked out!

                                             So happy you are with us,
                                                            Mom

60: Day 28 — Goodbye John and Amanda

Dearest Alex,

You have just cemented your place in my heart if you hadn't already. I slept like the dead. Even though there is no A/C in this apartment in Kiev, we discovered a ceiling fan (it has always been there — I guess we hadn't noticed it before) and that allowed a more comfortable sleep. So when I finally awoke I was so crumpled and rested, it wasn't funny. And anyone who knows me knows that I am not a morning person. And I had gone to bed with wet hair the night before — everyone starting to get a mental picture here?

So I stumbled out of the bedroom and found you in the kitchen, cooking breakfast. My heart stopped! I was able to crawl into the banquette and just sit while you served me a lovely frittata and toast with even a garnish of lettuce and tomato on the side. Then you cleaned up the dishes! If it wasn't true love before (and you know it was) it definitely is now. I was able to slowly become functional through breakfast and discovered that you had gone out for a run in the morning and then come back, showered, and then made breakfast. You had asked me about a run the night before and I had A1 translate that you could go as long as you took money and a cell phone. Everyone questioned my conditions but as I pointed out what would happen if you broke your leg and had to get a taxi or needed help? Of course at that everyone had to point at my knee!

I was so not into you going out alone. I usually would never allow G4 and Amanda to be out alone, but this again highlights the differences over here. You just feel so removed from your normal life. You seem to just function differently. And I was still not feeling like a full-fledged parent here. It felt more like you were the parent taking care of me in this country that I don't speak the language, understand the customs or know how to get around.

I am so impressed with you. You are like a little adult in the body of a teen. I hope that I can give you back some of your childhood. I also want you to know that you do not have to do anything back for us — there is nothing that you have to be grateful for or thank us for — *you* complete US. If you want to do these things, fine, but they won't make me love you more — I already love you bunches already just for the person you are.

So, sadly this is John and Amanda's last day here. They are flying back to the states today. They have a layover in Detroit overnight so they will not be home until Sunday. A1 came over and accompanied us to the airport.

It was hard to say goodbye to them, especially John. He has been my protector and partner in this venture and I feel so lost without him. I know that it is just a few days until I will get home, but then he will be gone on a business trip to Chicago for a board meeting. We will be back to the two ships that pass in the night thing, but this time here has been such a gift. It really has been with Amanda too, the lazy days as I call them when we could just visit you for a few hours were wonderful. Ok, I take that back—they weren't wonderful because we wanted you and were reduced to seeing you only a few hours a day, but they were wonderful in that the three of us got a chance to bond and spend time together that our normally busy lives do not let us do.

Anyway, after the soppy goodbye, I think you were worried about me because as we got back in the van to leave, you hugged me and asked, "Is OK, Mom?" You are so thoughtful and sweet! We went to an electronics store to buy A1 a gift—we have missed a lot of birthdays and Christmases so we bought him a tablet computer that he had wanted. Then Sergei dropped us off at a mall where we started to shop for some more clothes for you. Boy, that was hard.

What is it with teenage boys? Picky, picky, picky. These jeans were too formal, these jeans were too dark, those were too light. Even A1 was getting frustrated—he asked if he was this bad when we took him shopping when he lived with us, and I happily assured him that he was. And of course I have more recently been through it with G4. Yikes! Girls are easier—they can communicate what is wrong with the clothes—boys just mutter no and shake their heads. This wasn't language issues, this was teenage testosterone speaking. But we did manage to come up with one pair of shoes, one track suit, one t-shirt, and one pair of jeans. And boy were you beaming from ear to ear. It was worth the hard work to see that smile!

Then we went to see a movie, *The Avengers*. It was really good. And for me, very little dialogue so it was easy to follow! I was so proud of myself,

I even was able to understand a few sentences here and there and caught many words here and there.

Afterwards, we rushed in the rain to the subway station and took it back to the apartment. It had stopped raining pretty much when we got off the subway. I guess the rain cloud is just following me everywhere on this trip no matter what country I am in.

Once we got back to the apartment, you wanted to go to the market to get food to make dinner for me. You are definitely a keeper! But I wouldn't let you go alone — I was worried about you — I know you are fourteen, but you will have to cut me some slack. I know I let you go out on a run, but there you shouldn't have interacted with anyone. I think it will take a few weeks for this overprotectiveness and momma bear outlook to burn out. Also, I am out of my element here. Seemingly easy decisions are hard to make when you feel the power is not in your court. So for some reason, running alone was OK in the morning, but going out the market alone was not.

We shopped and then came back to the apartment. I had great notions of getting work done on my next book, but then decided to Skype and got sidetracked. G4 and Grandma were able to say hello and G4 was able to carry the computer into your new room to give you a look at it.

Once we were off the computer, you told me a story about your dad. You told me that your dad baked bread (I am thinking in a bakery or restaurant) as a job. When you were six, you got to go into work with him and he showed you how to make bread. Then you told me that he also showed you how to cook the meal that you were cooking for me now. It was a potato dish with onions and mushrooms. I was so surprised and honored that you shared the memory with me. Thank goodness you served the food and asked to go Skype your friends and ran off with the computer and your plate of food so that you missed me blubbering into my food feeling humbled all over again. The meal by the way was delicious!

I felt so bad that you cooked, so I roused myself out of my pool of tears and washed all the dishes. It was the least I could do. I then wrestled your dirty laundry away from you so that I could wash it and then hopped in the shower. I have figured the way to get a good night's sleep without air conditioning is to take a cold shower before bed—it drops the body temperature enough to let you get to sleep.

I have also discovered (actually I simply asked) that you have a girlfriend who is seventeen and the older sister of a set of boys who came to Utah last summer with you and are somewhere in the process of being adopted.

Anyway, time to turn in. It has been a great day and a fun one. A1 will come back tomorrow and visit before he leaves for Poltava to see his girlfriend and parents, and we have things to do on Monday like our embassy visit. There is the possibility that we can change our tickets to Tuesday if we get all of our paperwork done at the embassy Monday, so let's hope!

Bye for now (seems silly when you are right here—but that is good problem to have).

Mom

61: Day 29 — Goodbye to A1

Dearest Alex,

Ok, so it appears that I got some information wrong. Don't you just love language barriers? Anyway, out of the blue you came and flopped down on the bed next to me last night and immediately started in with the fact that I had gotten it all wrong — Olga was not your girlfriend — just a friend who is a girl. Then I asked if you had a girlfriend and you turned all red and said, "No, no, no." You were adamant; however, I'm not sure I believe you. Remember, I have seen with my own eyes how teenage girls throw themselves at you!

Anyway, I had another great night's sleep and woke up this morning to find that you were still asleep. Thank goodness, I was beginning to think that I had adopted a robot who didn't sleep. And once you get to know me better, you will figure out that sleep is the ultimate goal in my life! I think I missed out on too much in the years around medical school and residency and it elevated sleep to a very important place in my life.

So, I snuck out and started to get ready trying to stay quiet. You finally got up around 9:00 am and said that you wanted to go out running, so I let you. I hope you know how difficult it is for me to let you do that. But after making sure that you had enough money and the phone, I let you go. I know that everything is overwhelming at times and that you need to get away. Exercise is probably a really good way to deal with everything. But when you came back a suspiciously short time later with a grocery bag from the market — I realized you had fooled me — you went to get more food at the market!

Anyway, you were hot and sweaty, so I cooked breakfast for you. Not as good as yours I am afraid, but hopefully you liked it. Then we did a little English work and pretty soon A1 came. He had downloaded movies onto DVD's in Russian for you, which was really nice of him. I want you to have some ability to keep your language and I figured reading Russian books and watching movies in the language will help.

We had Sergei drive us downtown and got caught up in the marathon that was being run there today. We couldn't make it to the center of the city, so we got out and walked through a really pretty park by the river and then walked over to Khreschatyk Street. It was the starting and ending point of the marathon. There were bunches of people milling around, very fun, but hot. Then Sergei picked us up and drove us to another place by the river with all sorts of cafes and a boardwalk area. It was a lot of fun. We ended up at a sushi restaurant of all things and had a lovely lunch.

All too soon A1 had to leave. He is on his way to Poltava to visit with his parents. He has been saving up his vacation from work. So we walked to the subway and he pointed us in our direction and off we went. It was sad to say goodbye to him, but as always we will keep in touch.

I am so proud of you and me — we navigated the subway by ourselves and found our way back to the apartment completely by ourselves. Ok, it was really you. I am no help at all in the navigation area! No problems at all. It was so hot and nasty though that all we could really do is collapse in the apartment and cool off with the fans. It must be lethal here in the summer.

You have been yakking for the past hour or so on Skype with your friends. I am tempted to shut it off as it is getting expensive and I want to interact with you, but I know your opportunities to talk with friends will end soon as it will be more expensive from the states. You also asked A1 today if you thought we would be bringing you back this summer. Yikes! I don't think so. I am so homesick it isn't funny. And while we have had a record breaking FAST adoption — I still don't think that the memories from this trip are going to fade in my mind anytime soon. It has not been hard, but not easy either. The emotional side of things is overwhelming at times. There have been times that I have not wanted to be the adult — I have wanted to curl up in a little ball and have someone else be the adult and take care of me!

It is hard to put into words. I talked to the Radzinski's this morning on the phone as they are still in Mariupol. In fact, Becky and I were just talking about this very subject, the difficulties of going through this process. It is impossible to articulate the visit here. It is definitely not a vacation in any way, but you have the lack of responsibility of home that a vacation brings. You are not a parent for most (actually all of the trip) because either you are just visiting the child a few hours a day, or when they are with you, you are still on their turf, helpless with the language barrier. Even though

I can speak and understand a little — it doesn't seem to help. You just can't seem to impose normal controls or expectations because everything is unfamiliar and a little skewed. We are in an apartment with a kitchen, yet you can't cook like you normally would. This is just one of the things. You can buy everything you need here but somehow it is more difficult to meet your needs. I don't even know if I am making any sense but that is just the reality of the way I see it.

This whole trip has been really trying for me, but I keep having to remind myself that your tough period is yet to come. I know that I am wanting this time to end as quickly as possible but then on the other side, you want to stretch it out. Seems difficult to be so in love with someone that is on the opposite side of the spectrum.

So, I am anxious to get home and start making you part of the family. I know the bonding has started here, but I think it will go so much faster in America. Hopefully, you will feel less of the pull of your friends and Grandma there. I know that we are asking so much of you—something I know I couldn't have done at fourteen. And you are doing it with such grace and maturity that it sometimes floors me. I have been so appreciative of how protective you are of me, especially when we are out and about. But at the same time, I want you to feel that protected too, and I think I can do it much better at home.

Tomorrow we have the doctor's appointment and then on Tuesday, the final embassy paperwork!

Love you always,
Mom

62: Day 30 — Everything is done!

Dearest Alex,

The paperwork is all done! I can't believe it. You are officially ready to leave Ukraine. Getting everything done has given me a new perspective. I was initially fussy that we couldn't leave tomorrow and had to wait for Wednesday, but now, I feel like I can handle anything. We will just have a fun day tomorrow, you and me, and enjoy your last look at Ukraine for a while. I am absolutely committed to coming back in a year or two, but I need a little break. Ok, truthfully, more than a little — it might be a year or two before I can do this again.

We started out way too early this morning. You were up at four in the morning. Why??? I will have to get used to this. You were running, doing pushups and pullups and all other sorts of heinous things that are painful at best but early in the morning are horrid! Then you came back and woke me up at six thirty because you knew that I am not a morning person. You were so cute, trying to get me out of bed and then gave up and said, "ten minutes more, Mom," and went off to the shower. I managed to rouse myself, but it wasn't pretty.

Sasha came to get us at seven thirty and we were off to the doctors office to get your immigration physical. There was another adoptive family there who had adopted four (yes, everyone heard me right) unrelated children, under the age of six, with medical problems). They looked so tired, I felt so sorry for them. Three of the children came from Mariupol (obviously a different orphanage) and one from Donetsk. I typed on Google Translate to you that even though I loved you, I could not have handled four of you at once!

Once we were done with the physical, it was off to the SDA. Then we waited a long while in the unbelievable heat for Sasha to complete his business for some other families. I wanted to walk around with you, but you were busy listening to music on your iPhone, so I left you in the car and walked around. I found a few little things that I enjoyed dickering with the sales people to get. Then after about thirty minutes I went back to the car, at which time, you hopped out wanting to go buy some souvenirs for yourself, by yourself. This independent streak you have is a mile wide! Anyway, I let you go, watching you from afar.

We went to lunch at this point, everyone was pretty hungry. Every other time we have gone out—they have taken credit cards. Do you think these people did? No, of course not. Every other time we have asked the driver to lunch, do you think they wanted to? No, of course not, but today, of course. I had pretty much spent all but 200 hrivnas, and now had to feed four people off of this. I can't win—poor Sasha had to kick in. We are such lame people when it comes to picking up the tab! Anyway, it was a nice lunch, then off to the American embassy.

In contrast to the last time we were there, this time it was a ghost town, no one in sight. We went through security and went into the immigration visa area and waited. You were so antsy. Every two minutes, you were asking, "Go now, mom?" I realized real quick I am going to have to teach you delayed gratification, as well as doing things as part of a family.

Anyway, we were called up after about fifty minutes and the same gentleman who helped us before was there again. He checked all of the paperwork and then told us to go wait for the customs officer. Again, you were all antsy and wanted me to just go up to the window and I had to keep holding you back! Finally, we were called up and a final review of paperwork told us what we already knew, that it was complete.

Then we were told it would be at least an hour maybe two and sometimes people had to come back the next day. Yikes. Here I was trapped with you in a building with nothing to do and no electronics allowed, and there weren't even other people to watch! I tried quizzing you on your English words, but you gave me a look like, "Please, I am not five. I don't play I Spy." So I dropped that. But we got lucky, after only about twenty minutes we were called up and given all of our paperwork. It was an exciting moment for me. I don't know if you realized it at the time, but that marked the end! The absolute finite end of everything. You were now officially ours in both countries and it is a done deal. No going back.

I hugged you and kissed you, which earned me a roll of the eyes, but I didn't care. I know I was embarrassing you in front of others, but I was too happy. We walked out of the embassy and got in the car to go back to the apartment where you promptly fell asleep, deeply, and started snoring. It was so cute! I even snapped a picture and put it on facebook. I have to start amassing embarrassing photos sometime to show your girlfriends, don't I?

And speaking of girlfriends, you came clean with me today about Olga. It seems she is your girlfriend, even if she is an "older woman." You told me, "Love doesn't know age," and you are right. I know that sometimes love can strike young, so I won't tease or make fun. But I know that this must be very hard for you to leave her. You wanted to get her a gift to send to her, so when you went out to the market, I gave you money to get a small trinket. Tomorrow we will take it to the post office and mail it to her. I will help you there, but it is up to you to write to her and keep up the relationship. If you don't, it doesn't stand a chance!

And again, you were in and out all afternoon. Going to the small market nearby, wanting to go play soccer with some neighborhood boys, etc. I really don't like you going out alone, but at least I can watch you play soccer from the apartment window. You are like holding on to smoke. But hopefully, once I get you home, this will pass. I know as we get closer to leaving, you are getting more agitated, and I understand that. But somehow, I have to learn how to say no to you. You give me those puppy dog eyes and say, "Mom, I love you," and I am so busy trying not to cry that you are off before I can stop you!

Well, I am making dinner now, so I must go. It is hard to fill you up like any fourteen-year-old boy.

More later,
Mom

63: Day 31 — Leaving tomorrow

Dearest Alex,

Day 31 — last day in Ukraine. I can't believe it. What a journey it has been. In one way, I am so sad to leave tomorrow but in another way, I can't wait to leave. I miss home, my other son, my bed, big salads. What will I miss — the people, the cheap beer on draft wherever you go for pennies, the chance to practice my horrible Russian on unsuspecting people, and the friends we have made here.

I truly feel that between our last visit to Ukraine in 2007 to visit A1's family and this one, I have experienced living here, more than an extended visit. I would move here in a heartbeat if I could just ensure that certain amenities (like air conditioning, a good mattress, and year-round lettuce) were available. Rest assured that if you ever want to move back some day, I will support it and come with you for a while, but I have a feeling that once you get entrenched in America, you will want to stay. Maybe I am wrong, but we will see.

Now that this whole thing is done, I am relieved, energized, happy, and sad all at once. It has been a journey that our family has shared with you and countless others and I am sad to see it end. I am relieved that nothing really went wrong, and energized to be able to start the next phase of our life together.

Last night, you were late coming in from playing soccer and I was getting worried and then mad. When you were fifteen minutes late — I was frantic. Then you came in and brought me a rose! You had been saving all of the change from our purchases (you have been handling the money since I am not very good with it) and you took it to buy me a flower. You are so sweet (and crafty) — you knew that would soften the blow of being late. And you were right — I couldn't get mad after that!

Rest assured that you can throw almost anything at us and we are staying right by your side. Maybe no one else has stood by you in this world, and I am sure you can't fathom anyone doing so in the future, but we are committed and we will be right there next to you!

Today we are going out to buy you some music. There are a number of bands whose CDs you really can't find in America, so we are going to get some here. Then off to a post office and then early back to the apartment to pack and get to bed early for our flight tomorrow. We have a pick-up to go to the airport at four thirty in the morning. Yikes! That is really early. But you and I can just snuggle up and sleep on the plane all the way home. We were lucky to get pretty good times—we have a two-hour layover in Amsterdam and a two-hour layover in Minneapolis but other than that—straight home we go!

Love you bunches!
Mom

64: Home at Last

Dearest Alex,

Well, we got to the airport this morning early for our six twenty-five flight. I for some reason couldn't sleep, maybe it was the clock watching, but I was awake at two thirty after having gone to bed at eleven thirty. Very yucky.

But I have to fill everyone in on last night. It was the funniest, saddest, and all around weirdest night that totally captured the essence of this whole adoption thing. When we got back from shopping at four in the afternoon, you hadn't been there five minutes when you were getting ready to go out again. I, of course, didn't want you to go. I knew Sasha was coming over at five to square up money and that we had to get to bed early to get up uber-early. You said six, I said five and finally we settled on five thirty. Then you were off. Well, being a good mom, I decided to go spy on you. So about five minutes after you left, I got some of the garbage together and was going to go outside under the guise of looking for the garbage. Lame, I know, but moms will do anything for their kids!

So, I got to the front door and couldn't open it. I had never even opened the door of the apartment myself as someone else was always in charge of the keys. I figured you had locked the door on your way out, so I turned a few knobs and, no luck. By this time I was starting to get a little frustrated because I knew my spying was in jeopardy and I was hot and sweaty. Now a word about the humidity level. It had been raining off and on all day. The temperature was not too hot but the air was saturated with moisture. Any movement, and I mean *any* movement resulted in torrents of sweat running off of me. Minimal movement was what was in order, and here I was wrestling with the door! And if you all know me, which by now you do probably more intimately than you want to, you know that I am the kind of person who hates to sweat. In fact any activity that might cause sweat is immediately boycotted. I might glisten occasionally if it is really hot, but that is my limit.

So here I am swearing at the door, at you, at Ukraine, and basically at everyone in my life and the door still doesn't open. I went into the living room area and stood in front of a fan for a few minutes to cool off and got my temper under control. I reasoned that the door had to be able to be opened, I just needed to approach it in a scientific manner. So once cooled down, I readdressed it calmly and confidently. There were two locks and I kept trying them in combination. And guess what, no luck—I just could not get it open. I realized then that you needed the key to get it open. So I was out of luck, no spying and no getting out of the apartment building if it caught on fire. You also had taken the phone with you (because I always made you take it when you went out alone) so I could not contact anyone.

Then the doorbell rings—it's Sasha! That's right. Now what was I going to do? He is standing outside saying let me in. I am yelling back through the door—I can't. Thank goodness he lives close by and was able to go get another set of keys. The apartment actually belongs to his father-in-law. So he was able to get in, only to discover that indeed I was not locked in, I am just an idiot that can't open doors.

So, he asks where you are, I look like a massive parenting failure because I can only say I don't know. And I look like some crazy woman, sweaty and disheveled. I was ready to cry at this point. He and I talked for a while, basically him lecturing me on keeping a tight rein on you. Then he said that he felt he needed to call the orphanage director and have her talk to you and threaten to take you back. I just about keeled over. That's all I needed right there, to scare the crap out of you that if you don't behave I will abandon you too! So I begged him not to. I need to bond with you, build trust, and threatening you is not the way to do it. So we talked some more (or rather I listened), and then you finally came!

You came in holding something behind your back, but I was so relieved that you were back that I just ran up and hugged and kissed you. Then as I was gasping and choking on a cloud of cigarette smoke that surrounded you, you brought out roses from behind your back—beautiful ones! Hard to see as I was spluttering and gagging on the smoke but appreciated nonetheless. I think Sasha was surprised.

Then he lit into you and told you not to go out anymore. You looked crestfallen. I knew you had come home only to give me the flowers and then were wanting to go out again. You talked with him and then before I knew it, were gone again! Sasha explained that you had a friend nearby that you were hanging out with and just wanted to go say goodbye. I guess that explains the smoking too. I didn't always smell smoke on you, and I am ashamed to say that I riffled through all of your things while you were gone to see what I could find—which was a big, fat zero. You were just being a bad boy when you were hanging out with this friend.

I was feeling a little low at this point, as I was disappointed that you had not shared your friend with me. He would have been welcome to come over and visit—under my supervision would have been best—don't you all think?) It really highlighted to me that we are going to have work on trust and communication. But you finally came back. And when you were walking back, the heavens opened up and you got drenched—hah—a little part of me was snarky and said serves you right.

But you came back, I was happy, and Sasha left. Then you pointed to your stomach, settled in with a DVD in Russian we had bought earlier at the mall and off I went to cook a dinner with the little remaining food we had left. Well, evidently it was not enough because about forty-five minutes later (after I had cleaned up and done all the dishes) you came into the kitchen all dressed saying, "I go out. Get more food." I just about died. I was already changed into jammies and was helpless once again as off you went. I couldn't very well deny you food could I? And to be honest, I was tired, it was raining, and you were just wearing me down.

You came back about fifteen minutes later, riddled with smoke again, plopped down a grocery bag in the kitchen and off you went to finish your movie. After I stopped coughing and choking on the smoke, I cooked you *another* dinner and then cleaned up from that one too. I forgot how much fun it was to have a growing teenage boy around. G4 went through his growth spurt early and had been out of it for a while. Oh the joys of parenting a teenage boy.

At this point I was sooo sweaty—nothing like a humid day with now the heat from two dinners to add to the discomfort. I kept repeating to myself, "Tomorrow it ends. Back on home turf. Just keep your cool." I finally got everything cleaned up around eleven and finished the last bit of packing. You were fed, happy, and content watching your movie and gave me the winningest smile as I said good night. You couldn't even rouse yourself out of your self-induced torpor to hug me good night, I had to crawl through cords, chargers, iPads, and computers to get to you. Talk about being comfortable.

I think this sums up the relationship really well. You are becoming closer to me day by day—I already know that I adore you—those bonds are strengthening—but there is a long way to go. Maybe most of it is communication, so I promise to work on my Russian as you work on your English. I will also work on changing that bad boy persona at home, but for now, just realize that I love you the way you are. No changes necessary.

Now that brings us to this morning. I was up, albeit grumpy and looking like the wicked witch, with bags under my eyes big enough to check as baggage, by three thirty. Sergei was coming at four. I snuck in and tried to wake you up. You opened one eye, said hello and I thought were going to get up. I checked back ten minutes later to find you sprawled flat on your back again. So I tried again. Same thing. Finally, I was getting fussy and stayed until you actually sat up. But I think you were sleeping sitting up! Anyway, Sergei came a few minutes early and really started fussing at you—so you got moving, dressed and ready in record time.

The drive to the airport took about an hour. When we checked in they took an inordinate amount of time perusing your passport and then asked me for the 'papers.' Thank goodness Sasha had warned me about this and I was ready to whip them out. Then we went to passport control and again they took forever. I think the guy read every line of the judgement and then asked you questions. We were getting quite the grumpy line of people waiting behind us.

The first leg of the trip was uneventful. You slept and snored all the way to Amsterdam, only waking up long enough to eat and drink. But before the plane took off, I detected a little forlornness in your attitude. I know it must be hard, and I wish I could talk to you and help you understand that you are not losing anything—you are simply adding, but once again I find myself helpless to communicate these feelings to you. I think deep down you know they are there—but it will be a while before we can let them out with words.

Then in Amsterdam, we had to go through another passport check.

When the airport official came up to us, he asked me if this was my son. I choked as I realized, this was the first time I was going to voice aloud the words that I knew in my heart, had worked so hard to be able to say, and was so proud to be able to voice. I told him, "Yes, this is my son!" I then told you in Russian what I said and was rewarded with a great big smile. I think I could have flown home right then and there on happiness. You seemed to be better and happier—maybe it was the sleep that did it. Or maybe those ties that bound you to Ukraine were melting away—but you were smiling more.

The trip to Amsterdam was long, long, long. And you were hungry the whole time—again, joys of parenting a teenage boy. But we joked and laughed, and you ate! Then I got really tired and it was cold in the airplane. We snuggled under a blanket together and I slept on your shoulder for a few hours. I am glad you are a cuddler; both G4 and Amanda are totally lacking in that area!

Anyway, the electronics gradually failed one by one on the long flight and soon you were left with just listening to music. We had bought a book at a bookstore for you to read yesterday, but you kept saying later, later. I have to learn how to resist you. I think you are fast discovering that I am the weak link in the parenting chain. G4 and Amanda figured it out long ago, it just took them a while to do it. You have caught on faster because I am sure that you are testing me. I know you are—I didn't fall off the turnip truck yesterday—but that is OK. Test away—nothing will diminish the feelings I have for you or unglue me from your side. Some day you will realize that.

Anyway, we talked and joked around for a while. You have a great sense of humor! You seemed very comfortable and happy and light-hearted. At one point you just leaned over and said, "Mom, I love you." Boy you sure know how to tug at the heartstrings.

When we arrived in Minneapolis, we had to go through customs, making me very nervous. I was concerned about the paperwork and getting through immigration. We stood in line for a while and then were ushered to a customs official. He asked for the paperwork from the embassy and then started asking questions about the adoption. He asked you a few questions and when you were reluctant to answer (I think you didn't understand him) he started shouting at you like you were retarded or deaf. I was so irritated. You are perfectly smart, just not able to speak English, and shouting at you isn't going to make you understand English any better. Higher volumes don't convey meaning! But we got through customs and were awarded the coveted immigration stamp on your passport.

We went to the plane for Salt Lake City and just relaxed, knowing we didn't have too much longer. I was just staring out the window on the plane, thinking about the first day that I met you and how I knew instantly that you were the one for us! There was no question in my mind, and there still isn't. Anyway, we finally arrived at home. You and I were so tired that we could hardly walk straight. We got home in about an hour, but you had succumbed to your tiredness on the car ride home and slept for most of it.

We were excited to see your new room—it hadn't been finished when we left yet. Grandma and G4 helped finish it and get everything settled for you. It looks great and I think you were happy to see it as well. You immediately settled right in and started playing and investigating everything—running back and forth touching everything like a kid at Christmas. You also seemed happy with our new dog, which was really gotten with you in mind.

We had a nice dinner together, then celebrated with a cake that had Welcome Home Alex on it. G4 had some presents for everyone that he distributed, then we gradually scattered and then hit the sack one day at a time. It is great to be home and to be able to sleep in my own bed

Great first day home. Hope you liked it too!

Love,
Mom

PART FIVE:

FINALLY HOME

Easing the Transition

We have covered the details of packing, travel, culture shock, and some of the issues that you will start to face overseas in becoming parents of an internationally adopted child. There are some areas, where I had been intentionally vague, that were covered in more detail when you read the account of our trip to Ukraine. Certain aspects are just clearer when explained in context and also vary so much from country to country and with the individual situations.

I do however want to talk about the transition that you and your child will have as you plan your return to America. Those first few days after leaving the orphanage will be key as they will set the tone for a while to come between you and your child. This is going to be hard for you as you are going to be out of your element and trying to navigate a foreign country with only minimal help and understanding. You will feel out of control and it is only natural to try to assert that control over your small sphere where you have influence.

Think of this now from your child's point of view. The first few days of any experience are going to be hard for anyone, but leaving the familiar for the unfamiliar must be very trying when you are a child. The younger they are, the more tenuous their grasp will be on the situation, which could good and bad. It could range from, "I am being kidnapped" to "who cares as long as I have a cool toy to distract me." For an older child it could range from a complete understanding of what they are leaving and the ensuing depression of leaving friends and maybe family, to the excitement of a new opportunity.

You however, will be getting more and more excited as you contemplate the end of your journey and getting back to normal. This might put you in direct conflict with the desires of your child and could set up a rift that is bigger than the one that just exists naturally. So how can you fix the situation?

Well, the quick answer is that you can't. Sorry to be so blunt, but it's the hard truth. However, there are some things that you can do that will make the time easier for you all and put everyone at ease.

Immersion in the Culture

The first is to work on cultural immersion, which can start with language acquisition. This is a nice give and take where the child can actually be put in the driver's seat. Exchange words for things that you point out. Make a game of trying to remember words. Sound out words on signs and in stores. Even simple interactions will start building bonds together.

Make sure that you do this in a fun way, and make sure that it goes both ways — don't insist that the child learn everything in English and you nothing in their language. In fact, with Alex, I told him I wanted to learn Russian and made him think it was all one direction, me learning, but then I repeated the words in English several times and then I would say them in Russian also.

Next, make sure you spend time eating local foods, shopping in local markets and doing everything you can to soak up local culture. All too soon this will be lost and you will feel bereft if your child longs for something that you don't understand. To this end, you can talk to as many people as you can, your facilitator, friends you have made, or anyone that can understand you. People are usually very willing to share about themselves and their country — so ask away. Ask waiters, salespeople, and anyone else you can find. You can ask about holidays, food, pastimes, or anything else you can think of.

Also, take the time to people watch. Go to a shopping mall, park, or other public area and simply soak up the ambiance and the people. There will be things that you notice that then you can ask about of file away the information. One thing I noticed early on when watching the Ukrainian people was how the little children were dressed. Under the age of seven or eight, they were bundled up to the point that even on a sunny, warm day, they had on tights, boots, hats, gloves, and heavy coats. We asked about this habit, as we had seen some children I swear on the verge of heat stroke, and were told that it was a cultural belief that you couldn't allow small children to get chilled. They might have serious health problems if they weren't kept warm.

At first this seemed strange, but now is not the time to react to these differences, just study them and remember them as best you can. I pulled the above example out of my hat once when Alex was not doing well and was missing Ukraine desperately. I bundled him up in a warm, fleecy blanket telling him that I had to keep him warm and toasty to stay healthy. He almost immediately settled down and I realized that by validating something that he knew to be true (warm kids are healthy kids, whether it was really true or not) that I reduced some conflict in his mind between his two states (that of being Ukrainian and that of trying to be American). He was subconsciously being assuaged that America is not all that different so it must be OK.

I know this is a simplification of the issue, there are many things Alex has had to work through and they are not all fixed with a warm blanket, but I think you can see the idea. Even just a verbalization of a custom can be enough. I know also that the Ukrainian culture values soup when you are ill. I am not a big soup maker, and once when Alex was feverish, I remarked, "Oh boy, I wish we had soup because I know that is good for you, but I don't have any. Here take this grilled cheese sandwich because it is warm like soup." While again, this may seem simple and almost childish, Alex accepted the sandwich and internally accepted the lack of soup.

It is hard to imagine the psychic distress these children are under with an international adoption. They are bombarded on all levels and anything you can do to alleviate this will go a long way to easing the transition. And while you would think many of these things could be communicated, the reality is that much of it is subconscious and you will need to drive the process.

Contact with Friends

The second thing you can do to help transition is to allow your newly adopted child contact with their friends. This will be somewhat age dependent, as younger kids will not be able to do this as easily, but the teens will love it. They will want to share their new experiences with someone, and unfortunately, your understanding of the language won't be good enough to do that. Also, you were there with them, so in a way, you don't count. Don't forget too that their adoption gave them a sense of status in their orphanage community that they won't be able to experience without contact with that community.

This could be a sticky situation if there is family involved, so be careful with who they are calling. The last thing you want is a complicated entanglement of a family member either feeling remorseful about letting a child go, or seeing dollar signs with rich Americans. Also, if there is a love interest, it could get too sad for the child. So make sure you monitor the interactions and ensure that they make your child happier not sadder.

Transition Troubles in a Foreign Country

The good times of transition do have a flip side. You will be anxious to start building your life with your new child, and then to have this limbo time where they are not focusing on the new but looking back at the old can be frustrating. You are all of a sudden a new parent, but really don't feel like one. The facilitator and their staff is on the down side and are not as helpful or attentive as before. After all, the adoption is finalized and there is just some simple red tape left before going home.

You will feel frustrated, homesick, and out of control. You will want to start right away with the regimen you had planned for your child, but find yourself unable to because of so many factors, language, culture, etc. So how can you manage these feelings and avoid the beginnings of post-adoption depression that can so easily set in at this point? After all, you have done most of what you went overseas to do, are probably running out of emotional reserves, money, and time off of work. You are missing family and friends at home and are now really just realizing the enormity of the task that you have taken on.

NO PANIC!

Help! I'm depressed and feeling sad that things are so difficult when they should be so great. Do I have Post-Adoptive Depression?

There is nothing wrong with these feelings if they are fleeting and aren't causing you difficulty with your daily life and interactions. As I have been detailing, the whole process is extremely taxing upon a family and you are bound to havesome negative feelings. But, post-adoptive depression does exist and according to various studies can be seen in fifteen to twenty percent of adoptions. Don't rush to diagnose yourself, though, give yourself a break and some time. Get back home and into your comfortable place before you worry too much. Make sure you are taking care of yourself physically with good nutrition and rest. But if you do know that you have depressive tendencies, have had problems in the past, or are having difficulties in just doing basic life tasks, then you might want to seek the advice of a health care professional.

So you will have to change gears and move away from your normal "get things done mode" to a different plane. You will need to slow down and accept a lack of forward momentum. Just like the people watching described above, you will need to sit back and spend time thinking about how to engage your child on a personal level. This doesn't mean with education or language, but one on one as a person. Things like telling stories, even if they are hard to understand, playing games, shopping together, and getting out together.

This whole experience was good for me, as it gave me a place to channel my energy and thoughts and feel empowered, where in so many other instances, I felt so powerless. I also think that it helped Alex understand that I was interested in him as a person and interested in things that interested him.

While I state that this might have been good for me, it was extremely hard to do. I love progress, the feeling of accomplishment and checking off lists. Sitting and doing nothing is not a favorite activity. It seemed like such a different time compared to the rest of the adoption process, where there was a lot of activity and tasks to be accomplished. Here there was very little to do but wait.

Remember I talked about patience earlier? Well, draw upon that well now and take a deep breath. There are also some ways to manage this time. As I mentioned, I started looking more carefully at the country and people around me. I took notes, caught up on my writing, and made sure I was paying attention to Alex. I watched him carefully and tried to get to know him as a person. I watched what he ate, how he acted, and what he seemed to enjoy. I turned a frustrating limbo of time into something that I felt I could look back on and see accomplishments during. It wasn't easy, but I do think it helped in the long run.

And finally, the down time helped me to understand the stress the whole situation was causing and feel better about allowing more freedoms as a parent than I probably am normally comfortable with. In this situation, enjoy the feeling of a loss of control, and don't worry about consequences. Not much will carry over, if anything at all. You might be more lenient on buying presents, outings, eating sweets, and so on, but anything to build good feelings and positive interactions will go a long way to easing the strain of the situation and put you in the driver's seat for a better experience stateside .

Do Not Hit the Ground Running
After the limbo I have described above, once you land back in America, you will want to hit the ground running. You will have stacked up activities to accomplish after your long absence. You will want to get going on these right away and the natural tendency is to think that everyone will follow right along with you. Caution, caution, now, think of a blinking yellow light. Slow down.

First of all, you will be exhausted and so will your new family member. Take enough time to rest and recover from jet lag. Make sure you have someone cooking healthy meals and that you are having adequate opportunities for rest. Even when you feel that jet lag has improved, take an extra few days to lay low and get your bearings back. Imagine how stressful this is for your new child and make life pretty low key. Don't try to rush around, but rather ease into tasks and spend a lot of time just relaxing, much like you did overseas before you came home.

Ease into the parenting transition also. Your child will be naturally worried about how different things will be, so don't place them into situations where you will be laying down a bunch of rules or behavior guidelines right away. Let them feel life is fairly much the same and introduce things slowly. This goes for introducing family and friends as well. They will be dying to rush over and meet your new family member, but you will have to regulate the process. There might be no need as your new child might be thrilled to meet and play with other family members, but more than likely, they will be scared and feel out of place. A slow and measured introduction with low expectations are a good place to start.

Explain to friends and family that the transition period will take a long time and that they need to respect your wishes during the time. Giving them some concrete things to do will help make them feel useful, but at the same time, will allow you to control the environment around your new child. Giving your new child concrete things to do will also help them by focusing on themselves and not on the big scary unknown.

For example, if friends want to meet your new child, you might have them over in small groups for a specified ten or fifteen minutes at a time, explaining the importance of keeping the time very short. You might also prep your child ahead of time to make eye contact, shake hands, and say a few words. Then they could be excused. This would give your friends a look, give your new child a specified interaction of short duration that helps teach good manners and then an out in which they can go back to familiar places and not feel overwhelmed.

This might seem rude, but giving everyone guidelines will help them feel more comfortable and avoid awkward situations. You might even coach people as to please not ask questions like, "How do you like America?" or "Do you love your new home?" These questions will only lead to problems; what child could say wholeheartedly yes when they are overwhelmed, probably still in shock and getting used to a new place?

However, there could be instances in which you feel perfectly fine with having people interact with your new child and even welcome it. These decisions are really up to you and the child at this point. Experts will have opinions on 'nesting' with your new child and when to introduce them to your wider community, but only you and your child will know when this is appropriate. This is where all the time you spent observing and quietly assessing your child overseas will come in handy. Hopefully, you will know them enough to be able to say when things can move faster.

But remember, there is an ebb and flow to this as well. There could be a time where you think these interactions are fine and then another time when they aren't. This is normal and natural and reflects the up and down of integration into a new family and the transition process as a whole. It is not a nice, neat linear line. It looks more like a scribble from a two year old on graph paper and it will feel like you are riding a roller coaster on that scribble.

So relax and enjoy the down time. There is no need to rush back into your life, as it won't be the same. You will have a new life now with a new family member and as much as you would like things to go back to normal, they can't. You are going to have to find your new normal and it will take time.

Managing Emotions

I made a tough decision after coming home from Ukraine, and that was to end the letters to Alex. I enjoyed writing them but now once Alex was home, the letters became more informative than anything else. I continued writing the blog for a few months more, but now it is more now for others than for Alex. I decided to make the letters from the blog into a book just for him and finished up with a sappy letter just for him and me, and will give it to him for a present someday.

However, these letters have been so incredibly helpful to me in managing my emotions, and writing them for Alex was very cathartic. There was so much that I wanted to share with him but was unable to, early on because of our physical separation, and later because of the language barrier. But more importantly, I was able to order my thoughts and emotions as I as writing about them. Having to go through this process made me see things with more clarity than I would have otherwise and I think this was helpful. It allowed me to modulate emotions more than I probably would have been able to do otherwise.

I would recommend to everyone going through the process of adoption to do something like this. Even if you are super busy, some kind of record is a wonderful tool. I have enjoyed going back through and reading about everything that happened. You forget the small details, and reading about them brings back so many memories for me.

If you are really busy, there are alternatives to writing. You can make voice recordings, or even just mark details on a calendar. Anything will be better than nothing. Trust me on this! As I have gone back through and reread the things I wrote, I pick up things that I didn't realize at the time I was knee deep in emotions.

This was new to me, as we weren't a family of particularly high emotions. I wasn't used to being so worked up all the time and on edge. However, just when you are so worked up and on an emotional roller coaster, is just the time when your children need to see a parent that is calm and in control. These new family members are drawing upon you and your family to fill their emotional reserves that are probably dry with the stress of the adoption, new family, and new country.

You want to be able to fill them up with emotions of happiness, love, self-control, and confidence, not uncertainty, fear, and loneliness. But if I was to take a survey of the feelings you as a parent are managing right at this point, the top ones would be uncertainty (how am I going to parent this stranger), fear (did I do the right thing), and loneliness (none of my friends or family quite get what I am going through).

So, how to hide and ultimately remove these more negative but common emotions you will be feeling and replace them with the positive ones you want to convey? Well, let's first start with understanding where they come from and then by looking at them one by one and demystifying them.

CAFS—Chronic Adoption Fatigue Syndrome

Just because you have arrived home doesn't mean that everything returns to normal immediately. There are some after affects that last for a while that contribute greatly to the emotions that are running rampant through you. I want to describe a syndrome that we suffered during this adoption—Chronic Adoption Fatigue Syndrome.

At first we thought it was just jet lag, but rapidly realized that four weeks into the trip, jet lag should have resolved. Then when we got home and were still super fatigued, we realized it had nothing to do with the travel and everything to do with the emotional withdrawals that were taking place from our bank. Of course some of this fatigue originated from physical causes. I have a couple of theories—just bear with me.

While there are many lovely things about Ukraine (the people, the food, the culture) there are a few things that you can do without, and chief among those are their beds and pillows. The mattresses are on average half an inch thick, just foam, and often lumpy. This is universal, whether it is an apartment, hotel, or anywhere. The pillows are dense, heavy, and the wrong shape — square, not rectangular. You might as well just pull up the nearest boulder for all the comfort they provide. This combination makes for bad quality sleep. You need about two hours to get thirty minutes of real sleep.

The next is the North Pole—like almost twenty-four hour daylight. I know that Ukraine is north, but people, it is not above the arctic circle! Why does it get light at about four in the morning and stay light until ten? And we were there in April. Does the sun never set in the middle of summer? And with this known issue, why are there no blackout drapes in the windows? Gauzy curtains might be beautiful blowing in the breeze, but do nothing to aid sleep when the sun's rays are burning holes in your retinas.

Then there is the emotional factor. No matter how prepared you are — these kids have the ability to just wring any staying power you have out of you. You will be assaulted on every level with emotions that you thought were behind you in your unstable teenage years! You will be frustrated, worried about money, in love, homesick, happy, and sad, all at the same time. At the same time you feel like you are stuck in a wormhole without any way to get out. You hear about a light at the end of the tunnel, but it doesn't feel like you will ever reach it.

And finally, the time zone trouble. You want to keep in touch with home, which means staying up late to try to catch them in their morning or getting up early to catch them at their night. Then you are tired and have down time during the day which lends itself to naps! Then you get in this weird sleep cycle that seems a few hours on and a few hours off. There really is no cure for this one, but it is a killer.

Well, I think this just about summarizes the Chronic Adoption Fatigue Syndrome. It doesn't go away when you get home, but after a couple of weeks or so, it gets better. But you will find yourself going to bed earlier than you did before — I think this whole process actually ages you by a few years.

Dealing with Disappointment

All humor aside from my examples above, being out of your element in a foreign country and trying to complete your forever family are enough to stress anyone out, and when you add to it the uncertainties you face throughout the process, is there any wonder that some negative emotions may surface?

Add to this the fact that you may also be dealing with some disappointments and you have a recipe for very negative emotions that will be hard to cover up and control. So how do you defuse them? The first is simply by recognizing their existence. You need to be aware of the physical demands that have been placed upon you with travel and such and realize that that in itself will cause some problems. Nice thing about those causes though is that once you can get home and rested, over time this will fade away. Also, making sure that you are as healthy and well taken care of as possible is another way to combat these emotions.

But these negative emotions can be caused by other things as well. When you are frustrated with language, concerned about parenting, and realizing that your child isn't the little angel you had expected, well, the uncertainty, fear, and loneliness will kick right in.

I hit this wall when I was alone in Kiev with Alex after John and Amanda left to go home. The adoption was final and we were just awaiting embassy paperwork and the medical, but I looked forward to the time as a great time to start bonding with Alex.

I hit a low point in the apartment when we were having trouble communicating and Alex was just skyping away with friends forever. I was getting irritated but couldn't effectively tell him why. Then when I tried, he would comply for a few minutes because he thought I just wanted his attention for that time and then go right back to what he was doing. I was flouncing around and muttering that we were bonding like oil and water. I was so fearful that we would never be close, but then I calmed down and tried to look at his behavior and figure out why this was happening. After all, he hadn't been around me long enough to actively dislike me yet, so why was he ignoring me? Then I got a really good idea. I figured out that he was keeping me at arm's length because he felt that if I knew everything about him, I would probably not want him. His friends already want him so they were the safer bet.

So instead of just remaining fearful and uncertain, decided that I needed to take action. Having a plan to success is a great way of feeling like that success is almost at hand. I started a campaign of understanding. I told him (as best as I could through Google Translate) that nothing he could do or say would change my love for him. I know he has never really had a mom and everyone he has had has left him — so why would I be any different? I know it will take him a while to get it but I think at least I have started him figuring it out. He had been ignoring me for his friends not because he liked them more that me, but because of a lack of understanding and communication. Well, once a little of this got through — the floodgates opened and he started talking more to me. I felt a lot better and felt some of the fear and uncertainty wearing off.

And now this is where the faint of heart need to sit down and take a deep breath. I am fairly sure there has been adult type behavior going on with him and his many girlfriends if you get my drift. Also I found out he was a smoker and a drinker and I am sure has several other vices.

Wow! I was not prepared for this. I had just felt a minor level of success at conquering some of my fear and anxiety to now be battling anger, frustration, and disappointment as I realized my little angel had a really tarnished halo. He had already experienced so much of life, how was I going to make any effect? Where was the innocent little boy that wanted a family, not the hardened street urchin who could take care of himself? Also, what was I bringing into my home and how would I deal with it? I wasn't a smoker, had never been a smoker and didn't know anyone who was. How in the world was I going to pull off stopping his smoking. Let's add inadequacy to the pile of emotions that were stacking up.

But I just put on my best game face and just said OK and went on to the next thing. I didn't want him to get a shock value out of it. I also didn't want him to get the idea that this changed any of my love for him. All I said was never smoke around Amanda because she has asthma!

But after thinking about these things for a while, and wallowing in my grief for a bit, I realized that this was Alex's "bad boy" persona. Probably a defense mechanism against the world he was trying to fit into. And there was no one guiding him in the right direction. Well, I comforted myself with the realization that he has a guide now. As feeble as it sounds, it helped me deal with the information I had gotten. I directed my anger outward against a corrupt and broken system that left a child having to experience these things at a tender age.

The disappointment I was feeling also needed to be acknowledged and understood. There is nothing like thinking you had one kind of child, then to turn around and discover that in fact you have someone totally different. This is also where not having expectations about your child will be helpful. Or at least having flexible expectations. Once I forgave myself for having these thoughts, I realized that the process of understanding what Alex had been through and what his life was like before us was going to be a long one and one that I would have to take slowly. I also realized that there would need to be a grieving process as I let go of certain ideas and accepted new ones. Just articulating these facts was in and of itself helpful.

It is important to be able to roll with the punches that come your way. It is hard enough to help your children adjust to a new life; you will have very little time trying to adjust yourself. The less you have to do for yourself, the more you will have time to devote to your child.

It is important when trying to manage these negative emotions that you focus on the positive things and the future. I knew Alex was a wonderful kid, I was not really worried, just heartbroken that he has not had a strong loving guiding force to protect him from things that could hurt him. He has had to confront adult decisions without help and that just seems so unfair. I think I was finally realizing how immature Alex was in some respects for his age (which he is in one way—survival mode took away normal maturing) but how unfortunately mature he was in others. Even though his was a great orphanage, I think these kids were exposed to the seedier side of life before they went in and once in I get the idea they were still vulnerable to others preying upon them from the outside. So I decided that I was not going to lecture or chastise, simply lead by example.

So, the best advice on managing these negative emotions—just be understanding with your kids. They are coming from a different culture with different priorities. Add on top of that the circumstances with which they have navigated their life, and you will find a wealth of differences between your ideals and their actuality. If you can try, don't pass judgement on them. They will react negatively to it and if it is perpetuated, and will give up trying to live up to your expectations. The best thing to do is to start with a blank slate. Understand what went on before, be clear about expectations going forward, and try to forget the in between time.

I felt like our time in Kiev was our in between time, where we were learning about each other, but still not understanding what each other wanted. We were still following old habits. It was hard for me to accept this reality, but once I realized the dynamics of the situation, I understood that it needed to happen this way. I could start working on behaviors at home, but overseas, where I was not always the one in control, it was best to let some things slide and concentrate on building love and understanding than to worry about specifics. Also, I realized that learning to control my own emotions was learning to control my actions first. When I acted like I was full of positive, uplifting sentiments, my thoughts were often ordered that way and it helped keep the more negative emotions at bay.

Developmental Stages

Being an adoptive parent will push you outside of your comfort zone and cause you to become an expert at many subjects that you probably never thought you would learn. You are already a master at paperwork, waiting, traveling overseas, and navigating stressful conditions. Now you need to become an expert in child development overnight. You won't have the natural progression and the pace by which development occurs in biological children. This doesn't mean that it is always easy in biological children, but there is a sequence that can be expected and anticipated. In older children that have been adopted, the natural sequence has probably been disrupted by abuse, neglect, institutionalization, or any number of other factors. This will mean that you will have to be ready for a non-sequential pattern as your child settles in and begins to focus on growing physically and mentally and leaves behind just trying to survive.

Dealing with older adoptive children cycling through the developmental stages of childhood is very much a process that takes a lot of patience. I think many people just chalk this cycling through developmental phases as immaturity and a mercurial temperament, but there really is a predictable pattern behind their actions. Ok, maybe not predictable, but understandable.

I first learned about children needing to go back and relive developmental stages to resolve unfinished or unfulfilled problems when I was a pediatric resident caring for victims of abuse, so I was familiar with the concept and what it looks like. But what I didn't understand at the time was having to go through it personally and developing the ability to spot the stages when you are so close to the situation.

Normal Developmental Stages

So, for those that are unfamiliar with the concept, I will backtrack and give a crash course on developmental stages. All children go through normal developmental stages as they grow and mature. And, to be perfectly accurate, this continues into adulthood as well. There is nothing magical about children that makes them the only ones capable of moving through stages of life. The difference is that they pass through many more stages in a compressed amount of time, making it a continuous process.

These developmental stages can be broken down into physical, emotional, and mental stages, each with a reproducible timeline in which each stage needs to be accomplished and conquered before moving onto the next stage. Usually it is a nice linear, predictable process.

Now some children seem to skip stages, for example, crawling, moving right from sitting up to walking. The muscles of crawling need to be developed before the child can walk, but some kids go right to walking. It is not that they skipped the crawling stage, it is just that they found a way to develop those muscles and necessary skills in a way other than crawling and were able to progress to the walking stage faster. Some kids have trouble getting to a next stage because of problems with a stage prior. For example, in order to learn how to speak, you need to hear sounds first before you can start to imitate them, and children with chronic ear infections can't hear, so will have speech delay.

NO PANIC!

I am so worried. I don't have biological children and I am not at all versed in children's development. What can I do?

No panic! This is an easy one to fix. There is so much information available now for free even. Just googling child development will bring up a plethora of resources. If you prefer a print version, look to the American Academy of Pediatrics. They have numerous resources and books they espouse that cover child development. Don't just focus on early childhood though, make sure to look at elementary and older ages as well.

Just like everything else you have had to do in the adoption process, you will need to educate yourself about these developmental stages. You don't need to become an expert on them, but just skimming through an understanding will be helpful. After all, your children will be picking up past stages they might have missed as well as progressing through stages in which they are normally reaching. You will have to understand both and be able to separate them in your mind as well as integrate them into your child.

Non-Linear Development

The clinician in me could go on and on about developmental stages and normative milestones, but lets get back to adoption. Kids that have had trauma in their early life (and I think this would apply to every kid that needed a new family) won't have been able to go through developmental stages normally. This will mostly apply to the emotional stages, but it can cross over into the physical and mental areas as well if it was severe enough trauma or at critical stages of development.

In addition to this fact of abuse and neglect affecting developmental stages, there is the fact that you all are new parents to this child. Whatever stages they did get through were not with you. While there is no repairing this fact, to some extent, you will see your child going back over some of these developmental stages as a part of the process of bonding and attaching together.

I also need to make the point about the process of cycling through developmental stages with your adopted child that they will not occur in order. They will randomly pop up and will serve to confuse and frustrate you. You will be dealing with one developmental stage of a teenager in one minute, then you will be dealing with another one of a toddler in the blink of an eye. This will make you think you are losing your mind, when in actuality, it is perfectly normal.

Kids will start displaying symptoms of developmental stages without even thinking about it or understanding why they are doing it. It will look like immaturity and might even frustrate the child themselves as they don't understand where their behavior is coming from.

When we first arrived back in America, Alex could not be separated from me for more than about ten or fifteen minutes. If he went out bike riding, he would come back home and have to make eye contact with me and touch me. This was a toddler stage of development, learning how to separate and feel safe in surroundings, and understand that even though you can't see something, that it is still there. This showed me that something happened in his life around his toddler years that caused him to not be able to complete this stage of development. There is also a component though of having to attach to me as a new mother. I think some of this stage is going to show in any adoption because of that fact.

Well, over time the timing between his contacts with me spaced out until it reached the thirty to forty-five minute mark, where he completely dropped the behavior. I figured that he was secure and happy and was fine, but just recently it started back up again. There was no explanation that I could see for it, but I just went back to my way of dealing with it, making sure that I was available at all times to give him the reassurance needed. I stopped separating from him like I had started doing when the behavior had extinguished before. I can only say that, obviously, we needed to revisit this step. There was not the closure that should have occurred before.

I felt a little bad until I realized that none of this was my fault or problem. It was simply that way that things had to be. I could fuss, complain, and moan all I wanted, but until Alex had move beyond this phase, we couldn't either. Realizing this brought me a measure of peace while I considered that in fact I was so blessed to be able to do this with Alex. I had missed so much of his life and truly grieved about that fact. Now I was being handed an opportunity to make up some of this time. Inconvenient, sure. Frustrating, you bet ya'. But absolutely priceless. I feel so lucky in a way. And once I started looking at it this way, it allowed me to reexamine many of his behaviors that I found irritating or troublesome and understand them better.

Common Developmental Issues

So what are the more common developmental issues that you might find yourself facing with a new child. I can't possibly cover every one, but there are many that are commonly seen and can help you start the process off. Once you get used to looking at your child's behavior in this paradigm, it will become second nature and you will internalize it.

The most common one is my above example with separation anxiety. Stemming from two places, both perhaps a disrupted bond with primary caregivers when young and also a need to bond with new caregivers, can make this severe. As I described above, this usually extinguishes itself, but it can take quite a while.

The best way to deal with this one is patience and love. The more you fight it, the more desperate your child will become to stay with you. So when in a situation where your child has to separate, like at a park, or school, you will have to accommodate them as best as possible. Like I mentioned at the park, I would sit in one space where Alex knew exactly where I was and then he could stay with me or separate as he wanted. I didn't send him to school, instead choosing to homeschool, so I didn't have any school separation problems.

Several parents that have sent their children to school have developed tactics around the separation anxiety. In the beginning they would wait for the children, sending them only part of the day. I would counsel against doing something like volunteering in the classroom as this will habituate your child to your immediate presence. If you are looking to be able to leave them, then start with saying you will wait outside in a specific parking space or such. Then you can gradually increase their time away from you and maybe even start running errands during this time. As long as you ease them into it, allowing them to express their anxiety and acknowledging it, you will gradually work beyond it and be able to go back to your normal schedule.

Some parents have managed this with technology. They have asked schools for special permission for the child to make a phone call to them during the day and maybe even go to the school during lunch to see their child. There are all sorts of clever ways to connect with your children even though you are separated by circumstances.

With older children, it is important also to verbalize what is going on to them. They will probably not have the self-insight to know why they are unable to separate or are feeling anxious. By explaining why they are anxious will help validate their feelings and not feel bad or immature for having them. It will assuage them and allow them to start dealing with the feelings and develop coping strategies instead of hiding them or acting out.

So, what happens when a child can't deal with the anxiety or is having trouble ever separating? At this point, you might need to start looking at outside help to assist your child.

Another common developmental issue is mistrust and lack of empathy or self-centeredness. It is unusual to think of all of these being related, but they are. Humans move from being totally dependent on others and self-consumed to being more independent and empathetic and outward facing. If in early infancy, basic needs weren't met, then a basic mistrust of caregivers sets in. This basic mistrust blooms into worrying more about meeting personal needs and less about worrying about others. If basic needs are met and there is that expectation that they will be, then a child can more easily start to focus on things outside of themselves.

Many adoptive parents of older children complain about their lack of empathy and lack of concern for anything other than themselves. But when you look at childhood development, you can easily see that needs unmet during infancy will snowball later on. To this end, the first place to start is to smother the child with meeting their needs. You will need to regress them a little for this but it will pay off.

How can you do this? Start with thinking of them like a royal guest in your home. Breakfast in bed, plumping up their pillows, covering them with fuzzy blankets, letting them pick favorite meals, no chores, picking the movie for family movie night, etc. However, this very easily could result in a pampered, expectant child and that would be counterproductive. So, as you are smothering them with the basics in spades and wallowing them in hedonistic delights, you will also need to start a campaign of getting them to understand what you are doing.

As you bring them breakfast in bed, you tell stories about when your mom or dad would do this for you, or as you are snuggling them up in a fleecy throw, you explain to them about how you like to be snuggled up with a good book and you thought they would like it to. You should carefully accompany each gesture with an example of your or someone else's empathy and generosity that matches the gesture in some way.

Modeling how much you enjoy doing things for them will show your child how fun it is to think of others. Also by caring for them, you are helping to meet their basic needs and more. You are starting to build the trust and meet those needs so they can move beyond that stage of development.

Gradually move beyond doing things for them and suggest they do things for other family members. By relating this back to the child though you will help create a continuum of understanding. Try maybe something like, "Remember last week when I made you your favorite meal for dinner. Well let's do that today for your sister." By evoking positive memories in your child, you will be able to push them forward into an area where they are less comfortable.

With Alex, I did most of these things, including daily massages. I used to massage both of my biological kids after bath time when they were infants and have fond memories of that time. So, when Alex was settling down to go to bed, I would bring some lotion in and flip him over on his back and give him a back rub. Now I am not skilled in massage, but the calming affect of the movements and the lotion and the time together was really key to our bonding. I told him how I used to do this for my other two and why I did it and then we would talk about a variety of subjects.

I found that Alex loved to mimic the things I did for him to others. Most children are this way, loving to copy. And while it starts as a love of copying, it will gradually turn into caring about others. When I would bring him breakfast in bed, he would look for ways to bring others food, and so on.

Now, there are times when a child is so mistrustful that more than just this approach will be needed. In this case, your child might need help moving onto another developmental phase, but this is a starting point.

Another very common problem adoptive parents find in their children is acting out behavior based upon low self-esteem. A child might exhibit this by lying (I can't achieve on my own so will make it up), stealing (I can't be successful by myself so will just take what I want), and general negativity (I don't feel good about myself, so I will bring everyone else down). These behaviors and others are rooted in an essential negative view of self and low self-worth. This can come from either circumstance as they were abandoned or from direct communication where they have been told they are worthless or unwanted. It can also come from experience, as things like a disrupted family life leads to poor school performance which leads to a feeling of being stupid. There are so many ways this message is repeated to children over and over, both verbally and non-verbally.

Overcoming it will be difficult and time-consuming, but an exercise that needs to be started. This one developmental stage more than any other will probably not be fixed in a short time and might even never fully be dealt with, but if strides can be taken to allow a child to move on, then their future will be brighter.

So, where to start? The first place is to reinforce their worth to you. You can't say enough that you love them, value them, and think they are wonderful. This will be ridiculed and rejected early on but keep on. You will wear them down eventually. It will also set up a conflict within them as you are saying things that are in direct opposition to what they believe in their hearts. This conflict will cause them to be even more negative for a while until it is repeated often enough. After all, once something is repeated enough, you start believing it is true.

The next step is to allow your child to have a series of small triumphs. They need to be meaningful and celebrated. This could be praise over learning English, mastering a new habit, or just looking nice and smiling. Don't overdo the praise, but let them feel the glow of accomplishment. You will need to watch them closely and praise things that might seem ridiculous to you, such as remembering to brush their teeth without being asked or making their bed in the morning. Rewarding the good behavior and ignoring the bad will hopefully extinguish the bad and keep the good coming. But this is a slow process and one that will take more than just the ordinary opportunities that life presents.

You will have to manufacture opportunities for your child to "win" so that you can praise them. These can be simple at first and aligned with things your child was already doing. For example, asking a child to bring their laundry downstairs when they were already heading downstairs for something else, could then be praised later as a child helping you with the housework by bringing the laundry down. These might seem ridiculously simple, but added up over time will allow your child to grow into helping and positivity naturally.

A child's natural tendency is to want to please and earn praise but only without too much effort. If you can play into this, then later you can ask tasks that are involved and more difficult that will merit more lavish praise. All of this is a continuum and will be building layer upon layer.

Be careful to praise only what the child actually does though, as this helps develop a realistic sense of self-esteem. You don't want to create an inflated and erroneous sense of self-worth which is no better than a bad sense of self-worth.

Hopefully, this quick overview of missed developmental stages and their consequences has helped you to understand the importance of being able to move through the stages and complete them. Even though it is frustrating and looks like immaturity, it is important to allow a child time to go back and complete a stage. This will only increase your bonding with them and allow them to move forward.

When to Discipline

This is a difficult subject for a parent to deal with, as they are never really sure how to deal with a behavior problem or how their adopted child will accept limits until several questions are answered. The first question is whether or not a certain behavior or problem is adoption related or not. If not, parent away as you would any other child. No repercussions or careful treading needed. If yes, then you need to answer whether it is related to developmental issues that occurred before you as the new family were in the picture. If the answer is yes (and the answer will probably always be yes), then you have to stop and take stock. What developmental stage was not met? What particular need is the child trying to meet and where will successful completion of this stage take you? Having an end point and goal will be helpful to you as a parent in keeping the faith when things get rough.

I recommend familiarizing yourself with normal childhood development and then without looking for solutions, examine your child's behavior and try to figure out the stage missed yourself. It will bring a lot of insight into your child as you do this. There are certain common reactions to situations that experts see over and over, but generalization can be troublesome. The behavior that your child is exhibiting is a unique combination of their background and your input as the new family. Your understanding is key to the situation. That being said, just identifying the stage and understanding it is going to do nothing for the behavior. It will have to continue until the stage is resolved. In my case, there was nothing I could do to stop Alex from needing the reassurance, so I had to adapt the situation to meet his needs. But if the behavior is something that you can't tolerate or deal with, you will need to get inventive. If I knew that I was not going to be able to be consistently available for Alex, I would try to set expectations ahead of time, or adjust my schedule to accommodate his needs. Short of that, I would try to get someone else to take my place, with varying levels of success.

Many people will ask however, what happens when I can't help my child move beyond a developmental stage? What happens when I can't identify what need is not being met? What about the situations that are totally disruptive to us and others in the family? In these situations, I would not immediately throw in the towel and run to an expert. Of course, you might need professional intervention, but still go through the steps as much as you can on your own. After all, you will know you child better than anyone else. You know their unique background and your family dynamics, all of which are instrumental in their reaction to situations and how they are navigated. This insight and knowledge will allow you to incorporate the advice given to you by the professional all the more effectively.

You don't have to tolerate everything your kid dishes out, but it sure makes it easier to do so when you understand its origins and reasons. And knowing that there will be forward momentum and a new stage when the old stage is completed is a powerful motivation to help your child keep moving forward.

PART SIX:

BECOMING ONE

65: Settling in

We slept like the dead that first night, but woke up refreshed and ready to tackle the day. Alex was happy and bouncy that first morning. He, Amanda, and G4, spent the morning playing video games. We were a little bummed—John was out of town at a business meeting in Chicago, so we felt a little incomplete. The boys tried to go bike riding, but the bikes had sat in the garage for so long, they needed a tune up. So I loaded them in the back of my van and took off with Alex in tow. Alex has grown since he was here last year so we are going to have to get a new bike at some point, but we are feeling a little poor after all the expenses from adoption, so we are going to put off that purchase for a while. We have other bikes.

Then Alex wanted to go to the grocery store with me and then we stopped by the bank that had helped me get all of the money for the trip together. The women at the bank were all giggling over him and gawking at him; I think he was a little embarrassed.

We finally got home and Alex played around with the kids all afternoon. Victoria (our neighbor) came over to translate for us, but it turned out to be more of a fun visit than a necessary translation visit. She and Alex chatted for a while about inconsequential things and when she asked him how he was and if he needed anything, he said he was happy and didn't need anything.

John got home about nine o'clock that night, so it was nice to all be together. He sat down with Alex and laid out our strategy on calling to Ukraine. We are going to allow him a twenty-five-minute once-a-week allowance to call his girlfriend and Grandma (hmmmm—let's think how he is going to divide that—one minute to Grandma and twenty-four to girlfriend!) If he wants more time to talk, he will have to earn the money to spend on the phone calls. So, we let him have a freebie this time and call Ukraine—and guess what—he spent all twenty-five minutes on his girlfriend.

Then both boys got a lesson in shaving with a straight razor (G4 had been using an electric one that crapped out. Poor Alex really needed it—he looked like ZZ Top almost. He was so excited that before bed, he rushed off to shave! And that brings up an interesting point, about showers. In the three days he has been here, he has showered five times. Maybe there wasn't a chance to shower much at the orphanage, but he is making up for it here.

Today, he didn't wake up until one in the afternoon. I was concerned that I needed to check for the development of bed sores. I was at the Tae Kwon Do studio with Amanda when he woke up, but my mom called me and told me he was up and mentioned that he looked a little lost without me. I came home shortly thereafter, and when I walked in, he jumped up and gave me a big, crushing hug. He must still have a little anxiety that I might not always be there.

His room had been a pigsty with all of the suitcase contents spread around, but on his own, he cleaned it up today. I was proud of him, I didn't even have to ask him. Then he got ready and I took the three kids into John's office. I was a little worried about doing that. A lot of people at his work had been asking about Alex, but I am very concerned about him feeling like he is being shown off and paraded around. So I suggested that we take the kids to the break room where there was a pool table, a ping-pong table, and a Playstation. Then John told everyone Alex was there, so they could come in to meet him. I think that was far less threatening for him for people to come to him rather than the other way around.

He was playing with G4 and Amanda while John and I were able to visit with everyone. It was a lot of fun; however, I did notice that every few minutes he looked around for me and wanted to make eye contact with me. He needs constant reassurance that I am still there and available for him. It was so sweet. I realized how strong our bond was, and I need to make sure that this bond grows with everyone in the family.

Afterwards we went to the AT&T to get his iPhone activated. Since we do not have a home phone, everyone needs a phone to be able to communicate. He was excited and started calling all of us immediately. He will rapidly be filling up his contacts with friends, I am sure!

So, to wrap up, I can only say that Alex is a delight in every respect. He is still my "bad boy". He wants to drive my car, he sneaks up on me and scares me all the time, he plays his music too loud—all the normal teenage boy things. He is always smiling and happy and active. We are so happy to have him here and are so happy to share his delight in everything new. We are starting to work on family attachment things, like learning to sit at the dinner table until everyone finishes. He is such a good kid, he observes a lot and many times we don't even have to say anything. But when we do, he just follows along with what we want! He has been such a delight!

66: Happy Mother's Day!

We have been home for four days now and are still settling into a routine. Some things never change—I am back to sitting for hours on end in a taekwondo studio watching Amanda. After almost a year of being a black belt recommended, she has earned the right to undergo the last step next weekend and get her first Dan rank black belt. She is spending hours preparing for it and is very excited.

The first two days we were home, Alex and I pretty much just spent sleeping and eating. As I get older, it is harder and harder to acclimate to travel! But I noticed that even Alex has had trouble switching between time zones.

On Saturday, John took G4 and Alex to do paintball, since my bad boy has an unnatural fascination with guns. Maybe this will be therapeutic for him and get it out of his system. This is so ironic since I am the ultimate pacifist and don't even believe that guns have a place anywhere in our society! Guess I have just seen a few too many gun shot wounds in the ER when I was working. They had a great time, coming back covered with bruises and welts! It was a little more barbaric than Alex thought it would be and I don't think he will be jumping to do it again anytime soon.

As I was reflecting this morning, things with Alex have almost been too easy. I know we are probably in our honeymoon phase now, but so far anything we have faced has been so minor it is almost laughable. I think I am living in a state of concern as I wait for something bad to happen. I read too many blogs early on and I think I was too well prepared for the worst to happen. But on the other hand, I think that it was helpful in a way to deplete me of any expectations I might have had of what kind of experience I would have over in Ukraine while adopting, and what kind of son Alex would be.

He seems so carefree most of the time, but I noticed that there are times when he is a little sad and downcast. After paintball, he came home and went bike riding, and then we all ended up in a huge water gun battle that was a lot of fun. But almost like a switch going off, he clammed up and went down to the basement and started boxing like a fiend on our workout bag. He seemed like he wanted to get out some aggression. I know that still misses his girlfriend and friends very much, and I am sure at times being here gets a little overwhelming. When I called him to dinner, he refused to come, so we left his plate at the table and kept trying to get him to eat. (I was a little miffed, after scouring cookbooks to find a meal he would like and then spending two hours making it.) When he did finally come upstairs, I could tell immediately that he was unhappy, he is very expressive in his face. It almost seemed like he was reacting to how much fun he had had that afternoon; he was almost acting mad at himself. I think he forgot about Ukraine for a while and it scared him and made him feel guilty.

But then we had an unexpected bonus! We received a surprise visit from the Bahr family, and he was roused out of his funk for a while to came and visit. They are a family that hosted a fifteen-year-old girl from Alex's same orphanage the same time we hosted him the summer before. The nice thing is that they are Ukrainian, having been born in Kiev, and still having family over there. So Alex was able to chatter away in his native language. But in a way, I think that he was almost more sad afterward—I think it reminded him of all that he had lost and the difficulties ahead with a new language, culture, and family. I think all of this combined with being physically tired and a lack of food, made for one quiet and grumpy little boy. He ate a little for dinner then (actually only the salad that Vira brought over) and then called out to me, "Night, Mom." This is highly unusual, as he usually comes and finds me, specifically seeking me out to say good night. I went to him, and I think this was another test—he was waiting at the top of the stairs to see if I would come to him or just call out good night as well. I gave him a big hug and told him that I knew he was unhappy and that I was sorry. He threw himself into my arms and gave me a big hug and told me he was tired. I told him I loved him and toddled him off to bed.

This morning, after a good night's sleep, he was back to his chipper self. John cooked with all the kid's help a huge breakfast of belgian waffles, fake sausage and fresh fruit smoothies. It was delicious. Alex sat with us at the table for almost the whole meal without wanting to bolt off as he usually does. Then we got ready and went shopping. Everyone was surprised that I chose shopping for him and G4 as my mother's day activity, but the more clothes they have—the less I have to do laundry! G4 has grown again—unbelievable but true—and of course Alex only has a few things. So, off we went to Park City outlets to get some serious shopping done.

I think Alex has finally gotten the hang of shopping. He got into the spirit and started really picking out clothes and trying them on. He was less picky, thank goodness! He even picked out a suit and tie, I was so surprised. When he tried them on and came out of the dressing room, he was so handsome! I almost started crying but I knew that would irritate him so I busied myself with checking the neck and sleeves and generally fussing so that I could concentrate on the details and ignore the big picture that was making me all emotional.

He made out like a bandit with bags and bags of clothes. John scored a major triumph when Alex didn't want to try on a pair of jeans that he begged and pleaded with him to try on—and guess what? He loved them!

We went out to eat and had a magnificent lunch and then walked up and down Main Street in Park City. He wants to send a card to Olga, so I bought him a nice card with a celtic love knot on the front that says, Two Hearts—One Soul, on the front. He was very happy and definitely approved. We came home and just like a little kid, he had to go change into one of his new outfits. He went out bike riding, but as always, he only went ten or fifteen minutes before he had to come back and assure himself that I was there.

We have just been schmoozing around the house, playing in the back yard, letting the chickens roam and generally doing nothing important. When it got dark, I wanted to type this blog and this little weasel had appropriated my computer to listen to some music, so we reached an accord. He is sitting next to me playing Call of Duty 3 on the Wii system, with headphones plugged into my computer playing music on it, while I am typing away. Amanda is working at the table next to us on her black belt poster presentation, John and G4 are making a cake for Grandma and myself for dessert and Grandma is enjoying a glass of wine.

I have been giving Alex's schedule some thought. He needs to start doing school work, so I think I will be starting with English again sometime soon. He also is very athletic and has expressed interest in kickboxing, so I will investigate that as well. I am a person that likes to have a feeling of accomplishment at the end of every day, but in this case, I will just have to be happy with the fact that Alex's accomplishments are going to be more family and language oriented than anything else.

I really couldn't be happier and more content on this first mother's day with everyone around me. I feel so happy and blessed. I know that we will have more bumps in the road, but I hope that I am learning him as well as he is learning me and that we will work things out. I have found so far that the few times he has been sad or down, just to acknowledge it and tell him I love him has been the best medicine. Hopefully, as time goes on, he will realize that we are definitely here to stay and will support him no matter what.

67: School begins

School started this morning! Alex tried to get out of it, but I persevered. I put both him and Amanda at the table and started her working first. She is pretty independent, so I just let her work quietly while I devoted the lion's share of my attention to Alex. We started with a placement test from Teaching Textbooks (homeschoolers know this is the best math curriculum ever). I printed out the Algebra 1 test and had him work on that. The word problems, he obviously couldn't do, but some of the purely mathematical expressions, he knew exactly what to do with. He got several right, and several more wrong, and then we got into an argument! He kept saying, "In Ukraine…" and then I kept saying, "Math is math…" so I ended the math lesson! But at least I did get an idea of what he knew and where his level is. I think I am going to start him in Algebra 1 and then move along faster once he gets English better. I don't want to hold him back, but I know there have been some gaps in his schooling.

We then moved on to English lessons. He is doing really well; however, I think I am going to break down and buy Rosetta Stone English. It isn't my favorite program, but for purposes of getting him conversationally fluent, I think it will be the fastest way, and the easiest for me. He can just work on it at his own speed, leaving me free to do other things. But for now, we are just using the workbooks that I bought in Ukraine. They have all the instructions in Russian. I am not thrilled with the way they present information, but it has been pretty good so far, and they do have some grammar in them. So far, I would say that Alex is understanding about twenty-five percent of what we say in everyday conversation and about fifty percent of what we slowly try to say to him alone.

We worked for only about a half an hour, as we were interrupted by the sprinkler man and the window man—argh! Every person coming to the door set the dogs barking and distracted Alex too. It will take some time to get him accustomed to working without getting distracted. But it was a good start this morning, and one we can build on.

Then it was time for grocery shopping. Just Alex and I went this time. We have been to the store for a few items and quick visits, but this was our first big stock-up-on-food outing. Yikes, that was an adventure. He wants all kinds of junk food that I don't want him to have, but at this point, I am going to pick my battles one at a time. I gave in to most things, but let others go. I just trust that in time, when I can explain things to him, we will gradually get him over to our way of doing things. I did buy him a half pound of sandwich meat to make some sandwiches—and guess what—it is gone already! He has had three sandwiches today, plus a lunch! Oh, teenage boys with hollow legs.

Amanda had to go to the studio for two hours this afternoon, so Alex came with us and while she was there, he and I ran errands. We went to the post office to mail a letter and small gift to his girlfriend and buy some International Return Coupons, so that she can write him back. We then went to the Social Security Office to apply for his social security card. Even though we checked the box at the embassy when we did the paperwork, they told us to still apply at our local office. I had to show them the judgement, his passport, my passport, and fill out an application. Relatively easy, compared to the adoption paperwork.

We have just had a quiet afternoon, some Wii, some bike riding, more school work, and me cooking dinner. I wish I could make school work fun for him, but I figure if I make it non-threatening then he will be more willing to do more to catch up!

68: Sore muscles and tickle fights

Monday night Alex had his first kickboxing class. We found a gym twenty minutes away that has classes, so I made the trek up there with him. They were very nice and accommodating. He really enjoyed the classes. When we got there, the wife of the owner/chief instructor was behind the counter and was asking about his background in the martial arts, which of course I could not answer other than to say I didn't think it was much. Her sixteen-year-old son, Nicholas, was listening in and stepped up and volunteered to be Alex's partner in the classes. What a wonderful young man. He really liked Alex and they had a lot of fun together. At the end of the two hours, he came over and told me how much he enjoyed working out with Alex and how he would like to get to know him better. I was really impressed.

However, the mom was a different story. In between classes, when there was a little break, she calls everyone over in a circle and points to Alex telling everyone, "This kid is from Russia, he doesn't speak English, so be nice to him." I was a little angry because the last thing Alex needs is to be stared at like some freak side show attraction. It is funny how people react to him. I wish they could all be as nice as Nicholas and as accepting of him like it is no big deal. But there will always be those that want to point him out or be like the customs officer in Minneapolis who was shouting at Alex like he was retarded just because he didn't speak English. I think I am going to have to develop a little routine when I introduce him to people to help stop occurrences like this. I am not sure what to say or how to convey the information, but I am tired of people reminding both Alex and me that he has not always been mine.

Anyway, it was quite a workout at the kickboxing class. Alex has a lot of natural talent and wants to continue classes. But the next morning, boy was he sore. He came limping upstairs and could barely hug me! I fixed him a big breakfast and over the day he gradually worked out the kinks. We are going back tonight for more punishment. Maybe all this sitting and vicariously exercising between him and Amanda will do me some good!

Yesterday, I did get a little miffed at him. He is so easy to handle and really we are having no issues, with a few minor exceptions. He doesn't seem to have any concept of a family yet, or the fact that he has to subjugate his desires for others in the family. Amanda has been begging him to come to one of her karate classes with her, just once, to introduce him to her friends and work out with her. For whatever reason, Alex doesn't want to. And here is where the language barrier gets really frustrating. I don't know why he doesn't, but anyway, I got mad at him yesterday after begging him just for Amanda. He knew I was mad at him and later relented. He came up to me a few hours later and said, "I love you mom. Is OK?" Of course he knows that I can't resist him. So I gave him a big hug and told him that I loved him. We reached an agreement that he would just come to the class, meet everyone, and then leave. So that is what we did. But I do see that we are going to have to work on this concept with him. He has never had a real family unit, so I am not surprised. I was talking to another mom who is adopting from the same orphanage about this yesterday, and while I know that all these adopted kids have different backgrounds, and that they have had different family situations, the one thing they have in common is a disrupted family sense. So, I think all of us will have to deal with this in one way or another.

The first family thing we worked on was sitting at a table while eating with others. Alex used to like to bolt off when he was done, but now he seems to get the concept that we all sit together until the end of the meal. We are lucky that he is older, because many of these things like this we have not been telling him, but rather modeling the behavior that we want. This way I think it makes it more gentle — I worry that if I say anything it will be taken as a criticism and interpreted as an, "I don't love you."

We are trying to use this on other behaviors that we don't want, like violent video games. I am a Mario Kart kind of parent and he is a Call of Duty kid. So when he asked for it and several others, I only bought him the teen rated Call of Duty and when he plays it, everyone else just kind of wanders off. Pretty soon he will figure out that this is not what everyone likes to do and I think it will extinguish itself. And if it doesn't in a couple of months, his English will be better so that I can explain it better, without hurting his feelings or making him feel like he is flawed for liking something that the rest of us do not approve of.

He is continuing to test me a little. When we were in the supermarket yesterday, we ended up on the aisle with beer. He asked me if I wanted to get some, but I said no. Then with this sly look at me he told me, "American beer better. Ukrainian beer bad." I looked at him and saw that he was trying to get a rise out of me! I just shrugged my shoulders and said, "Well, I liked Ukrainian beer, but you won't be drinking any beer in America. Hey, do you want these potato chips?" He kind of looked confused for a minute because he was trying to get me mad or say I wouldn't love him if he drank, but when I made no big deal about it, it totally deflated his sails.

John and Alex had a lot of fun last night with a tickle fight and wrestling. I think it is good for him to have time with John since I am with him all day long. Between homeschooling him and everything else, we are joined at the hip. It is nice for him to have some time with John to bond with him as well.

Before I went to bed last night, I brought Alex into our bedroom and sat him down on the edge of the bed with me and with a combination of charades and Google Translate told him that I understood it was hard to be in a family sometimes. He emphatically shook his head no. I then told him that I get mad sometimes like I did earlier, and he acknowledged that. Then I told him I loved him always no matter what. He threw himself in my arms and gave me a big hug and told me he loved me — so all in all, it was a successful parenting moment.

69: A thought on language

I know there are a thousand different ways to teach a new language and every family will be different, but I want to share what we are doing. In the beginning, in the orphanage, we started with flash cards that we had bought at a local bookstore in Mariupol. It was a great way to interact and to bond early on. It helped me learn some basic Russian words and Alex to learn some English words. Then once we left the orphanage, I graduated up to a workbook that I had bought in Mariupol that had instructions in Russian and exercises in English. This is more of a self-study thing but he seemed to like it.

At home, I soon realized that I needed something a little more to add to the conversational piece of this. So, I broke down and ordered Rosetta Stone English. It came in yesterday, and Alex seems to love it. He admitted to me that he was up to four in the morning doing it and when I went downstairs this morning to get him up finally at noon, he was sitting on the couch doing it as well. So I think it's hit. I guess he likes the visual component.

In addition, I have opted to not get a tutor. On the first day home, I invited Victoria, our neighbor, over just to talk to him, but he seemed like he didn't really want to talk in Russian — or let me rephrase — there was nothing he was dying to tell me that I couldn't understand. He and she just chatted for a while. Then he spoke to the Bahr's when they came over this weekend. And then a girl that had been adopted by a local family from his same orphanage several years earlier called him on his phone. I thought they would yak away, but he spoke for only two minutes and seems very unwilling to speak in Russian and the few times he has, he seems a little sad afterwards. He seems OK watching the movies I got him in Kiev before we came home, or talking to friends, but otherwise, he seems to be unwilling to engage much in Russian. I wonder if it makes him homesick?

Anyway, because of this, I have opted not to have a tutor in the house. We are just trying to muddle through on our own. I don't know if this is good or bad, but it seems right for him. There was one time in the grocery store when Alex wanted a special sweetened milk that I didn't think we had in America, so I called Victoria and she was able to tell him that we can't get it here, but other than that, we haven't really needed help.

Alex is pretty open with us and if he needs something, he will usually speak up and try to ask for it. So this might not work with kids that are a little more shy, or unwilling to try out their English skills, but for now it works for us.

70: Jealousy and building trust

We are continuing to build relationships here. Alex was fine yesterday, but then some jealousy reared its ugly head. Or at least that is what I think it was. He was in a fine mood before kickboxing yesterday but then Amanda had a serious asthma attack at her Tae Kwon Do studio necessitating me to stop there before taking him to class. Her master knows her well and had started the appropriate medications, so by the time I got there, she was fine. But I think that Alex was aware of how worried I was. Then on the way home, I was on the phone with her master and I really felt him withdraw from me. I think he understands intellectually that I have other children, but emotionally, we have been so connected that I think he resents it a little bit. Maybe I am off base, but he went straight to bed last night and wouldn't even say good night to me! That is a change, and I think I was getting punished a little.

But this morning, he seemed back to normal—playful and happy. He seemed over his pique. We went to the doctor this morning and got him started on his Hepatitis B vaccination series. Then we got his foot x-rayed to make sure that the broken bone had healed properly (which it had), and then got my knee looked at and x-rayed. I have torn two ligaments and bruised the back surface of the patella, but it is healing, and hopefully it will continue to heal without incident.

We have had a few problems with Alex trying to call Mariupol without permission. He keeps trying on his cell phone, but smartly, we blocked international calls! He used up the rest of our Skype credits without permission as well calling Mariupol. It was only four dollars, but still, John landed on him pretty hard, telling him that we have to be able to trust him. We have agreed to let him call once a week, but more than that no, unless he comes and asks and can provide a really good reason.

For now, we have opted to let John play the heavy and me to be the accepting, loving one. I usually would not condone this type of parenting—I think that a united front is the best defense against children. But in this case, it just feels right for me to be the forgiving one that has trust just because he is there. I want him to know that there is nothing he can do to get rid of his forever family, we love him just the way he is.

But at the same time, I think having to earn John's trust provides a little incentive to work hard and try. I am so concerned that he will think we will abandon him too, that he will lose the motivation to change and try to be a part of the family. So this feels like a good compromise. And so far I think it is working.

When John confronted him about the phone calls, he was chagrined and got *really* quiet. We have seen that shutter come down before. And he was quiet with me until he realized that I was treating him the same. Once he realized that I wasn't mad or upset with him, he loosened right up. I don't want to be naive, accepting all of his bad behavior, but I do want to give him a refuge.

71: Major breakthrough

Ok, well, maybe not a major breakthrough, but certainly a good one! We have had a busy couple of days here, preparing Amanda for her black belt test. She has been spending hours in the studio and that has taken me away from everyone else in the family, as her medical conditions mean I have to be there with her. It culminated today in an eleven-hour day at the studio.

The boys were asleep when I left this morning with her. When John could finally rouse them out of bed, they went up to REI in Salt Lake to buy some kayaking equipment that we have needed that was on sale. Grandma helped spell me at the studio, as sitting there for hours gets long and tiring. Amanda did great though; she had one bad asthma attack, but we were able to keep it under control. She had so much fun overall, the culmination of five years hard work.

The boys came later in the afternoon and sat quietly and patiently throughout the whole ceremony, which was running very late. Then we all came rushing home for a party that we were throwing to celebrate Amanda's accomplishments and to help introduce Alex to some other teenagers. Everyone had a great time, dancing and playing around. Alex is certainly getting comfortable and feeling at home here. He seemed really happy and carefree.

But, to get to my breakthrough. After most people had left, Alex came and grabbed me and took me outside to the porch and told me to sit down and talk to him. He handed me his phone and pulled up google translate and pointed to it. Then he asked me about girls and dating and relationships and wanted me just to talk to him. So we spent about forty-five minutes just talking together about dating, girls, and so on. It was a great segue into parental expectations. He was very open and really listened to what I was saying. He had a lot of questions and I think I was able to answer a lot of them. I guess he has never really had someone to talk to like that and was really wondering about one girl in particular in our neighborhood that he had met. He was asking a lot of questions about love and relationships and about parents. He was scared about having to deal with a girlfriend's parents, and I can understand it. He probably has never had to deal with other parents before!

Then about an hour later, I went downstairs to clean up and found him moping around on the couch downstairs. He was looking really sad, so I went over to him and asked him what was wrong. He told me, "Nothing." I of course told him that he was telling a lie—that I knew him really well and that he was unhappy at which point he smiled and said, "Yes, Mom. You know me." I felt triumphant at this admission!

I talked some more to him and asked him if he was missing Ukraine and Mariupol. He emphatically said no. So I had a flash of brilliance and asked him if he was lonely. This was the ticket! He said yes and then shrugged his shoulders. I wrote on google translate that I knew he was having a hard time but I also reminded him that he has only been here 10 days. I tried to reassure him that he would have friends but that it would take time. I told him that we loved him and just wanted him happy, and not to be impatient. After he had been here some more time, I assured him, that it would get better.

I don't know if I made him feel any better, but I did get a smile out of him. I hugged him and told him I loved him, then hugged him again. He clung to me and I almost started crying, but knew that I couldn't! We just sat for a minute or two holding each other. Then I told him that I loved him again. I told him to go listen to some music and forget about everything for a while. He smiled and said good night.

I feel like we are cementing a good relationship together. He seems more confident in our love for him now and seems to be homesick less. I think that the culture shock and language barrier will be the next big stumbling blocks, but I know that in time, we will be able to get over them. I think that this was the first time that I was able to really portray some of our family values to him and help him understand some adult type issues. He has obviously had a lot of "adult type" experiences but not the understanding that goes along with them. I feel like tonight I was able to fit some of that into the conversation in a very natural way that didn't sound preachy or dictatorial. I hope that I was able to make him feel empowered to do things right and to really understand what he was feeling and how to act on it. I hope more teachable moments like this pop up because I feel like a giant step in the right direction was taken. He is such a wonderful kid—I just sometimes can't believe how lucky we are to have found him!

72: Mommy flips out

I flipped out last night. We had had a good day overall, but it was pretty much marked by everyone doing their own things. We brought the motor home to the house to wash it and prep it for a trip over Memorial Day weekend. John washed it while the boys peripherally helped. Amanda was so sore from the day before that she pretty much was a couch potato on her computer. Grandma went to church and then shopping. And I cleaned the chicken coop and then flitted around from person to person making sure they were OK.

By dinner time, I was so irritated. I felt like we were six roommates living under one roof but not committed to each other. I finally got everyone to sit down at the table outside together to eat a nice dinner that I had cooked, but the moment Alex was done, he bolted. G4 drifted off to play video games, Amanda played with the dogs and John cleaned up the table. Before I knew what was happening, I was sitting alone outside as the sun set getting more irritated by the second.

I marched inside and lo and behold found everyone else downstairs in the family room. John and Amanda were each on their own computers, G4 was reading a book, and Alex was cleaning up his room. Even though they were physically in the same place—there was no interaction taking place at all!

I just flipped out and started fussing at everyone! When not one person looked up at me—I really flipped out and started shouting. Finally, Alex came out of his room asking, "Mom OK?" to which I replied, "No, Mom *not* OK!" I told everyone that this had to stop. We were a family and had better start acting like one! No more solitary activities unless there had been a family activity first.

John started translating for Alex on Google Translate and to my utter annoyance, everyone started laughing at me. I did the only thing I could—I picked up a pillow and threw it at G4, who happened to be closest. Then he retaliated by starting a tickle fight, which then degenerated into everyone getting into a free for all tickle fight. And BTW—Alex is the most ticklish kid I have ever seen.

I don't know if anyone will pay attention to me in the future, but at least I felt a little better that we were interacting together. I guess in the end I got what I wanted. But I do realize now that we are going to have to work on it harder. G4 and Amanda have been so accepting of Alex, that they have not gone out of their way to do extra things with him or treat him special. Good I guess in one respect because they are so accepting, but bad in another way that they need to treat him a little special until he is fully integrated.

The language barrier is tough at times, because a lot of the things we do together as a family rely on English — I didn't realize how much until now. So we are going to have to keep working on it and find things. In a way, I wish he was littler because it would be easier I think to play simple games — but teens are harder to amuse.

Alex is handy around the house though. We developed a massive leak under the sink this morning and I (in classic, helpless female style) was standing there wringing my hands and putting out towels to mop up the water, when he came upstairs and found me. Immediately he requested a flashlight and tools and ten minutes later he had tightened a connection that was loose, tightened the whole faucet mechanism and fixed it. That saved a call to the hubby!

He still is a little imp though — this morning school work was not high on his list, so he has been trying to circumvent me at every opportunity. I finally had to sit next to him to get him to work! But overall things couldn't be better. I know that I am impatient to get back to normal — whatever that means — but I am going to have to give it a little time. I know it will happen. But in the meantime, I need to think of family activities not based on language.

73: Daddy flips out

Copycat! I had a bad day and now John thinks he can have a bad day too! To be fair, he had had a hard day at work and was tired, but he was really set off by Alex playing music way too loud and not telling us he was going out bike riding. But instead of saying anything and having a hissy fit like I did, he goes to bed! Definitely his way of dealing with irritation—withdraw! Mars vs. Venus I guess.

But, I really think that he is not being given much of a chance to bond with Alex. His job is very high-powered and he works long hours, and I am home with the kids all day and homeschooling them. I am also a little bit of a momma bear and get in protective mode, which probably does interfere with anybody else getting close!

But anyway, back to my story—after John went to bed last night, G4 and Amanda followed close behind and left me with Alex—one hungry kid. So I made him dinner and then he grabbed my hand and led me outside to the back porch and the chaise lounges saying, "Go outside. Nice sky and stars. You I talk." And we did. We spent about two hours out there just stargazing and looking at the mountains. He was asking questions about our upcoming camping trip this weekend and then told me about the times he went camping with his dad. He told me they used to go next to a big lake. He liked everything about it except the bugs and sleeping on the ground. He will like camping in our motorhome!

We talked about Halloween—he was asking about the traditions over here. He had seen all of our creepy decorations in the storage closet and was wondering about it. I described to him our haunted house and he got very excited. Right up a fourteen-year-old's alley! Looks like John has another partner in crime—I am more of the dancing pumpkin and Casper the Friendly Ghost kind of person, while everyone else in the family is a scare the pants off the crowd kind of person. This is why I give out the candy!

It was a wonderful time together—I have come to treasure these talks we have. I am sure they will get better when his English gets better but companionable silence is OK too. I feel like he really wants to share things with me that he might be reluctant to share in front of others.

This morning, we went to his kickboxing class at 9:00 am. I told him—this was true love! Getting out of bed voluntarily at eight in the morning to take him somewhere! I took a coffee with me and finished it quick in the car—and was still moaning. So Alex looked at me and offered me the rest of his coffee. (He loves coffee as much as the rest of us—it's not a grown up drink here. The kids and I all love it.) I felt a little guilty because he hadn't eaten breakfast yet, but then I grabbed it! I needed the jumpstart and I rationalized it that I was driving.

We had a good day, but he has become a little resistant on schoolwork—he only wants to do Rosetta Stone English. I have let this slide a little, but soon, I will have to address it. We did a little Algebra, but right now, working on English is my priority. But in Alex's defense, his English is coming along great. He is talking so well and is trying to communicate now in bigger sentences.

This evening, I took Amanda to Tae Kwon Do and then to Karate (curse her for cross-training)! It was four hours sitting in two different studios. I asked Alex if he wanted to go with me, but he said no—which I was a little surprised at—but happy that he would have a little time away from me. John came home and he, G4, and Alex, had dinner and then started on a building project. We have decided that our chickens need some enrichment in their run to keep them mentally alert (we want smarter eggs) so Daddy John showed Alex how to use a saw and build things. They were building a sort of climbing device with toys hanging down to engage the chickens.

When I came home, Alex came running over, busting with a story to tell me. He had gone bike riding earlier before the building project with his new friend (the sixteen-year-old neighbor that inspired the conversation about dating earlier) and then when they came back, she waylaid him with a water gun and they had a huge water fight with her sister and G4 getting involved. He was so happy—it was great to see him so animated and talking so well.

Currently, John and Alex are playing a video game together and competing to see who can kill the most zombies—ugh!!!! But they are having fun and laughing and talking together. My system of weaning him off of violent video games is working in part. He still hasn't abandoned them, but there are times when I catch him playing other sorts of games that are more acceptable in my mind. I guess only time will tell if I am right about this approach.

So, back to Dad's earlier fit—I think he just needs to be patient and I need to back off my protective, hovering mode. Once Alex has a chance to bond with him like I have, I am sure that he will have a better understanding of everything. I had cast John as more of the discipline person, but I have started to take some control—I mentioned that he had to tell us when he goes out and that there were times to play loud music that we were fine with and times when people needed to talk and the music needs to be shut off. He is such a good kid—he complies with everything (at least for now). Tonight he asked permission to go out—he didn't forget!

Now, one last thing. I walked into Alex's room tonight putting some laundry away while he and John were playing video games, and just about died of a stroke. I know my kids are messy—but this took messy to a new level! He is always cleaning up his room, I just don't see how it gets so messy. I guess I have to be happy he is doing some minimal work to keep it clean, otherwise we would have a reality TV show on our hands—"Help us find our son in his room!" It was so bad that we had to stop the video game and stage an intervention. He was laughing so hard at my reaction that it was hard to clean up—but we finally got things somewhat under control. I think this is my next thing to work on. . . .

74: Nothing like a mopey teenager

Today Alex had a mopey session. We had a great morning, he cooked a wonderful breakfast, had some great school work, but then got really quiet. He retreated to his room, listened to music, and punched on his boxing target for a while. I figured something had triggered a bout of homesickness that he needed to work out, but for the life of me, I can't think of what.

I was feeling a little helpless when he was mopey, so I decided to try to intervene. I knocked on his door and when he let me in, I told him that I knew something wasn't right. He tried to bluff that he was OK—but I called him on it—and that roused a smile as he knows I know him. He wouldn't tell me what was wrong, so I just hugged him and held him and told him I loved him. I told him that nothing would change how much I loved him and he told he that he loved me. I just held him and squeezed him until he started squirming. I know that I can't totally fix all his homesickness, but I hope that letting him know that I am sharing his hurt and that I love him will make him feel a little better. I know that this is all a process of adjustment for everyone and there will be ups and downs. I love the ups and hate the downs.

He smiled a little and seemed to be better, but I could still tell that he was overall quieter and sadder than usual. Thank goodness, a neighbor that Alex really likes came over and asked him to go bike riding (of course it is a girl). He was snapped out of his mopeyness right away and perked up.

As the day wore on, I cooked dinner and we all sat down to a family dinner. Poor Alex sat there like he was at his own execution! His mopeyness had returned! Ack!!! He wouldn't eat dinner and just sat there very quiet and downcast. Finally we took pity on him and released him from jail and let him go. He did volunteer to clean up the dishes though. Then John had a great idea and got all the kids and himself playing poker. They played just with poker chips—not money. This really perked Alex up—lots of smiles. He was back to his joking self. And just like the "bad boy" that I know he is—he of course knew how to play—he did quite well and cleaned up. After winning all the money at the table and looking like a satisfied cheshire cat, he and John played more zombie shoot 'em up video games.

More tomorrow . . .

75: A day in the life of Alex's stomach

I know we are not the only family that is amazed at the capacity for food these kids have. And remember, I have a six-foot-four, sixteen-year-old son that I fed—and Alex is outpacing him at a phenomenal rate!

This was just an ordinary day—I just happened to pick today to keep track of what he ate.

Breakfast—two bowls of cereal (newly opened box this morning), banana, juice, large coffee

Snack—half a bag of chips and dip

More snacks—juice and the rest of the box of cereal

Then standing at refrigerator complaining there is nothing to eat.

Lunch—three cups of potato salad, two pieces of white bread, three pieces of semolina bread, four large slices of gouda cheese

Snack—half a bag of grapes, juice

More snacks—two sandwiches

More snacks—two large cokes (twenty ounces each)

More complaining there is nothing to eat.

More snacks—two pieces semolina bread and four large slices gouda cheese, juice

Dinner—Spaghetti with meatballs, mac and cheese, cauliflower, two pieces ciabatta bread

And it is now just ten at night and if you have been paying attention, you know that dinner number two and three are coming in the next few hours.

I need to get a job to pay for this kid's appetite!

76: Yikes — help me out!

We had a great day. Okay, mostly great after I recovered from a heart attack when Alex had another talk with me. Normally these go well, but this one degenerated after he and I were talking about G4's dyed green hair. I mentioned that I wanted G4 to pierce his ears but he wouldn't do it. This opened Alex's eyes as he lit up and told me he wanted to get one ear pierced. I am all for it but John reined me back in and correctly told me it was something that Alex would have to earn in the future. Alex was a little miffed at that, but took it in stride. Then he asked if he could have a tattoo.

After I picked myself up off the floor, I must have looked freaked out because Alex asked, "You OK mom?" at which I screamed "NO! You could gat Hepatits C and DIE!" I am a mite freaky about infectious diseases and I just can't trust tattoo parlors. I scrambled for the computer and typed on google translate as fast as I could no tattoos, not now, not ever! Then he started laughing and pulls his sleeve up and shows me a homemade tattoo on his shoulder! It is very small, almost indistinguishable, and didn't take very well, but he was describing how he and his friends got together one night and did this. I swear, I am not going to be able to survive any more of these "talks." My heart is going to just give out one of these days!

The only other major thing today was an orthodontist visit where I learned that we were going to have to pay equal to the adoption fees all over again in his mouth! Four wisdom teeth need to be extracted like yesterday and there is another tooth that had a bad filling that needs to be pulled, and then braces with coils for about two years. Yikes!

But I can tell you, it is all worth it when you have an experience like I did tonight. Amanda and I were at her karate class tonight, which is just about a mile from our house, when Alex rides up on his bike. He said he just wanted to say hi, then he said he was biking home. I got a text about fifteen minutes later saying, "I home." Then it was followed up by, "I love you." Things like this are the cure for anything! They make your heart sing. I love you Alex, more than you will ever know!

77: First family vacation

We had decided after coming home from Ukraine that we needed to get away from all the distractions of modern life. We wanted to leave behind internet and cell phones and video games. So, we planned the trip, loaded up the motorhome, and took off for Wyoming.

We are having a fun time in Jackson Hole. The weather hasn't been great, but as our first objective of the trip was to spend family time together, we have just tolerated the weather and focused on the family. I think Alex really got into traveling in the motorhome—he settled in on the couch with headphones on, listening to music, and playing games on the iPad.

Our first day here we walked down to Jackson Lake and spent some time poking around. Alex took me by the hand and led me aside from the rest of the family and told me how much he loves lakes and mountains. He said he likes the smells, the water, and the views. I guess he has some happy memories of times with his dad. He had told me before of camping trips to lakes with his dad.

It was a beautiful lake with a pebbly beach with all kinds of stones lying around. Amanda has been trying to learn how to skip a stone for a while, so she decided this was a perfect place to practice. The first stone she ended up throwing right into Alex's stomach, so that ended her throwing for the day. Then G4 tried and winged John's temple. After that, we put an end to the stone skipping for everyone before we ended up in an emergency room. Not a Gardiner family talent I guess.

We are staying in the Grand Teton National Park, but unfortunately have not gotten to see any Tetons yet given the fog and cloud cover. However it is still a beautiful setting. We have gotten to see a lot of wildlife, like bears, elk, deer, etc. Alex is making good use of his camera, taking it everywhere and taking pictures of everything. He loves wildlife and is always on the lookout as we drive around.

Yesterday we spent the afternoon in Jackson, poking around the stores and visiting the sights. In the evening we went to a chuck wagon dinner and listened to a country music band perform. We discovered that Alex hates (and I mean hates) country music! It wasn't hard to pick up on when he held his hands over his ears when the banjo started! He kept asking when it was going to end and when were going to go. We were cracking up—it was funny to see him so horrified. I don't think he realized this whole part of America exists.

The food was great though, real home-cooked country fare. We got Alex a steak and he scarfed down all of it—our veggie patties were good but not on that magnitude. So far he seems OK with being vegetarian most of the time at home. And of course when we go out, he is a carnivore extraordinaire. We decided that we would handle it this way, our rules (no meat) at home, but when we go out, he can choose what to order. It seemed like a good compromise to communicate our values without pressing them too intensely on him. And he is at the age too where you just can't tell him what to do. Imposing something unilaterally on him might make him rebel, and I really don't want to deal with that. I also don't think it is right to impose our values on him; I want to share my values with him, but ultimately in life, he will have to choose for himself, and I know if I am too heavy handed, the choices will not be those I want him to make. The only thing I can do is to model the behavior I want and to encourage those steps in the right direction.

We have pretty much adopted that attitude with most everything with Alex. We have talked to him, shown him what we value, and modeled what we value, but we have not imposed on him. I think that this is unique in older adoptions, where the kids come with an identity and values partially formed. With younger kids, this is probably not as much of a problem since you will have a chance to have them grow up with your value system in place.

It was snowing really hard when we left the chuck wagon show and John was a little worried about driving off the road in places. It is only about a forty-five-minute drive normally, but with the snow it took about an hour and a half. It was pretty much a whiteout, and the snow was accumulating so fast that you could not clearly make out the road in front of you. Thank goodness John is a good driver, calm and cool in these situations. We made it back to the motor home without incident.

Alex, Amanda, and I were tired and started to zone out—good thing G4 was in the front seat with John to keep him awake! It was so cute — Alex reached for my hand and squeezed it and then settled in and fell asleep still clutching my hand. I tell you all — he has a way of worming in and just squeezing my heart. He is so sweet and so nice and so loving, I still can't believe that he wasn't snapped up right away when he went in the orphanage.

We have had a lot of fun together as a family here. The forced confines of the motorhome are actually good for everyone. Alex has been working really hard at making a conscious effort to be part of the family. He has been in a great mood here.

On a funny side note — I have been learning how Cyranno de Bergerac must have felt like. Alex has gotten the idea of texting to friends and has several that are regularly texting him. The problem is that he doesn't always understand what they are saying or how to write back. So he will get a text and if he does not understand, he will give me the phone. I will translate and then we will decide what to answer back. If he can write it — he will, but if not then I have to write it. Especially with the girls, I am having to remember back to my teenage years to help advise him what to say. There are times the process is so onerous and he wants to do other things, so he just tosses me the phone and says, "Text for me. Say what you want."

His conversational English is coming along great. He was able to call a friend that he met last year when he was here that is going off to college next week and set up a get-together before he leaves. He was able to have a pretty good conversation! I am so proud of him. He seems to relate better to older kids anyway. I think some is the life experience he possesses and some is due to the fact that the older kids are more tolerant of his language problems and willing to take extra time to understand him.

Today we went whitewater rafting. It was a cold experience — the water here is forty-three degrees in the Snake River! We got wetsuits and splash gear so it wasn't that bad. It was a great experience. Alex had some trepidation initially but I think he really enjoyed it. We put him and G4 in the front of the raft; that way he got good and wet and really got to experience the rapids. It was a relatively short trip — eight miles — but we had some good class three rapids and a couple of class four. Everyone was sad and didn't want it to end. After the bus took us back to town, we went and got some ice cream—I mean, really, what is a better way to celebrate the great outdoors and exercise than with some calories, fat, and sugar?

We stopped on the way back to the motorhome and tried to take some family photos. We set the camera up on a tripod and used our remote control to get pictures of all five of us. If I thought it was frustrating to get a family photo with two kids—multiply that—with three it was impossible. It took us forty-five minutes to get a picture where everyone looked halfway decent. We would take one and see that Alex looked away, or I had my eyes closed, or G4 looked goofy! They were so funny that we ended up by laughing so hard it was impossible to line us up to get a good picture. But just when John and I were about to give up, we got a great one!

I have to say that the forced confinement has been great for bonding. In the mornings, we have been lazing around. Alex has been sleeping on the couch that pulls out into a futon. It has been so cold in the mornings that when I come out to check on everyone, he has patted the bed next to him and snuggled up with me. He knows how to get to me, I love to snuggle and have always decried the fact that Amanda and G4 do not cuddle. We spent two hours snuggled up this morning and dozed off and on. Okay—to be truthful, I dozed, all warm and cozy, while he played on the iPad. I could just stay like that all day, and I think he could too.

I am learning about him day by day. I know that he chews on his bottom lip when he is thinking or concentrating or unsure of himself. I know that he loves skinny jeans and adidas track clothes. He is very picky about how his shoelaces are tied. He loves to take showers—sometimes two or more a day, and he often forgets to brush his teeth at night. He is proud of his muscles and has me check them at least once a day to proclaim how strong he is getting. He loves learning English but hates schoolwork. He loves teasing people (like his sister) but has such a tender heart that if he thinks he has gone too far, will jump in immediately with an "I'm sorry." I know he bites his fingernails but is trying hard to stop. I know that he can't wait to learn how to drive and wants a car when he turns sixteen. I know his favorite thing to do is bike ride and second favorite is to listen to music. In third place, is hanging out with friends and learning English. And I know that I love him to distraction and can't imagine life without him!

78: Last day of vacation

Well, we had a great day today. We stopped in a small town (Victor, Idaho) and had the best huckleberry shakes I have ever had. We love the huckleberry flavors around here! As we were in the soda shop, we noticed that up on the wall were a bunch of different kinds of money tacked up. We asked about it and the lady behind the counter couldn't say exactly why it was started, but she said it was a tradition now for people from different countries to leave currency behind from their country. Alex has been toting around about fifty hrivna (about six dollars) since we left Ukraine so we went to get some and gave it to her to tack up. They had money from Sudan, Iraq, Hungary. So now they will have Ukraine!

After there, we went to the home of a friend that John works with. He owns a large ranch in Alta, Wyoming. He owns several horses and had them saddled up and ready to go when we got there. G4, Amanda, and Alex went out on a trail ride with him. His property backs up on Grand Teton National Forest. Amanda said it was some of the most spectacular scenery she had ever seen. The kids had a great time and spent about an hour out.

When they got back, Mr. Wilson took us on a tour in his truck around the area. His family had homesteaded the area in 1888 and had farmed the land ever since. They currently raise sheep and grow alfalfa. His three-year-old grandson wanted to go along on the tour but there wasn't enough room in the truck, so he was put on Alex's lap. Alex has a way with kids too and within five minutes the little tyke was out cold, all snuggled up in his arms. Alex is so gentle and nice, it was so sweet to see him cuddling that little boy. After the lovely tour, we said our goodbyes and headed out again. We made it to Pocatello, Idaho—home tomorrow.

79: Talk about ruining a good thing

Officially, I feel like the world's worst mother. We had such a great vacation with great experiences, and then we go and ruin it. We had to break the news to Alex last night that we might be moving sooner than we expected. We were hoping to wait it out until September or so, but it looks like we will need to go sooner than that to get established before G4 starts his semester at the University of Washington. We knew we would be moving this fall when we hosted Alex last summer and told him as much. But I am pretty sure that with all of the excitement and assorted activities, it got lost in the shuffle. We have talked a lot about how we move a lot, but I think that the reality is hard to visualize when you have never moved before.

G4 started college at fourteen and did transfer applications over the winter while we were working on paperwork. Quite the grind to do both things at once, critiquing essays and getting papers notarized—I am surprised we survived the winter. Now he is just sixteen and a junior, ready to go to top-level university, and we have decided as a family that we all need to be there with him. He is just not old enough to go off on his own. Add onto that the flexibility of John's job, and off we can go! After going through all his acceptances, he finally decided the University of Washington was the place. Seattle! I am excited—I am always up for someplace new, but apparently Alex is not.

And of course, why should he be? He has already gone through so much change and now we are trying to take away the only consistent things in his life right now. We told him that we loved him and that he could come visit his friends as often as he wants, but that was not cutting it. He was as sad as I have ever seen him last night—it broke my heart watching him. I just wanted to cuddle him and tell him it would be OK—that he had to trust me. But I know that nothing got through. He put up a wall and it was impenetrable. I just held him tight and tried to telepathically message my love.

Today was a little better. He told me this morning that he was not happy but he would try to be. He humbled me all over again. I know that I would not have had that in me at fourteen years of age. He has been a little mercurial today with his mood up and down. He was happy to be home but then got mopey again. He actually walked out on me during one conversation and then ten minutes later turned around and launched himself into my arms saying "I love you." Then a half hour later it was, "I no go. Utah my home." I told him, "No, you are my baby and I am never leaving you. I am your mom forever." To which he then smiled and said, "No, you my baby. I love you."

I know it is hard for him and that he is trying as hard as he can to accept the situation. I just need to get better at coming up with ways to help him adjust and realize that we stick together like crazy glue!

80: Things calm down

Well, Alex seems more resigned to moving now. He has even been joking a little about it and using it to get his way with things. I know he is manipulating me a little, but I am just content to let it happen. I have to get through to him that I have unconditional love for him and no matter what happens, he is my baby forever!

We got passes to Seven Peaks water park and spent a good portion of the afternoon there yesterday. It was fun just kicking back and sun bathing and visiting with friends.

He seemed a little quiet this morning, but was back to his normal self after a furious session working out and kicking and punching the kickboxing target! He really seems to need a physical outlet for his emotions. Once he works out the aggression, then he is back to his old self. I knew he was going through something this morning, but I couldn't put my finger on exactly what it was. It is so weird being connected to someone so deeply that you know their every emotion, but you can't tell why because of the language barrier. Alex is also very resistant to getting help translating, preferring to either work it out himself or try to communicate with me directly.

We are back to our old issues of trying to integrate Alex into the family as quickly as possible, but it seems very hard to do. He is very used to doing things on his own, and coupled with the busy lives that everyone else in the household is living, it makes for a lot of solitary time. He also needs time away from us, just bike riding or running, where he can get away and not feel the smothering presence of all of us. Unfortunately, that leaves the rest of us, when we can get together (like at the dining room table for dinner) feeling bereft without his presence.

I feel in a way like I have two families right now. One made up of myself, John, G4, and Amanda, and the other myself and Alex. I am the only bridge between the two and it can be draining at times. I want us all to feel like one cohesive unit but until the language barriers, culture shock, and other things settle down, I don't see it happening. This isn't necessarily a bad thing though. I think the time that Alex takes alone is good for the rest of us to keep connected and in touch with each other. I have very ambivalent feelings about this. On one hand, I want us all to be together, but on the other, I don't want to change the way things were and potentially have the rest of the family feel slighted with the attention Alex is taking away from them. I know that I am just being impatient and that integration will occur with time, but it sure is hard to wait it out.

I was talking to Becky Radzinski the other day and she gave me a flash of insight. She rightly pointed out that Alex probably needs a physically demonstrative sign of integration into the family. So, I went out today and bought another little boy sticker to add to the family stickers on the back of my car. So, we will have a big ceremony tonight to put it on the back of the car. I hope that by starting to do more things like this, we will help Alex realize what he means to us and what it means to be in a family.

The other thing I need to work on is building bridges with G4 and Amanda. They are both so driven and on a master plan for their lives, that they have very little time or tolerance of others. G4 with his focus on academics won't let anything interfere with schoolwork. Thank goodness, he is on summer break now, but he still studies and pursues knowledge like it is imperative. Also, even though he is only a year and a half older than Alex, he seems worlds apart. Maybe this is just from having been in college already. He is so independent and just at a different stage in his life.

Amanda and Alex are closer, since she spent time in Ukraine, but still are not as close as I would like to see. She is so busy with her Tae Kwon Do and Karate, and her Olympic dreams, that she is only available when she isn't training or doing schoolwork. She is very self-motivated and basically schools herself and will make sure her work is done first before play without any real urging from me.

Even though we have been extraordinarily lucky without any signs of sibling rivalry, I want the kids closer. I have to come up with ideas of things they can do together that can help them bond closer. I guess I should have thought of this sooner, but I just thought that kids would play together and wouldn't need any nudging. In fact there are times that I just stand back in awe of G4 and Amanda and how well they have adjusted to Alex. They have been so welcoming that it is hard to believe. I keep asking them about the situation and giving them opportunities to talk to me, but they are really fine with everything. They are the best kids! In fact I feel so blessed with all three of them.

Otherwise, things still are going well overall. We have had very few problems in the grand scheme of problems and Alex and I have such good open communication and understanding of each other that I feel really stable and good about the way things are progressing. He barked something at me this morning (he demanded breakfast) and when I brought it down, I just gave him the plate and walked off—which is highly unusual. Usually I would sit with him while he ate and make sure he was OK and touch him on his shoulder or kiss him. Instead of saying anything about the imperious tone he took with me, I opted to give him what he had demanded just to let him know that he would be taken care of no matter what. However, I didn't follow it up with the usual niceties, subtly saying to him—you no give, you no get! He knew something was up and called as I walked away, "Mom, MOM!" I turned around and before I could say anything, he launched himself into my arms and kissed me saying, "Thank you, I love you." He knew I wasn't happy about how he had acted, and was offering up his form of apology. He knows me as well as I know him, and that is helping where communication is lacking!

81: The good (science experiments) and the bad (my cellphone)

My cell phone has decided that it does not like for me to have a complete conversation. It will drop calls at random times (usually at a crucial point in the conversation) or randomly not vibrate or ring with calls or texts. This happens in direct relationship to the importance of the call or text that I am expecting. Anyway, when something simple like this goes wrong in the midst of all that I am dealing with in the family, it tends to be like the metaphorical straw that broke the camel's back.

On Saturday, Amanda was in the studio for five hours, and in between, we took all the kids to a new trampoline park that opened up. They had a lot of fun, but got really tired out. Then it was rush, rush, rush to get to the airport to welcome another family bringing their kids home from Ukraine. Alex knows the boys and was excited to be able to meet them. It was the Radzinski family who was over in Ukraine with us for a while. They were bringing home Sergei, a good friend of Alex's, and his little brother, Max.

Alex seemed completely at ease at the airport. I was worried that he would not be happy in his role of experienced adoptee and would withdraw, but rather the opposite, he seemed happy to help Sergei and the make the transition easier. In a way, I wish we had had some of this support for Alex when he and I arrived home. But as usual, I stand in awe of how strong emotionally he is. We stayed at the airport long enough to welcome Sergei and Max and let the boys visit for a while, but I knew how tired they must have been, so we left as soon as we could.

After getting home finally that night, Amanda and G4 crashed, so Alex, John, and I ended up outside again for another "talk." This was the first time for John to be involved in these talks and I think he realizes now why I love these times so much. Alex's English is getting so much better. He is very comfortable speaking to us, but was explaining that it is harder to speak to others he doesn't know as well. When he meets friends of ours he just clams up. He isn't able to communicate as well as he can with us, but we reassured him that it would come in time.

Alex talked for two hours straight. He was just full of info that he wanted to share. We heard about trips that he had taken. He was in a competition group of dancers that competed in a competition in Kiev. I am pretty sure that I understood that his dance troupe won first place. He also told us about visits to St. Petersburg with his dad and Grandma among others. We heard about his time on the streets and run-ins with police. He opened up about his struggles with smoking and why he stopped. He talked about friends that he had and their struggles with drug use. It was great to see how open and honest he is with us. We just listened and commented appropriately — not really reacting or judging. I felt so honored that he would share this information with us. I know that it takes a lot of strength to share these memories, and I am so happy that he felt he could share them with us.

He seems very comfortable with us now and is definitely hanging out with us more each day. Yesterday in fact, he just hung out in the living room for a while playing with his dog while John and G4 were talking. He helped me cook dinner last night and hung out in the kitchen for a while as well.

Schoolwork was kind of forgotten this weekend, so yesterday, I decided we needed a little science to liven up our life! The kids and I went out and got a bunch of different kinds of sodas and mentos. I hope everyone has done this — it is so much fun. We have a special geyser tube that fits on two liter bottles to make it even more spectacular. We must have set off ten bottles! It was so much fun — Alex had never seen anything like it and enjoyed participating.

I need to keep doing more things like this as he and I work on English together. He is not big on formal work, so if I can keep him engaged with fun things, I will teach that way. He definitely seems to like my unschooling style. And even last night as he and I were sitting outside while he ate dinner number two at eleven thirty at night, he mentioned that it was back to the books today! So he is gradually learning our ways!

I am surprised how great he is doing and how resilient he is. He is still worried about moving and last night was talking about it again. He is having a hard time understanding why we would want to move and is going to miss Utah — but I keep trying to reassure him that it will be OK. I don't think we will have problems once we get moved, but until then, it will be difficult. I hope he trusts us enough now to take care of him. I keep reinforcing the concept with him that we are a forever family and that he is stuck with us as well. I don't want him thinking that there is a choice here! He is ours and we would be devastated without him. Very quickly, he has wormed his way into our hearts and become an integral part of the family.

G4, Amanda, and I were talking yesterday about how great it has been to have him here. They are getting closer to him day by day as he is to them. In fact, they are really treating each other like siblings now—complaining about each other! G4 was complaining about the music Alex listens to while he was complaining about G4's trains. They were laughing and joking with each other. Amanda was joking around with him as well—as they were each trying to proclaim they were the strongest. Poor Alex just doesn't stand a chance yet until he grows more! The kids agree with me that he has completed this family in a very special way.

82: Setting a few boundaries

We finally decided yesterday that despite all of Alex's protestations that he did not need translating help, that there were some things that just needed to be communicated and couldn't wait for him to learn English. One of these issues revolves around his teeth and the other is our upcoming move.

So, we invited Victoria and she graciously translated for us. There is going to be major dental work going on, starting with all four wisdom teeth. The top ones are growing near his sinuses and the bottom ones are starting to get near the nerve—so these need to go in the next few weeks. Then there is a tooth whose viability is in question that might need to go and be replaced with an implant—and then of course there are braces. But I didn't want him to be scared about all of this and to understand that we would not let him be in pain. So I think it was good that he understood. I really think he knew most of this anyway from talking to me—but with the help of a native Russian speaker—I think he will be more confident about what is going on.

We then moved on to our move. While he is still resistant to the idea, he did say it would be fun to move around and experience new places. He is so resilient and amicable—I am amazed at times. I think understanding things a little better gave him the ability to deal with the move better. He was smiling through the whole conversation and was joking around. I think he is in a good place regarding the move. We told him he could personalize his room when we move and he was excited about that. He wants to paint graffiti on the walls and ceiling. We said OK as long as we can OK the design first.

There was a little kerfuffle about an earring. He wants his to get an earring (and I think he would look darling with one) but John has appropriately said this is something that needs to be earned over time. He has tentatively said sixteenth birthday. John also pointed out that with an earring we would be having even more trouble with girls chasing him than we already have! Alex was a little put out, but I think understood that we meant it.

We also had to communicate that there was some music that he listened to that was inappropriate. There have been two songs that we have nixed out of all the rap music he listens to. He made some snide comment that it was because we were old! We fussed at him about that one, and were able to get the point across that when racial slurs come into songs, that is where we draw the line. I am even getting into rap and starting to enjoy it! We made sure to tell him that he was lucky to have us as parents—as a lot of parents would not tolerate any of the music he likes.

It was a great talk—I felt like he is starting to push back against some of our controls and I am glad to see it. We are pretty permissive overall, but when we have limits, they are in stone. But seeing him push against them shows me that he is confident in our love for him. He is starting to realize that we are there always and he does not need to treat us special for fear of losing us. I love how comfortable he is with us now. I know this is a long process that will take years, but so far—I can feel it starting and it is so rewarding to feel.

Right now we are in kickboxing class and I am watching him die from exhaustion! Amanda is at her TKD studio again and then we are going over to a friend's house to let Alex visit and relax. More later . . .

83: Our first fight

Alex and I had our first fight two nights ago. I think it scared both of us down to our toes. It was so stupid—a combination of tiredness, hunger, and misunderstanding. I guess I hadn't realized how much we were walking on eggshells around each other. It feels ridiculous to love someone so much and think you know so much about them but really in some areas, you know nothing at all.

Well, this fight was predictably about food. It was about dinner of all things. I had started preparing dinner and was doing that while trying to get some laundry done when Alex barged into the laundry room and told me he was hungry. He went on to demand that I go to Subway and get him a sandwich. I explained to him that I was already cooking dinner and wanted him to wait with everyone else to eat. I explained that I would have dinner on the table in about thirty minutes. He looked so forlorn that I relented a little and told him to get a small snack to tide him over, but I really wanted him to wait for a meal. I knew what would happen if I gave in totally and he ate a sandwich. He would then claim he wasn't hungry when the meal I had prepared was ready and wouldn't want to eat with us. At least if he came to the table hungry, I had a better chance of him eating with us.

This didn't seem to go over so well, as he made a rude comment in Russian. Unlucky for him I understood what he said. So I got nasty with him and snapped at him to to watch his language. Everything seemed to deteriorate from there. His chin stuck out and I could see him settling in for an argument. I really wasn't in the mood, so I took a deep breath and walked away. I counted to ten to calm down and then went back to folding laundry and then cooking dinner. Dinner was a little tense that night, but I just wasn't in the mood to give in. I usually do, but for some reason it felt right to stick my ground on this one. Don't know why—just felt from the heart the right thing to do.

I think he was really worried about the fight, as I have never walked away from him before. Later in the evening, I was back in the laundry room, folding laundry, when he came in and put his head on my shoulder. He nuzzled up against my neck and I turned around and hugged him.

He said, "Is OK mom" and I sighed a huge sigh of relief. It was *scary*—I think we both worried that this was it, the honeymoon phase was over, and either he wanted to leave or that we would want him to go—but when we got over our snit and calmed down and realized that everything was OK, and we still loved each other—it was a really special moment. I think Alex is really starting to realize that he can't get rid of me—no matter what!

We have had a busy couple of days. This morning it was dental visits for the two boys. We needed crowbars to pry them out of bed to get to the office by nine. I have learned now that all appointments need to be made after one in the afternoon. But after several hours there—I needed to be resuscitated after finding out all that is wrong. Alex has nine cavities and needs one root canal and a crown. This is on top of the four wisdom teeth that need to be removed and braces. The dental bill just for the cavities and the crown will be around $2500. After the $1500 for the wisdom teeth and the $3000 for braces—we will be living in a cardboard box!

I know I have said it a million times, but I am so gratified to have Alex in our family. He makes me laugh (we had a big tickle fight this afternoon). He is so funny and playful, and yet helpful and considerate. He always wants to protect me and gets jealous when I am busy with the other kids, not really jealous—but he always reminds me with an "I love you" that he is still there! He is a *great* kid!

84: Sickness hits

Poor Alex was sick yesterday. I knew something was up when he got up and then went back to bed. He spent most of the morning in bed, as I shuffled the others back and forth to other activities. Finally at about two in the afternoon, I went downstairs to see what was going on. He was burning up with fever and was just looking pitiful. I felt so bad it took me so long to catch on, but there is the lack of communication for you. I bet he was starting to feel poorly earlier but realized that I wouldn't understand.

Anyway, once I realized how sick he was, I immediately swung into action with fixing the fever, hydrating him, and keeping him busy with movies on the computer. I was so worried because Amanda had a graduation ceremony that night to get her engraved black belt and we were all going to it. I knew that she would be upset if we all didn't come, but I didn't want to leave Alex alone either. So I decided to do what I usually do when the kids get sick—put the sick kids in mommy's bed and get them comfortable with everything needed at hand's reach. This led to another disagreement but it was only half-hearted. I took him by the hand and led him upstairs to my bed and fluffed the pillows and pushed him in. He kept saying, "No Mom, my bed. In Ukraine, no in Mom's bed." I said, "Tough—in America, get in Mom's bed. Amanda does it, G4 does it, and now you do it!" He finally smiled and let me fuss over him. I felt really bad leaving him but by this time the Motrin had started to work to break the fever. I left him a ton of food, drinks, iPads, telephone, and computer all within easy reach.

I left feeling bad, but I kept in touch with him by texting every thirty minutes or so. The ceremony was really great and I even shed a tear when tying on Amanda's black belt. She has worked so hard over the past 5 years and faced so much adversity with all her medical problems, I am so proud of her accomplishments.

By the time we got home, Alex was feeling better and was more active—moving out of my bed to play video games. Poor Amanda was exhausted and went to bed really early. Alex was hungry (sure sign of recovery) and we ended up outside again while he ate. John and G4 came out bringing out the good binoculars and we spent about an hour stargazing.

We even found the International Space Station streaking across the sky. It was a beautiful night, just the right temperature, without any clouds.

Alex was in a cuddly mood and just snuggled up against me as we looked up at the stars. He just kept saying over and over how he loved me — it was really sweet. I think he was so surprised that I wanted to take care of him when he wasn't feeling well. I don't know for sure, but I get the idea that he expected me to pretty much leave him alone! He obviously has not had much mothering in the past — but he will get used to my smothering ways.

I overheard G4 talking to a friend yesterday about having Alex in the family and he summed it up perfectly saying, "It's like he has always been there. He just slipped into our family and our hearts without us really even knowing. He has been a great addition."

85: The dam breaks

Alex is feeling better (physically that is) — thank goodness he seems to have a strong constitution. However, in the aftermath of the sickness, he was left feeling a little down and out. It came out of the blue. One night, he was in a great mood — joking and playing around. He and I tickled, wrestled, and talked for about an hour and then I suggested we call Mariupol. He couldn't get through to anyone, so he suggested we call A1. We had a great talk and then I suggested he call his Grandma. Famous last words. . . . He had a long talk with her and seemed OK, but by the next morning was sullen and fussy. By the afternoon, he was working out on his kickboxing target ferociously.

Finally, I decided to confront him. I cornered him in his room and asked what was wrong, and the dam burst forth. He asked in a very confrontational tone of voice, "Why me? Why money, documents, Ukraine, why me?" When I told him it was because we loved him, he looked at me and sneered, "You talk, everyday you talk. I love you, I love you, but is not real. Just talk. All women talk." I was stunned. It was so vituperative and mean-spirited, very unlike his normal demeanor. Before I shot back what was on the tip of my tongue, that he was being an ungrateful nasty little snot of a child, I thought for a minute and realized just how much this kid was hurting inside. I realized that he really didn't understand the reasons why we wanted him. He had no concept of a love that was so deep that we were willing to go to the ends of the earth to make him a part of our family. We felt he was really a part of us, even before he came to us. We knew we had more parenting left in us and once we met him, we knew he was going to be the recipient of it. All the love in Alex's life hadn't gone so well. He had lost everybody even though I am sure they told him they loved him at one point or another.

So, I just looked at him and told him that I loved him deeply whether he believed it or not. I also decided that this was the time to confront him so I said, "You could have said no." He looked at me and said, "I know." I also told him that I didn't like to see him unhappy, but that he was part of a forever family now and was going to have to learn how to be a part of it. I could tell that his emotions were running higher than I had seen before, so that gave me the strength to be not as emotional. We talked for a little more, but by then I could see that he was not in any mood to listen to more. I left him and continued about my business.

Thank goodness, I picked the right attitude because about an hour later, he came and searched me out and told me, "I happy mom, every day, I happy." He then asked me if I loved him and when I said yes, of course, he went off singing, "My mom loves me," over and over. I think he felt if he verbalized his doubts about the adoption that I wouldn't love him anymore. Hopefully, he will learn someday that I love him no matter what he says or does!

He had a great day after that—I think it reassured him that we were still there after all the drama of the morning. In reflection on his first month with us, there are a few issues that I need to concentrate on, like the messiness in his room. I wouldn't leave the house today with him until he cleaned out all the dishes! I told him that we were not running a restaurant in his bedroom! Next I need to start working on schoolwork!

86: Day 30 — Mom is out of reserves

We have had a couple of great days. I think ever since Alex verbalized his worries and frustrations, he has felt better. He has been in a great mood and is back to his old self. It was good for him to be able to express himself warts and all and realize that John and I were not going to back down or withdraw. We love him no matter what and are willing to listen to him.

However, while he is feeling better, I am starting to feel a little run down. It is getting hard balancing everyone's needs. Alex is taking a lot of my time. In fact, last night, he was downstairs playing a video game long after everyone else had gone to sleep. I went down to say goodnight and he asked me to stay with him. He wanted me to sit next to him. I told him I would for a little while and I pulled Amanda's bean bag up next to the one he was sitting in and sat down. He kept saying over and over, "Do you love me?" I kept saying, "Yes of course I do," but it just wasn't enough. I reached over and started stroking his hair and he quieted down a bit. Then I started falling asleep and the next thing I know, he had brought over some blankets and put them over me. I stirred a little and he said, "Shhh, you stay here with me." I stayed for a while but I really, really wanted to go to bed. I finally said, "I am going to bed." He fussed and tried to hold my hand to stop me from going, but I just didn't want to stay. I felt guilty and on any other day, I would have stayed and given him the emotional support that he needed, but I just didn't have it in me yesterday. He finally kissed me good night and went back to his video game.

This morning, Amanda had a hissy fit at her studio fussing about her uniform, weapons routine, and just about everything else around her. She normally works out a lot and is under a lot of pressure just with her training schedule and schoolwork, but it is magnified now with Nationals coming up. All of her medical problems are flaring up too, we were at the allergist's office Monday morning for three hours while she received an infusion of a new, experimental medicine to help control her cholinergic urticaria and asthma. Let's hope it ultimately works — but we won't know for at least two weeks. In the meantime, she is still on her cocktail of nine different meds that is only partially effective. So my resistance is at an all time low! Then I got set off again this afternoon by Alex inviting a friend over. I yelled at him that he needs to check with me first and make sure the house is clean—he just looked at me like I had grown three heads. He pacified me with a kiss and showing me how much English he had done on Rosetta Stone. I then went to make cookies and felt marginally better—baking is very cathartic for me!

The late nights with Alex and the early mornings with Amanda are wearing me down. I think that I need to take a mental health day. Also, all the emotional support that Alex needs can get tiring. I love providing it and am so happy that he lets me—but it does take a lot out of you. There are still all the attendant responsibilities of home and other kids, and then add this on top.

I need to go now—boys being boys—Alex and Sergei are needing me to take videos of them doing flips.

87: Mental health day

Well, I decided that I needed a break and took a mental health day. I was talking to John last night and trying to explain how I felt. As I told him, "There is a conduit between me and Alex that has opened up and right now, everything is flowing one way. I am going to bleed dry soon." So he suggested I try to take a down day and just relax.

So the next morning I proclaimed to everyone that Mom was on strike and they needed to leave me alone. I stayed in bed as long as I could stand it, then got showered, dressed, and moved out to the couch. I asked for a cup of coffee and basically hung out on the couch all morning reading a thoroughly useless but highly entertaining book (think romance novel).

When the kids started complaining they were hungry, I let them fend for themselves, which they did. G4 made everyone an omelette leaving the kitchen a shambles. I just ignored it though. I then made the supreme effort to go lay out on the chaise lounges outside and catch a few rays while sipping on a soda. The day was shaping up nicely. The kids seemed to understand that mom was offline and took it easy on me. They really left me alone and let me recharge my batteries so to speak.

Alex and Amanda hung out outside for a while, then went downstairs playing video games, while G4 worked on his model railroad. All in all they did a pretty good job of leaving me alone.

For dinner, I had G4 take everyone out for dinner and a movie, while John and I went out on a business dinner with some of his coworkers. I enjoyed the evening free of kids responsibilities, but ended up by talking about the kids exclusively anyway. Everyone always wants to hear the adoption story over and over, and in a way, we never get tired of telling it. But on the other hand, it will be nice when we can move on and not always highlight the differences between Alex and the other two kids. I long for the day when we don't think of life in terms of before Alex and after Alex.

88: Epic parenting fail

On Thursday, John worked from home so that he could go and apply for Alex's American passport with me. They require both parents to be present and they are only open from ten in the morning to four in the afternoon. Not the most friendly of offices! Then it was off the the dentist office for both Alex and myself. I had to get a filling redone and he needed his root canal. I went first and then it was his turn. He was surprisingly calm about it. The dentist allowed him to put his earphones in and listen to his music, so that helped out. They worked on him for two and a half hours! Ouch! But he was calm throughout.

The office was small, so I had to kneel on the tile floor next to the dental chair to hold his hand. He squeezed my hand a few times, but overall did really well. The bad news is that they were not able to finish the root canal and he will have to go back on Tuesday for the rest of the work! He was a little bummed about that, but lightened up after he asked for donuts and I took him by Krispy Kreme. Boy that kid can eat! Two dozen donuts and they were mostly gone the next day! I cooked him some homemade mashed potatoes and a veggie sautee thinking it would be easy to chew and he scarfed down every bite of that too.

On Thursday night, John and G4 went kayaking at Deer Creek Reservoir—taking advantage of how light it stays out late. I kept Alex at home; even though he wasn't complaining about his tooth, I knew that he would most likely be hurting. It was nice for the John and G4 to spend some time alone together. We were always worrying about Alex, but it is important to keep some private time with each child.

On Friday, Alex was back to normal. The housecleaners were coming and it was a frantic rush to clean up the house so that they could clean. I think Alex believes we are crazy to clean before they come to clean, but I haven't had time to explain that if there is clutter around, they just clean around it. In order to get a good deep clean, I need everything to be put away.

We went out grocery shopping with everyone and two carts later, was stunned by how much food we go through. I forgot what it was like to have a teenage boy that is growing in the house. G4 is out of the eat-everything-in-sight stage—thank goodness—but Alex is still in it. Then we went out to see *Mirror, Mirror* at the movie theatre that night. The boys thought it was stupid, but Amanda and I liked it.

When we came home, Alex needed dinner number two as usual, so I sat outside with him while he ate it. I was so tired and wanted to go to bed, but he begged me to stay. So I ended up by falling asleep on one of the chaise lounges. He went and got my computer and started playing a game. I woke up about thirty minutes later with a stiff neck and decided, enough was enough—I was going to bed. Now here is the EPIC FAIL part of the story. I said goodnight and went in the house, carefully and unintentionally locking the door behind me! I can't believe I locked my child out of the house! I went to bed and slept like the dead, while Alex was trying to call me all night to get in. He could have knocked on the bedroom window or called John, but he didn't. Finally at 5:52 in the morning, John's phone rang. Alex told us what happened and I ran to let him in. Poor kid was half frozen. I felt SOOOOO bad. Alex correctly called me a LOSER and what could I say other then, "Yes, yes I am!" He then announced he was going to bed. He slept until about two in the afternoon and when he woke up, continued to call me a loser, but he was smiling while he did it.

This morning (Father's Day) we were all going to go hang gliding, but as usual the kids wimped out. 5:30 am was just too early! So, I took John and had fun taking pictures. He did amazingly well for his first time and I think has been bitten by the bug! The kids all slept late, but took care of the animals, got mail, and so on while we were gone.

We are planning a cookout tonight—I am marinating a steak for Alex, my final peace offering for making him stay outside all night! We will rotisserie a pineapple, grill corn and have veggie burgers for the veg heads in the family.

Hope everyone has a Happy Father's Day!

89: San Francisco and a love/hate list

We had a long, boring twelve-hour drive to California, but once we got here, everyone lightened up. We slept late to recover from the drive. Despite a very late start to the day (primarily because Alex and I didn't want to get out of bed), we got a lot of sightseeing in. I drove Alex down Lombard Street, went to Golden Gate Park, ate massive sundaes at Ghiradelli Soda Fountain, went up in Coit Tower, bought sourdough bread at Boudin's on the wharf, and ate dinner and shopped in Chinatown. It was a really fun day, but the crowning glory was finding a Russian supermarket. Alex was like a little kid running up and down the aisles throwing things in a basket. I suggested he call his friend back in Utah (Sergei) and see if he wanted anything. Well, that resulted in another basket of things!

As we were fighting traffic and driving around, I was thinking of all the things I love about Alex. But I also have to be realistic—there are a lot of things I hate also. Then I realized, they are almost the same things, just in different amounts. So I will do a top ten love/hate list. This should cover the basics!

10. Smarts—Alex is smart. He is bright and quick, but he hates school work and hates schedules. The schedule part I am good with, but the lack of schoolwork has to change. He has never had to work really hard for anything in education and therefore thinks he can just slide through with me too.

9. Athletic—I am proud of how active and strong Alex is. Every day he wants to show me his muscles so that I can proclaim how much bigger they are. He is always biking, jogging, jumping on a trampoline, jump roping, or at kickboxing. However, the flip side is that he often needs someone to do these activities with him or drive him and sit and watch. This gets tiring (really fast). He was even suggesting to me that once we get home from vacation, that I should work out with him. I just said no, but I didn't have the heart to tell him that the only place I like to run is back and forth to the fridge!

8. Music—He really loves his music. I like this and have really enjoyed exploring new genres and introducing him to our music.

Our tastes are pretty eclectic, and he even liked some of the African music we listen to. But, even though I like his music, when it is so loud that my ears are ringing after getting out of the car? I mean, really?

7. Immaturity—I know that Alex had to grow up too quick, but there is a huge streak of immaturity there. It is almost like he stopped developing when he went into the orphanage. It makes for a fun little kid at times. I like that, because when you adopt an older child, you miss a lot. This gives me the chance to catch up and put my stamp on some parts of his growing up. But, the other side of this is well, immaturity. Sometimes, you don't have time to deal with it and it gets annoying.

6. Maturity—I know this sounds ridiculous coming on the heels of the immaturity, but there it is. These kids are an interesting mix! Alex is so mature sometimes. I can rely on him in certain circumstances because I know he will come through for me. But the other side of this is sadness that he is too mature and had to grow up too quickly. I realize that there is no going back on some things and I regret that I missed a chance to parent through them.

5. Hygiene—I love the fact that Alex is a clean person. We haven't had to deal with any major hygiene issues, thank goodness. However, he has to shower morning, night, and sometimes in between. And the money we spend on Axe body spray! He reeks of it every time he goes out. We are going to need to take out a loan to pay for the body care products!

4. Good-looking—Alex is a doll and he knows it, but I can't believe how irritating it can be at times. We were walking along the street after dinner tonight in Chinatown, when a car pulls up across the street. It was a red Corvette and had two pretty young blond girls in it. I was immediately on high alert. I noticed Alex perk up and look over, when to my surprise the driver winks at him. He winks back and then the passenger leans over and waves at him. He noticed me watching and just blushed and walked on without responding. I have a HUGE problem in my hands here! Sometimes I wish he wasn't so cute—can't wait to get those braces on!

3. Not being a morning person—I considered this for number 1, but even though I love sleeping, I will have to admit, there are things more important. But not many! I love the fact that Alex likes to sleep in as much as I do, but then when it goes into the late afternoon? Needing a crowbar to pry him out of bed at two in the afternoon is excessive! We will have to work on somewhat of a loose schedule at some point—like maybe up by eleven.

2. His sense of humor—Alex is the most fun person to be around I have ever met. He is happy go lucky and always up for a joke. Now that I know more Russian, I am picking up on all kinds of little jokes that he makes. He really is funny and once he knows more English, I know that he will fit in our family (with our heavy sarcasm) just fine. However, the flip side is the joking sometimes never ends. He doesn't know when enough is enough and has trouble settling down when it is needed.

1. Love—I can't say enough how I treasure his love. At least fifty times a day I hear the words, "I love you Mom." I feel so honored to be the recipient of his affection. I know that he does not give it lightly and I know that he really does love me. I am so thankful that he has the capacity for love and affection and that his scars do not run deep enough to have affected this. However, the flip side is the how much he needs in return! At least a hundred times a day he needs affirmation of my love for him. I know that he has not had much affirmation in the past and craves it. And I know that he needs the constancy of a family, but there are times when I need a break. The emotional burden is hard to bear and there are times when I feel like I bear it for both of us.

Funny how the best things about a person can also be the worst! But I am happy to be getting to know Alex so well. Everyday he seems more and more like a true member of our family.

90: My Heart Breaks

We have had a great, busy weekend in California. We are currently driving home—the interminable drive across I-80. Since I have time, I decided to use these miles to catch up on writing.

Alex really liked San Francisco. I'm glad, because we all love the Bay Area and come here for almost with any excuse that we can make. On Friday, I pried the kids out of bed and made it to the kick-off party for graduation weekend. Amanda takes a few classes at an online high school run by Stanford University. They have great online classes taught by professors at Stanford, but because it is an online school, it is hard to have get-togethers. So the graduation weekend every year is a big deal, as kids from all grades come to see their friends in person. I am also a member of the parent association and was on the graduation committee, so I was involved as well. And finally, this was the group of kids that John would have graduated with, if he had continued in high school instead of going to college early, so for all of us, this weekend had special meaning.

The kick-off event was at a Malibu Grand Prix, a place with go-karts, video games, and mini-golf. I was working the check-in table so I couldn't just hang out with the kids, but Alex and Amanda had fun and participated with the others. I was worried that Alex would feel left out, but it all worked out and he had a good time. The only down side was that G4 and I got so sunburned! Amanda was a little pink and of course, golden boy just looked great after a day in the sun!

On Saturday, I was up bright and early getting ready for a speaking engagement. The Solano County library system had asked me to speak (and it is great publicity for my book), they had ordered quite a few copies to stock in their libraries. G4 volunteered to go with me which I was grateful for. It is always good to be able to show off a successful homeschooling graduate!

We made it back to the hotel in time to change and then dash off to the graduation weekend event that I was running—Pixel Olympics! The Latin club had gotten together and built a trebuchet that they brought where we launched off raw eggs in containers as a physics challenge. There were some rocket launchers that worked off of pressurized air and a bunch of field games that kids, family members, and faculty participated in. Everyone had a great time. Alex was his usual darling self, charming the pants off of everyone. He and John threw around a football for a while, and then he hung around me, helping out. It was a great event overall.

We retired back to the hotel where we had two connecting rooms. The kids hosted a board game party in their room for the kids that either were to young or did not want to go to prom, and we hosted the adults in our room with plenty of good California wine! We had a great time visiting with friends and the kids had a great time too. Alex even joined in for a while with the other kids. Several other parents who we had known for a while remarked at how happy he seemed. They also noted how attached he was to me. As usual, every thirty minutes or so, he had to poke his head into our room and make eye contact or physically touch me. I think these good observations cursed us however, because soon I noticed that he was getting overwhelmed, too much fun and activity. He asked me to go down and sit outside by the pool with him. I felt something building in him and finally said OK. He was in a talking mood again.

He told me that I was a good mom to him. He then said his one mom (birth mom) and two mom (step mom) were not good. I really didn't know what to say. I just reached over and grabbed his hand and said that I was sorry. It didn't seem like enough. He went on to say his one mom left him and his two mom would beat him. He told me that every morning before he went to school, she would beat him. He was tearing up as he recounted when he was eight and nine years old asking her why she hit him all the time and her ignoring him. Then he told me that once she hit him so hard, he went to sleep. I assume he meant knocked unconscious. I was horrified but just squeezed his hand and said that I was so sorry. Then he told me that he took up boxing when he was eleven and got big enough so that no one else could ever beat him. My heart was breaking. I am sure I should have said more, but I was so choked up that I couldn't. I just hugged him and held him tight. I told him that I loved him and he hugged me back and said, "You good mom."

This morning however, he seemed surly and in a foul mood. I know part of it is a lack of sleep—we have really been burning the candle at both ends this weekend, but I think part of it was a protective mechanism. I think he was regretting telling me some of these things. He pulled me aside during the morning and told me, "You big people. All big people say they love, but love not real for them. Maybe one month, two month, but not real." I guess he was trying to say that adults really don't mean what they say. I can understand this better in light of what he told me the night before, but I was feeling a little raw myself. I just answered back, "I know how much I love you. I love you a lot and it is forever. I will not leave you or hurt you. I loved you the first time I saw you at the park last year." He grabbed my arms and looked into my eyes for a long time and finally said, "Maybe you love me." I just looked back at him but didn't say anything. He just kept looking at me and then said, "Probably you love me." I hugged him and just said, "Yes, I love you."

This interchange seemed to turn him around. I think he was feeling that if he keeps pushing us away, when we eventually leave him like everybody else, he won't be that hurt. I think the fact that we are not withdrawing from him is confusing. He is gradually starting to realize that we are here forever, but it is baby steps! He was in a much better mood for the rest of the car ride. He seemed happy and carefree again. At one point he just looked at me and said, "I happy." I wish that I could bottle his enthusiasm for life. I am still constantly amazed at his resilience and adaptability. I hope we are peeling away the layers of his scars and getting down to the bottom so that we can start healing from the inside out.

As I write this, we are in the Nevada desert with still too many hours to go on our trip. We should get home by 2:00 am and then starts the crazy training schedule for Amanda this week. We all fly out to Dallas Thursday so that she can compete Friday, Saturday, and Sunday at Nationals. We will keep you updated.

91: Things look up

We are all exhausted! We finally got to the house at three in the morning. We spent some time ogling the stars in the Nevada desert at a rest area and it made us late, but we couldn't help it, they were so beautiful away from the city lights. G4 was a trooper and drove the last two hours for us—Daddy John and I are not as young as we used to be and twelve hours of driving gets old!

We ended up by sleeping in a little more than we expected. John's office sent out a notice that their air conditioning was broken so he decided to work from home. I decided to just leave the dogs at their 'pet resort' since we are just turning around and leaving in three days, and Amanda's private lesson at eight o'clock was canceled. Thank goodness! We felt a little more human after sleeping in to nine o'clock, but are still pretty tired.

Alex has been in a great mood today. He was a little miffed early on because he wanted his friend Sergei to come over. But before we left on the trip, he was punished for being forty minutes late with Sergei on their last outing. We told him that as punishment, he would have to miss seeing his friend while we were home for these few days. He must have been suffering from convenient memory loss because he acted like he had never been told. He was trying to tell me that he lost track of time and that he could not teleport from one place to another! He actually used the word teleport! I was pretty impressed until I realized that he had probably just picked it up from TV or a movie. Then he tried to tell me that Sergei's mom, Becky, had said yes to them getting together. Smart thing I double checked that one—because that was a whopper of a mistruth. Then he started with the, "You no love me," and I exploded. I know the difference between manipulation and reassurance and this was manipulation. I tried to talk to him but he was playing on the computer so I took it away. Then the phone rang and it was Sergei. I told him that I was waiting to talk to him so he said goodbye to Sergei and put down the phone. I started to talk and then heard some noise and realized that he had not hung up but had just put the phone down and was waiting for me to finish like I was some kind of nuisance in his life. Well, I flipped out! I started crying and stalked out of the room.

I think I scared Alex because about five minutes later, he came and found me in my bedroom, crying as I was unpacking suitcases. Chalk it up to hormones, tiredness, or whatever, but I was stressed out. He pulled me close, dried my tears, and hugged me tight. He kept saying over and over, "I love you mom. You no cry." I calmed down and said OK, but he stuck to me like glue for about an hour, helping me unpack and put things away (ok more like watching me and messing things up — but he did help a little). Then later, he tapped his head and said, "I smart. You cry, you no love me. You no cry, you love me." I started laughing and said, "That won't work, I cry all the time." and he just answered, "Women!"

I had to take Amanda to Tae Kwon Do for training and when I got home, I found the boys all agog at a present John had bought for Alex. He had bought him an air pistol or something like that. Maybe BB gun? There was a paint ball gun too (I think). I don't know as I abhor all kinds of guns, play or otherwise. But it must be something good as they were all exclaiming over it and he was stroking it like it was a baby or something.

Then he convinced me to go out to the hillside with him and shoot it. I didn't want to, but I got the please, mom, please. So I went out. There is an abandoned building near our house where someone has spray painted an outline of a person on it. He took aim and was so excited to hit the head. Then he insisted that I do it — proud to say I got a perfect head shot. I think it surprised him, he said, "Wow, Mom." I told him that just because I didn't approve, didn't mean I wasn't capable! But I made sure that John gave him the talk of no aiming or shooting at any animals or property. The guns will disappear if I see that!

Anyway, all in all, I was pleased that he seemed to take the discipline well, and that he didn't get overly upset with me getting upset. He was concerned about me, but he also seemed more secure in his responses this time. We are definitely making progress!

92: Silver medalist at Nationals!

Amanda has been fighting a wicked stomach flu for the past 3 days. It had her so weak yesterday that she could barely move—but she was brave and went forward with the demo team competition. She is one of the highest ranking members on the team would leave the team a little bereft without her. She gave her all—I am so proud of her. Lesser kids would have thrown in the towel and given up. But she is tough and kept going. The team really pulled together and the seventh place finish is nothing to cry about.

Unfortunately, Amanda seems to have passed the bug to John, who is down and out now too. So I am the glue holding everyone together! Let's hope I don't succumb too.

Alex and G4 have been supportive and helpful, but I think Alex is having a hard time focusing so much on Amanda. I had to sit him down and explain to him that just because it seems all about Amanda right now, I still love everybody just as much. I lectured G4 as well and Amanda at the same time. I think it helped Alex to be lumped in with everybody and just be 'one of the kids.' I explained to them that at different times, each of them would have different needs and I would devote the necessary time and effort to that child to take care of them. Just because I was not focused as much on the others was not a reflection of my love for them. I went on to give them concrete examples of what I meant. I pointed out that when Alex first came home, it was all about him for the first month or so, helping him get settled. I explained to him that maybe he didn't notice it, but it really was that way. I then explained that now was Amanda's time, leading up to Nationals and during. Later this fall when G4 transferred to a new university, it would be all about him, getting him settled and into his classes.

I think talking about it so frankly was helpful and allowed all the kids to realize that I still loved them all the same. I think it also helps them learn for their own lives, how to prioritize and deal with the negative emotions that can surface in interpersonal interactions.

So with that, we were able to focus the rest of the trip on Amanda. She was still sick and weak, but at least wasn't throwing up any more. She started the morning with board breaking and placed 5th. She was a little disappointed, but her routine was flawless and well executed. I think that she was just outclassed by the older, more experienced competitors. It really tired her out though, and I was worried about the rest of the day. She is still so weak and hasn't been able to eat anything for about four days now.

Then it was time for weapons. She was competing against the biggest group that she had ever competed against, and boy did she rise to the occasion. She performed her heart out and had a nearly flawless routine with one tiny bauble on her one-handed throw. She didn't drop her staff, but it was right in front of the judges. By a mere .3 of a point, she missed out on the gold medal, but we are so proud of her and happy. The gold medalist executed a perfect katana sword routine, that was not very difficult but traditional, and the judges are always swayed toward the traditional in martial arts. Amanda was a little disappointed but given her sickness and the stress, I think this was phenomenal.

After the weapons, it was time for forms. Amanda was really nervous about forms. Her category was huge this year—fifty-four other competitors. She was really tired at this point and we realized that she had just about given all she had, but this girl keeps on giving. She went out there are made it to the finals! She made it to the final eight before being eliminated. We were amazed, it was her highest finish ever in a major competition in forms.

We are just all so proud of her and her dedication. Lesser kids would have quit and given up, but she just kept on plugging away this whole tournament. I know all the hours training that this child has put in and it showed. She has worked so hard every step of the way and I am in awe of her accomplishments. All the hours I have sat at studios, watching her, and driving her forty-five minutes away to train extra at other studios has all been worth it!

John is feeling better. Unfortunately, I seem to have gotten the flu now. It started yesterday with me throwing up before Amanda even started, and just got worse. I just came home after the competition and rested.

Today we fly home and get to start worrying about packing and the move. Now that Nationals are over, we need to focus on the next thing, which is moving and getting G4 settled at the University of Washington.

93: Eight weeks as a family of five

We got home from Nationals tired and recuperating from sickness. We had really been burning the candle at both ends and were feeling the results. I think also that the time we had been spending on traveling and Amanda had taken away from the family as a whole. I was so busy walking on eggshells around Alex, making sure that he was happy and then dealing with Amanda and her training, that I was not looking at the big picture of the family as a whole. I was overwhelmed with the details of getting her ready for her competition (like making hair pieces for the demo team) not to mention keeping the house clean for the showings we are having. It is all I can do to get the laundry and the dishes done some days. Also, in between there are dental visits for everyone and Amanda's medications—yikes! John was complaining that he missed having a wife around! I was always busy with something else, and he was getting lost in the shuffle. So, I have been really trying hard to come up with activities that all five of us can do together. We went to play racquetball the other day and had a lot of fun. It was a great workout and we all were able to participate. I suggested a comedy club last night that was also a lot of fun. Alex didn't understand much but he was able to pick up some of the physical comedy.

Then in the midst of all this, we found cigarettes in Alex's room! He can't hide anything worth a damn (excuse me—but it is true) and his messiness caught up with him. John hit the roof. We had a big discussion the next day in which he revoked almost every privilege that Alex has. Alex was upset, but John followed it up with a really nice metaphor for Alex about how much he was loved, and how much we wanted to make him a part of our family forever. He was really sincere and it was great watching Alex's face light up as he realized that discipline did not mean out of the family. I think he really thought that he was going to be sent home! It broke my heart to realize how tenuous this relationship still is. He has fussed a little at the constraints on him, but not as much as I would have thought.

We are now going to have to focus on packing and moving. John and I have to decide when we are going to Seattle for a house hunting trip.

As well, we need to get G4 to his orientation and registered for classes in this coming fall semester. At times it seems overwhelming, but I also love moving and cleaning things out. Moving always gives me a chance to have a fresh start.

I have also been trying to cook some of Alex's favorite foods. I made vareniki a couple of days ago from scratch. It wasn't as hard as I thought. I made two kinds, potato and cheese, and then cherry. We all loved them, they turned out really good. I think Alex really enjoyed them. Then the next day, I made a Ukrainian salad (kind of like a potato salad) that he also liked. I love cooking, and cooking ethnic foods is always fun. Being vegetarian sometimes limits recipes, so I have had fun finding Ukrainian foods that I can modify to our herbivore ways!

I can't believe that we are at eight weeks already as a family of five. It has been great, I can't imagine life without Alex. His English is coming along despite some of his new reluctance to do Rosetta Stone. He has completed this family and I am so grateful that he is with us. I love this little guy so much!

94: Trying not to be cynical

Alex hasn't asked to call Ukraine for a while, so two nights ago I suggested that he call. I don't know if I should have, but I figured I should offer. He called his Grandma, who just spent thirty minutes crying and talking. We have discovered that calling through Skype is the cheapest way to call, so I could hear her. She just monopolized the conversation. He was just placating her and when he got off the phone, he told me that she needed money for medicine and hospital bills. He also told me that she had not had enough money recently to pay for the upkeep on his dad's grave. I wonder how she blew through all the money we gave her when we left Ukraine two months ago? We had given her several hundred dollars when we were there, and we knew that we would send her more, but the reality is just now sinking in.

Anyway, he was very reluctant to ask me for money for her, but I could tell he felt obligated to do so. I was so mad; this is a burden that he should not have to bear. I was also mad at her — she really didn't give him a chance to talk about his life here. She didn't give him a chance to tell her if he was OK! So this is where my cynicalness is coming out. I should be more charitable, but it is hard — I think the first priority in all our lives should be Alex!

But, I tried to put aside all these feelings and feel more understanding of her situation. Thank goodness our friends the Morfords are going over to Ukraine. (Thank you Alisa and Marsh!) I rushed around yesterday, withdrawing money, and having Alex write a letter, so that they could hand deliver some money to her. I don't know how we will support her once we do not have anyone going over there. I do not feel comfortable sending cash in the mail and I do not think she has a bank account, but maybe this won't be a problem — I am not going to suggest Alex call her again. If he wants to — fine, but I am not going to push it.

I worry about this relationship with his Grandma. On one hand, we need to keep it up I think for him. I don't want him to lose all contact with his former life. I think some day, it will be important to him, after all, it is a part of who he is. On the other hand though, there is the concern that this was not a good relationship in the beginning, as is evidenced by the fact that he was in the orphanage! So, where does that leave him and us? And the quick answer is that I don't know. I am not sure how to navigate these treacherous waters.

I know that as teenagers, they are always looking to try on new identities. In some ways this is helpful to them in developing their own individual identities. After all, it's like trying on clothes; you have to try on a lot before you find the ones that fit just right. Many parents despair at this developmental stage that their teens go through, as often the first identities that are tried on are the exact opposite of the parents'. Then as the teens cycle through the different images of themselves, they usually end up somewhere close to how they were raised by the end of young adulthood, but sometimes not. It is a very individualized process.

Now, for poor Alex, we have all the normal dynamics of teenagerhood, and let's add onto that a new family, new language, and new country of citizenship. There is so much going on that it is hard to comprehend. I have noticed that to people that speak Russian or that have known him before, he still prefers to be called Dima, but with us he prefers to be Alex. This already highlights the divide that is developing within him. He needs to figure out who he is: is he Dima who is Ukrainian, or is he Alex, the American teen? Where do we as a family fit into this? Can we bridge that gap with him, or will he compartmentalize us into the American side? How much is it right for me to control? I can give him more access to keeping the Ukrainian side, or I can cut it off. When he is grown with a family of his own, where will he want to be? Will he have wished I was more of an influence one way or another?

For now, I have just opted to let him guide this process. I allow him to be whoever he feels like being at that time and try to deal with the jumping back and forth as best as I can. I will continue to try to support him as best I can, but I think that this is one place that he is going to have take some personal responsibility. If not, I can see him being a little lost later in life. I just hope with time, he can reach a place of comfort with the person he is currently, the person he was, and develop a clear vision of the person he aspires to be.

After the conversation about his grandmother ended, he looked so pitiful. I tucked him in bed and tried to say goodnight, but he just clung to me and didn't want to let go. He wanted me to stroke his hair until he fell asleep, so I gladly did. My heart was breaking as I looked down at him. He is such a little boy at heart and just needs so much love—I hope I am up to this task that has been set before me.

95: No Rest for the Weary

This week has been just a crazy whirlwind. I keep thinking that life will slow down at some point, but it never does. I guess I will just have to adjust my expectations.

On Monday, John and I had to go out to dinner with some of the people he works with. He has a team of about sixty people under him. His team has been working really hard and he wanted to reward them. He invited them and their spouses out to dinner and surprised them with their raises at dessert. They were really surprised and excited. Unfortunately, I had to leave Alex, G4, and Amanda to go to dinner. Alex especially was not happy for me to leave him. But G4 took him and Amanda out to the new Spiderman movie and he seemed to be happy.

On Tuesday, John and I had to go to Park City for a DNC fundraiser. We have donated quite a bit to the Obama campaign this year (yes, we are progressive, liberal, tree-hugging, democrats!). Joe Biden was speaking and we were excited to go. I met the most lovely woman there and hopefully have made a new friend. Also, after Biden spoke, he said he would take some questions from the audience. I raised my hand and was one of the three questions he took. Afterwards, there was quite a line to meet him in person and John and I were at the end of the line. He had to leave to have dinner with the hosts of the fundraiser, so he started to walk away, but at the last moment, he looked at me and recognized me as one of the question askers and motioned me over. He spent about ten minutes talking to John and myself hugging and kissing me—it was crazy! Of course, if anyone is wondering what my question was about—don't think too hard. What is the subject most of interest to me? Why, educational freedom of course! Homeschooling is not just the special interest of the right wing party, and I wanted to make that point.

Anyway, poor Alex was left without me for a second night in a row—he was a little miffed. But by the following day, I had a sore throat and cough—arghhhh! I tried to rest, but Alex wanted to go to the trampoline place, so I dragged myself out with him. At least all I have to do is sit. John came to relieve me so I was able to come home. Then after starting dinner, I went to put some laundry away in Alex's room and started hyperventilating at the mess. I could not resist it, but had to clean up. That was a forty-five minute ordeal. But I found a picture of his dad and him (at about age three) that was just thrown under some clothes. I found a picture frame and put it on the night table for him. He actually said thanks when he came home and saw that I had cleaned up—that is a big step—before he insisted on doing it himself and didn't want me cleaning.

Then about five minutes before John and Alex came home I finally sat down. He walked in and said, "I am glad you had a chance to rest!" Ack! I can't win.

96: Internal conflicts

Well, both Alex and I have been on a little emotional roller coaster recently and I don't see a way off. It is really like a real life coaster—thrills and scares, but one that will not stop and let you get off.

Alex is starting to have problems with how comfortable he is getting here, I think. Out of the blue, he said to me in the car the other day, "Good mother, good sister and brother, good father, I happy here." I was so surprised that I almost drove off the road. There was nothing that precipitated it and he sounded sincere. But just that same day, I was talking to him about English lessons and he got so fussy. He started in with the old routine that I hadn't heard in a while, "You not my mother. You no love me. I no want to learn English. If English good, then Russian bad." He would not listen to me that we would keep his Russian good and that he really needed to learn English, only good could come of it. I was really hurt by this—he has been really eager to learn English in the past, but the more I thought about it, the more sense it made. He has really left behind his old life. He is getting comfortable here, but still is not fully integrated yet, and I think feels a little adrift. He feels that by rejecting the new, the old will still be there. But what he doesn't understand, is that the old is fading away and there is nothing he can do about it. He can't hang on to it no matter what. My heart breaks as I consider this—I wish that he could understand that he has his forever home with us—I know that it is coming and this realization that is triggering these fears, but it is a slow realization. I want to snap my fingers and have it happen right now!

So, for now, to help, I am just laying off English and just loving him. So far, this has been a good fix for everything else that has gone on. But that brings up my conflict. I just love this kid so much that I feel everything so intensely with him. He and I have forged a really strong bond that is both wonderful and draining at the same time. I feel every mood swing, every frustration, and every happiness. It is great that we are so close, but I feel that at times it is too much for me. When I have to say no to him, it is like a knife in my heart, because I feel his pain. He still equates love with things and privileges which makes parenting very difficult. It is hard to say no to any kid, but this makes it soooo hard. I can be more objective with my biological kids, because I know their past so well. I know when they are really hurt and when they can handle things. With Alex, there is so much unknown, but the feelings are so intense and known. There are times he is hurting that I can feel it like it is my own, yet I don't understand why. This makes it so much more complicated!

There have been a few times when he is mad or trying to get a rise out of me that he will say, "You not my mom." This just cuts to the quick as I realize the truth of this—I am not his mom. On a piece of paper maybe, but I have not earned the right yet and I am not sure even how to do this or if it is even possible. I am trying to love him as best as I can, but nothing can change the fact that I am just another woman in a long string of women that have cared for him. Hopefully better than most, but certainly not anything special in his mind. He does care for me, I know that, but whether it is truly as deep as I wish—who knows? Something tells me that we will never be let into his heart all the way, and that is understandable. After all he has been through to even let us close is a miracle.

But there are times when I can forget this. We are at the trampoline place again and he struck up a conversation here with a guy who was a missionary in Ukraine. After Alex and this guy talked, he came over and spoke to me a few minutes. He mentioned that they were talking about school and the guy was wondering who was teaching him English. Alex told the guy that it was his mom and when he relayed this to me—he added that there was no hesitation—he said that he believes Alex thinks of me that way! These little moments can feed the soul!

97: All good things come to an end

We have been so blessed on this whole journey. I can't believe that the hosting program is starting again this week. To think, a year ago we were worried about whether or not Alex would want to stay with us for a little bit, much less even want to become a part of this family. As I think back on the events of the past year—I realize how far we have come. From the paperwork to the trip to Ukraine and then coming back home, it has been been incredible. I was looking at Alex last night as he was standing in the kitchen talking to Daddy John and realized that we are really a true family now. He is integrated—sure there are problems, there are frustrations, and there are still issues to work on, but as I was watching them, I saw how comfortable everyone was.

For everyone out there reading, I want to catalogue some of the changes that have occurred to make us a family.

1. Alex now routinely chooses to sit at the dinner table with the rest of the family. He will get his plate of food and plop down at the table without thinking about it.
2. Alex comes out of his room more to interact with the rest of the family and seeks out John actively when he is home to talk to.
3. He routinely asks about the plan of the day and is getting used to the things we do.
4. He has stopped asking incessantly if I love him—he might ask every once in a while, but for the most part it is *only* once in a while. I hope this means he is more sure of my love for him.
5. Alex is actively talking about the future—something he never did when he came here. He talks about getting his driver's license some day, getting a job, and life as an adult. I remember when life was only for the moment for him and he even mentioned to me once that he never thought he would get a future. He is actively thinking about the move to Seattle and learning a new place.
6. He is starting to suggest things for the family to do together. A few nights ago, he asked to watch *Ice Age* with everyone. This is a big step, as he usually preferred to do things with just me in the past. It is still mostly that way, but definitely improving.

We still have some things to work on, like his lack of interest in school work and his messiness. We also have to work on him still holding himself aloof at times and his reluctance to do some things with the family. However, for the most part, these are things that most teens struggle with. I am happy to say that a lot of these issues are normal teen things and do not feel like we are dealing with adoptive issues per se. I know that there will still be things that come up, but we feel like a family unit. I feel like I have three children, all the same, that need to be taken care of.

When I think of all the changes for us and him this past year, I can't help but feel overwhelmed at times. We have spent a lot of time and money completing our family, planning a move, Amanda's black belt and competition, G4's transfer applications and ultimate decision to go to the University of Washington, and a long trip to Ukraine. Alex had his first trip to America, got offered a family, had to wait, go to court and renounce all he has ever known, come back to America, and be immersed in an English-only environment, and learn how to be in a family. Wow! And we all have come through this stronger, tougher, more resilient, and still with a sense of humor and a lot of love. We are a great family and I am proud of all of us and what this year has brought us. We are a complete family now and I am so happy!

A few final notes—these kids that are adopted need so much love. They are like little sponges soaking up everything you give them and then needing more. I was talking to John a couple of days ago and I came up with the perfect summation. You can't love them enough, treat them nice enough, think about them enough, give them enough. There is no way that you can make up for what they went through before they came to you—all you can do is try. Alex humbles me in that he still has the capacity for love and affection after everything. I don't know if he will ever let me in totally, but the little he has offered so far feeds my soul. There isn't enough you can do in the understanding and empathy department—but they can sense you are trying, and that seems like enough.

PART SEVEN:

A NEW NORMAL LIFE

Getting Your Life Back — Not!

When you are overseas on an adoption, as I have mentioned before, you are in a time warp. Life seems to move at a different speed and there are different priorities. However, when you return home, some part of you expects life to return to normal. You feel like you should pick up where you left off. This can frustrate you to no end when you realize that you can't do that. Life has been inexplicably altered—for the better since you have a new family member, but you can never get back life the way it was before.

I think this causes a type of grieving period as you let go of the old and figure out the new. Even the most adaptable person is going to have trouble doing this. I wish that I had a prescribed seven step system for you to follow that would make this process easier, but I don't have any short cuts for you. The best thing is to be flexible and take time. Acknowledge that your life has changed and spend a little time reminiscing about the past. Don't romanticize it, but it is OK to miss it. I think a lot of parents feel guilty about missing their old life and look down upon themselves for feeling that way, but it is understandable.

Everyone in the family will be going through this process at different paces and it is important to realize this and not rush the process along. The primary caregiver will be the first to go through this process, since their life will be altered the most and the fastest. Therefore, once they get through this phase, the tendency is to have frustration with other family members who are still in the resentment phase of having their life altered. I know John had more trouble with this aspect of the adoption than anyone else and I know I got very frustrated with him as he worked through it. He verbalized several times how much he was resentful of the changes that had occurred in the family dynamics and wished that life would just go back to the way it was before our trip to Ukraine. He wasn't resentful of Alex per se, just what changes were wrought by his presence. There wasn't really anything that we could do about this, other than just acknowledge the feelings and try to work through them. Over time as we were able to get back into a rhythm of life, he felt much better. And once six months or so had gone by, this wasn't an issue any more as he had had time to adjust and accept the new normal and grow to enjoy it.

Kids will be the last ones to go through this process, and just when you think things are calming down and are status quo, they will pop up with their issues. I think this is because kids are pretty easy going and love a new playmate. Regardless of the age, it will take time for a new sibling to get on their nerves. But when it happens (notice I said when and not if) then they will start to resent the changes and will need to work through them as well. But by this time, hopefully you and your spouse have worked beyond this state and can help them.

You have to be able to let go of the past and embrace the new normal that is being created in your family. You won't be able to predict what this new normal will be, you will just have to wait and see what it is. You can of course put some ideas in place and suggest ideas, but how they will be assimilated into your family dynamic will be a product of you, your other family members, and your new child. Gradually with time, as our family has worked through these times, John has been able to let go of the past and embrace the new family dynamic. He has also been able to retain some of the parts of our old life that were really important to him. We used to have family movie night frequently all together. When Alex first came home, we gave this up partly because he didn't want to sit with the family, but also partly because his English wasn't really good enough. But as the weeks passed by, we were able to gradually bring this family time back. It wasn't immediate, and it took some time, but now we are firmly entrenched in family movie night again, with Alex even suggesting it at times and helping to pick the movie to be watched.

When new routines and habits emerge, you should recognize them and celebrate them. It is the beginning of making memories together as a new family. Make sure you point these times out to your new child and show them explicitly how they are becoming an integral part of your family. Let them even suggest new routines and even drive the process. This will help send a message to them that they are valued and wanted and a message to the rest of the family that the new addition is important and integral to the family.

Alex enjoys playing pool and several times he initiated a pool game with John late at night before bed. This was a lot of fun for the two of them and gradually it has become an expected occurrence several nights a week that they will be downstairs at the pool table having a great time until the wee hours. It was nice to see Alex initiating this routine.

This highlights an important point, that you can't try to drive the process all by yourself or with your spouse. You all are half of the equation, but the other half, the child, needs to be participatory as well. You can propose all you want but if you aren't met half way, nothing will happen. The same of course will happen on the other side as children try to share things with you. When you are open, it will be great, but when you aren't open, there won't be a two way street. This can actually work to your benefit though. You can propose and watch what is received well by your children and then begin to be able to get to know them better. You will become an expert at understanding what they like and don't like and what they value. Also, they will be doing the same thing with you as they see what things you are willing to share that they enjoy. When they see you reject something, they will know that you have a line that has been crossed. When this does happen, though, it is important to explain explicitly that it is the activity, music, or item you are rejecting, and not the child.

This happened with music with Alex. His tastes in music are far different than ours and in the beginning I was shocked at some of the music he listened to. But I forced myself to learn about rap and its origins and find some of his music that I was OK with. We listened together and he saw that I was open to his tastes. Therefore when some music was inappropriate, he understood that it crossed the line for me and was willing to give those songs up. At first, we told him to listen to them alone, that we didn't want to hear them, but later as he became more integrated, we saw that he was listening to them much less than before and eventually deleted them from his playlist. The desire to listen to those songs naturally extinguished itself as he began to slowly and unconsciously pick up the mores and values of the family replacing his own.

I had more preconceived ideas than I could count about adopting. But one by one, they have fallen by the wayside as I have been through this process. The most important piece of advice that I can give someone who is adopting is to leave their expectations behind, and this is all expectations, about your new family member, your family, your reactions, and your ability to parent the same. You will see quickly how the new member of the family will push or pull at your notions of family. And they need to be included in the picture that you are slowly building of your new family. Their input will lead to a stronger family unit than the one that you construct on your visions alone.

I had crowed about the fact that I would treat all of my children the same and quickly realized that I could not do this. First of all, my biological children had been raised with my expectations and history already communicated to them. There was not much they didn't understand or know already. Alex, of course, had none of this history and worse, had the expectations of others and another culture.

I realized with our first big talk with Alex that I was going to have to treat him differently and spend a lot of time trying to convey our family's mores to him. This really highlighted for me that this was going to be a long process and the end point we reached together would be one of mutual choosing, not the end point I had initially laid out.

It is important however to make sure that you are not judgmental or preachy when talking to your kids. This goes for your biological kids as well, but adopted kids have such fragile egos and are just building their sense of self-esteem and their place in your family. It is important for them to feel as if you are a partner in this process and not a dictator. Also, you will find that you might change some of your long-held beliefs and convictions when looking at the world through their eyes. It is a process of give and take, allowing you both to grow and change. The exciting thing about this growth is that you all will be different people at the end in ways that could only have happened from the association with each other. When you look back you will see the process of integrating a new family member changes everybody. So hang up your expectations of the way things should be or the way you want them to be and allow life to proceed organically and naturally. The path will not always be clear and might seem to loop back on itself, but the final destination will be breathtaking!

All this being said though, don't think that life will be all fun and games. There will be times that you want to scream. And this is OK too, after all, parents are only human as well. But maintain your sense of humor and be open with everyone about what you are feeling. Don't try to hide anything—it will sneak out somewhere. Acknowledging your frustrations and sharing them can be cathartic in itself as well as showing others where they could contribute to make things better.

Also, make sure you acknowledge that you are having problems within yourself with your feelings and not because of your child. Ultimately it might be because of them, but they don't need to be confronted with that. As I mentioned before, their fragile egos and unsure status in your family won't be able to tolerate the thought that they are responsible for any trouble.

However, don't make this an excuse for trying to hide your feelings. Kids are good at sensing when something isn't right and by being open with them, you are taking away the possibility that something could be misinterpreted. You are also mentoring how to problem solve in life. This is a key factor in trying to impart your family values to a child and allows you to show practical application of some ideas that you express abstractly at other times. When you show a child how you are working through problems or frustrations, you will be giving them the tools to do it on their own.

For example, there was a time a couple of months ago when I just lost it about how messy Alex's room was. He had always been a messy child, and I had gently tried to redirect him over and over. This had been only minimally successful, but on this one occasion, I couldn't take it any more. I blew up about it but was careful to point out that the reason I was mad was because my day was busy and I really didn't have time to pick up the laundry off the floor and clean up the dishes that were left in his room. I explained carefully to him that me having to take the time out to do these things meant that I wasn't going to have the time to do other things later in the day that he might want to do.

I took the time to explain why we didn't want to leave food on plates in his room and why I had to stop everything to clean up just then. He got the message loud and clear but didn't internalize it as it was his fault that I was mad. He knew that he had culpability, but it wasn't necessarily directed at him, it was a function of my busy day. We then brainstormed together and he came up with the solution that he needed to, that he needed to be better about taking dishes to the kitchen and cleaning up his laundry. We got to the place we needed to get to, but he felt more part of the solution than having the solution imposed upon him.

It is hard to give up control sometimes and it is hard to get used to a "new normal." You are not alone in this and you need to understand that just as your child is going through changes, so are you. Giving yourself permission to blow up about it every once in a while is helpful as long as you are aware of how you are doing it and trying to make it a positive learning experience and not a negative one.

Becoming a Family

There is no easy or quick way to become a family. Only time will allow this to happen. You need to be patient and accepting that for a while, there will be no cohesive family unit. For us, we decided to not push things too fast. We also realized how overwhelming all the family attention could be to someone who was used to taking care of himself and being the master of his own destiny. Alex always had friends around in Ukraine, but he controlled when and how he interacted with them. Now all of a sudden, there was a family that was controlling him.

We tried to give Alex space, but also at the same time, show him how the rest of the family interacted. The family vacation in the motorhome was a stroke of genius on John's part, as it gave us forced family times together, without any rules of engagement. When we conceived of the vacation, it was to spend family time together, but specifically away from attention of friends and family, internet, cell phones and so on. However, it ended up being a great kickstart to the family unit. It was a new destination that none of us had been to, so we all got to experience it for the first time together. This was a really great scenario and I think Alex felt more comfortable realizing that he was not being dropped into a well-oiled machine that was previously working well, but was getting a chance to become a part of a new family machine.

I will give a small spoiler here. Over the course of the first year with us, Alex has become fully integrated. Things that confounded us before, like how to get him to sit at a table with us, now are distant memories. He is now comfortable participating fully in family activities including sitting at the dinner table. Just by letting it happen slowly on his timetable was the secret to our success. He was easy and eager to do things as he felt comfortable. If your child is slower to warm up to things, or just more reticent in general, you might have to push a little harder or be a little more patient, but in general, kids will accommodate your desires when they are ready.

Specifically, I will focus on the dinner table issue. This was a big one for us. Early on, as I have written, Alex hated to sit down to dinner with us. I think it was for several reasons: he wasn't used to a family meal; in the orphanage they were allowed to eat and bolt; he didn't always like the food; we were a little overwhelming with the language etc. So, I started serving the food buffet style and once everyone had gotten a plate, we would move downstairs to the TV or to the game table. Sometimes he would bolt off to his room, but sometimes he would loiter and see what we were all going to do. But after about two months, Alex started getting his plate of food and then hanging out waiting for everyone else to get a plate to see where we would go instead of bolting off. Then the next step was that one day, he got a plate of food and then just sat down at the table. We all looked at each other and then sat down next to him and had our first family dinner!

Now, we can eat together easily, without any problems. We don't always sit at the table, but when we do, there are no issues of sulking or bolting off. We could have just forced the issue early on, but I think that would have caused a lot of resentment and possibly a long standing reluctance to have a family table. We could have just let him eat whenever, but then it would have been hard to ever get him at the table with us. So, by leading him with baby steps, we lowered the threat level and let him lead, so that when he was ready, he could demonstrate it to us. As I mentioned above, if your child is more reticent, you might have to nudge them along, but by doing it slowly and non-threateningly, you can avoid hurt feelings and future problems. So relax and let it happen—we are proof that it will happen!

Momma Bear

One of the biggest hurdles that we as a family have faced with this adoption is me! Believe it or not, I have turned into something of a momma bear where Alex is concerned. He and I bonded so intensely early on and he has become so attached to me that I have not really tried letting anybody else close. I view him as mine, all mine. Kind of like Gollum in the Lord of the Rings—Alex is my precious!

John really helped me realize this by pointing it out to me. And once he confronted me, I quickly realized the truth of his statements. It is so hard though; I think something that only adoptive mothers understand. I need Alex to be a part of me the same way he needs me and I think that mutual need has trumped the rest of the interactions with the family.

However, once I put my mind to the problem I realized that the bond between Alex and me doesn't have to trump the relationships between the rest of the family. But what compounded it in our case was the fact that everyone else withdrew instead of pursuing their relationships with Alex. This is not in a bad way, but I was so adept at talking with Alex and understanding his needs, it was just easier for the others to take care of other things and let me deal with Alex. It was also easier for John to just accept that I was taking care of Alex.

Once we realized the dynamic that had been set up, we went around changing it as best we could. Alex will still always be my baby, first and foremost, but interacting with others will not change this fact. When John has gone out of his way to engage Alex whether it is in a building project or playing games. He found that Alex was willing to be engaged and wanted to spend time with him. I think that made him feel better and realize that the closeness that Alex and I have will not intrude on relationships with others as it shouldn't. Adoptive kids need strong relationships with all of their family members to be feel a part of the family unit. Skewing this towards one or just some of the family can be dangerous, both for the child and for the family unit.

There are times that I won't be available for Alex the way I have been so far. In these times, he needs to have a solid base with others so that he can still feel taken care of and happy. I also want the others to feel that Alex is a complete member of the family, not just someone that is peripherally involved through me. What start out as little problems now can blossom into big problems later that will be harder to fix, so if you see anything developing that could be troublesome later on, try to stop it before it becomes habit. Once abnormal dynamics exist in a family, they are so hard to break. It is like kicking any other habit, the best way is not to start the habit in the first place.

So to solve this problem, I stepped back a little and let some of the things that I would normally do with Alex to be done with other family members. I have also encouraged others to engage him and talk to him. You can't step back and wait for your child to come to you, you need to be the driving force for them. They are not sure of what is in your heart, even if you have told them, so only by showing them can you hope to make them realize it. Once the rest of the family realized they had to go to him, they were more then willing. And in fact it has worked so well that now Alex will go searching for Amanda to play with or G4 to help him on something before immediately defaulting to me.

An example occurred recently when Alex chose to sit apart from the family while waiting for a table at a restaurant. Instead of leaving it that way, or only having me sit near him, everyone else got up and moved toward him. He was initially alarmed but them quickly realized that we just wanted him with us. He laughed and acted like he wanted to move again as a joke, and then started interacting with us.

It is these little things that add up to a lot when trying to show your new child how much they mean to you. Everyone needs to participate in this effort as well. And I have realized that I am a momma bear always, with all my children, biological or not, and will continue to be so, so watch out everyone!

Emotional Reserves

I have discussed a lot in this book the emotional toll that adoption takes on you. I really can't stress this fact enough. There are so many ways that it happens and you need to start this process with a full balance in your emotional bank and figure out how to replenish it along the way.

From the stress of making the decision, to getting the paperwork done, to actually going through the process to getting your child, and then finally integrating them into your home, there is not an emotional free moment in your life. They are not all bad emotions and stress—they can be good emotions too—but even those can take a toll.

Everyone has their strengths and weaknesses, but it helps to understand yours and figure out how to get your weaknesses bolstered up throughout this process. For me, my emotional weakness is not being able to deal with too many things at once. So, having to fill up Alex's well and the rest of the family's at the same time was extremely trying. There really wasn't anything I could cut out. I needed to be a wife and mother, as well as a teacher, housekeeper, and a mover—and all of those things needed to continue happening.

As I mentioned before, it is good to have a support system or some kind of place that you can deposit back into your emotional bank account. You can't keep drawing upon it forever without restocking. This will be important for your family to do as well. Everyone needs to take stock of how they are feeling and regroup when necessary. Too often I have seen people ignore their emotional account until it is too late and then they run into problems.

I think to some extent that the process of bonding and attaching to children drains your emotional reserves as well. I covered the basics of attachment earlier, but I think that Alex and I had a more intense, quick timeline that many others I have seen. There are many resources out there for parents that are having trouble attaching and bonding to their new children, but I haven't seen as much relating to quick and intensive bonding. It seems like to the experts, as long as bonding has occurred, you are considered out of the woods and sent on your way.

However, the intensity of a relationship can be too much sometimes and this needs to be addressed as well. These children need a lot of love and attention and when they bond to you, it seems like they can quickly become parasitic. It took a lot for me to recognize this as I was just over the moon about how close Alex and I were, seemingly without any effort or problems on either of our parts. We had an incredibly close relationship that I am so proud of. But once I realized how depleted I was getting, I knew that I had to act. I started pushing back on him a little and being more vocal about my needs. Sometimes this worked and he would acknowledge my needs, and sometimes he wouldn't, but it made me feel better. Also, just sharing this with my husband helped enormously; after all, he is my partner in all of this and my best friend. Being able to talk and share your burdens really does make them lighter to bear.

You have to remember that parents are people too, with all of their attendant foibles and faults. Too often during this whole process, I felt so much pressure to be perfect. I felt that in order to get Alex to love us, we had to be the perfect family. I felt that in order to help G4 and Amanda to accept Alex, I had to be the perfect mother. I felt that I had to be the perfect wife to my husband, making sure there was a meal prepared and the house picked up every time he came home from work. I felt like I could not disappoint Alex with any request to go somewhere or get something, and I could not disappoint Amanda with any missed training sessions.

All of these demands upon me let me get run down and focused too much on things like meals and cleaning, when I should have been focused on the people themselves. I have already covered the emotional reserves getting depleted but this can run far deeper. John complained to me that he missed me as a wife. When I responded that he had good meals cooked and laundry done he responded with pointing out that he would rather bring home a pizza once in awhile but have me available just to talk to. Amanda was noticing that even though I was taking her to every practice, I was not as engaged in the details of what she was doing.

I realized that I was so busy trying to do everything for everyone, that I was actually not doing as much as I thought I was. In the process of adoption of a teen, there will be adjustments and time needed to be spent with them that you didn't have to do before. Because of this, you won't be able to get as much done as you did before, but that is OK. Understand this and reach a level of comfort with it. Give yourself permission to let certain things slide and decide what you need to not compromise on.

I wasn't the only one to suffer from this; John felt it too. He wanted to continue his normal routine with G4 and Amanda, while continuing all of his previous responsibilities like work, finances, etc. He was getting very run down as well, staying up late and getting up early to go to work. He didn't adjust his schedule or expectations either and was depleted as well.

The best advice I can give to other parents is to let go of some things and focus on the important things. There is nothing as important as love and family, and these should be at the forefront of your daily activities. I know there are some things that can't be ignored, but cut yourself some slack.

And when you do mess up, beg forgiveness, but most importantly, forgive yourself. You are doing a wonderful thing, both for yourself and your new child, and you deserve credit for it. Pat yourself on the back and move on.

Developing a Thick Skin

Every day early on in the first few months Alex would say, "You no love me." He jokes most of the time and I just brush it off, but every once in a while I think it has a grain of sincerity and he really doubts my feelings for him. These times usually happen when I have to say no to him or after an emotional exchange. I know intellectually that he has a hard time trusting us (after all, no one has really stuck by him before) but emotionally, it is a little harder to process.

It helps to develop a thick skin and really try to figure out when these times are based in jokes and when there might be more behind them. For a long time I just tolerated the jokes and let them slide off, but recently I have been calling him on it and pushing back, saying, "I know you don't mean it." I don't mind the jokes, but there is a time and place for everything and I want him to know that not all jokes are funny!

For the other times, when I suspect a small grain of truth in it, it is harder to brush them off. I have talked to several other moms who have adopted and universally, we agree, there is a crisis of confidence phenomenon that affects adoptive moms of older children. I believe that it is rooted in the uncertainty of not really knowing your adopted children as well as you know your biological children. Because there is very little shared history, you are not really sure of what is beneath some of their comments or actions. This wondering can lead naturally to feelings of insecurity as a mother and then the whole thing can snowball from there.

The trick I learned is to nip the thoughts in the bud before they have a chance to gain any momentum. They can derail your best intentions with your new child and are not healthy for either you or your child. Trying to squelch them can be difficult though, and can take a lot of internal fortitude.

Some of the coping mechanisms that I have used or seen others use are:

1. Reminding yourself that not knowing your child does not necessarily translate into your inadequacy. It can give you motivation to learn more about them, but one does not not correlate with the other.

2. Understand that the verbalization of something like, "You don't love me," is actually an opportunity for you to reaffirm your true feelings for your child. It could just be a cry for help and reassurance that they need.
3. Communicate your feelings and verbalize the hurt you feel when they speak like that. I can't guarantee any results (it depends on their level of empathy) but at the very least it will help remove a chip from your shoulder. It also will help model appropriate behavior for them later on in life. Showing them how you cope with hurt will allow them to internalize this strategy, not immediately maybe, but someday.
4. Brush it off and simply ignore the speech or behavior. Realize that it is not you, but them and move on. Easier said than done, I know, and I was not ever able to do this very successfully, but I have seen others do this successfully.

Regardless of which strategy you employ, find something that works for you. After all you have gone through to get and assimilate your adopted child, hearing something like, "You no love me," can be devastating. You will need to be able to cope with hearing this and move on and not lose your direction.

There will be a lot of things you will hear and see from your child that you will not like, appreciate, or understand, but when you were not there to form their early years, this is understandable. Add a difficult family situation and maybe a foreign culture on top of it, and you can start to see where you will feel lacking.

The primary message I want to get across is that no matter what you hear, don't circle it back on yourself. You know what is in your heart and mind, and just communicate it through thoughts and actions consistently and frequently. When your child misinterprets it, remember that it is just that: a misinterpretation, not a rejection.

Getting Help

The process of melding together disparate people and creating a new family is exciting and wonderful. It will bring rewards that you never could have even imagined. But every once in a while there will be areas where you find yourself in need of help. It could be that the problems are minimal but that you are just without a place to start fixing them, or are too tired and emotionally drawn out to fix them yourself. There could also be problems that you feel ill equipped to handle or that are honestly larger and more complicated than you feel like tackling.

From choosing an agency, to doing the paperwork, to first getting home with your child, to making them part of your family, it all takes an incredible amount of time and patience. Sometimes on top of all of these stressors, you might have other things that complicate matters, such as learning disabilities, special medical needs, or attachment issues. Or you could even be dealing with more mundane issues like unsupportive family members, physical and mental exhaustion on your part, or financial woes.

Regardless of where the problems are coming from, if you need help, be proactive about seeking it out. Don't feel that you are inadequate by asking for help. For some reason, I have seen more parents in my private practice than I can count that feel like they have to be all things to all people. Well, I can tell you that this ends up by making you nothing to anyone.

By surrounding yourself with the appropriate support at various stages of the adoptive process, you can mitigate some of these areas of concern and set yourself up for success.

If you have to seek help during the adoptive process, you need to be okay with this and accept the help that is offered without resentment. You also need to be able to let go of guilt and remorse about seeking help as this will interfere with the healing that has to occur, both within you and your new family member. I will cover a few of the more common issues that pop up in the adoption of older children and will provide you with resources and perspective on how to handle them.

Help with Mechanics

The first place you might need help is with the mechanics of the adoption itself. As I covered in the early sections of the book, picking an adoption agency is an important first step. But while I talked about the mechanics earlier in the book, like track record, costs, and reputation, now I want to focus here on the human aspect. Do you like the people you have met? Are they nice and do you feel like you can talk to and confide in them? Do you think they will be understanding of your fears and concerns as you navigate a probably unfamiliar process? When things are taking longer than you want, or you are having trouble with the paperwork, these will be the people you discuss it with and rely on for feedback and support. Do you think they will offer that level of support you need?

Next, is the financial end of life. Adoptions are costly and the last thing you need is to be worrying about your next mortgage payment while you are trying to attach to your new child, or travel overseas to get them. As best as you can, try to have the financial end of things wrapped up before you get your new family member. In many cases, this is not possible, but you can reach for that goal. The other thing that is helpful is to have a safety net of another person (maybe family or close friend) that is your angel of money or sponsor. Ask this person to help out only if absolutely necessary. I know of one family who used a stepdad for this purpose when they were trapped in a foreign country with no way out, since the adoption had taken longer than expected and their resources were strained to the max. They also were dealing with unexpected medical complications in one of the children of the sibling group they were adopting. Being able to call on their stepdad allowed them to make travel arrangements back home without worrying about how to pay for it and since they had arranged for this ahead of time, they were able to ask for the help without guilt or worry.

Attachment and Bonding Problems

Attaching to and bonding with your adopted child is probably the most important obstacle to surmount in your family. This is not a problem that is solely relegated to adoptive families though. Even with a biological child, the parents need to bond with the new addition to be able to effectively parent and raise the child, and the child needs to bond with its caretakers to be able to be raised as a successful and contributing member of society. There are well-described instances where there are attachment issues in biologicalal children, both from the child's side and the parent's side. However, these are usually few and far between because the normal process of pregnancy, birth, and development proceeds very organically and naturally, allowing attachment to happen without many impediments.

In adoptive instances, there are many impediments that are placed in the way of bonding with your child that need to be overcome. Usually, these are overcome without much difficulty, but every so often, there can be some issues, spanning the spectrum from mild to severe, that need to be addressed. The key to navigating this issue is to have patience and understanding. There is no right and wrong here and attachment will proceed differently for every family. You also need to be brutally honest when evaluating the situation in your family and seek professional help as soon as you suspect something might be wrong.

To totally understand attachment disorders, let's talk a little bit about normal attachment and bonding. There are two sides to the attachment equation, the parent and the child, On the parent's side, attaching and bonding entails caring for your child, both physically and emotionally, being empathetic and reacting to their needs, being sensitive and responsive to your children, and being a consistent figure present in your child's life. On the child's side, it means being the recipient of all the above that a parent offers, and then giving back to the parent with expressions of social engagement, like eye contact, responding to their parent's care, and interacting appropriately with parents and caregivers.

Attachment and bonding are not the same as love, but often they are found hand in hand with expressions of love. You can see now looking at the list of what normal attachment entails, how this process could be disrupted in scenarios of abuse and neglect. Not all adoptive children are available because of abuse and neglect, but many are, and are at a high risk of experiencing problems with normal attachment.

In many of these children's lives there have been inconsistent caregivers, situations where their needs have not been met in either physical or emotional instances, and they have been placed in situations where they have not been able to interact with caring, empathetic, and responsive people. They have not been encouraged to respond back to caregivers either and have not learned or had modeled for them appropriate expressions of social interaction.

These scenarios are risk factors for attachment disorders that will manifest when you try to establish a normal parent-child relationship with your new child. Now every child will be different and their reaction to these adverse conditions will be different as well. The severity of the adverse interactions and the prevalence of them in early life, primarily from ages zero to three, will be slightly predictive for their risk of presence as well.

There is no litmus test to determine whether your child in particular is at risk for an attachment disorder, or whether they have one, but if you can get as much information as possible about their life before you, it would be helpful. The more information you have, the more likely you will be to correctly identify problems if they are present. There is nothing quite like being blind-sided with a situation when you were under the impression that there were no issues.

There is a tendency to over diagnose attachment in adoptive children at least early on, because their attachment is different from what is normally found in biological families. So, in the beginning, I would recommend reserving your judgement until you have had more time to evaluate life with your new family member. As I mention in the book, attachment is a process, and can move forward and backward on the spectrum as your relationship evolves, so don't be quick to jump on the bandwagon that there are attachment issues when it is just a temporary setback in your relationship with your child. Also, if you had an international adoption, think about the language barriers that exist when considering bonding and attachment. There are factors that could be mitigated with just simply understanding one another.

However, the sad fact is that some of these children are so damaged from early life experiences that they are unable to form attachments and to bond with their adoptive parents. In these cases, professional help will be needed. How can you know if your situation fits this scenario? Again, there is no definite answer that I can give to you, but there are some signs that will be present.

If your child is consistently unable to make eye contact with you, resists any type of physical contact, is not empathetic towards others, shows cruelty to animals or those weaker and smaller, or seems unable to follow social cues and interactions, you should seek a professional opinion. There could be others factors that affect attachment and bonding as well such as learning disabilities and other diagnosable conditions. A full evaluation is warranted to ferret out problems and get a clear picture of what you are dealing with.

NO PANIC!

I think we have an attachment problem, but I am not sure where to go to get help.

There are many resources out there. The first is the Internet, where simply searching for RAD (reactive attachment disorder) will yield plenty of information. There are also numerous websites and books that deal with attachment disorders. These sites, such as www.adoptive-parenting.com and others, will have listings of resources and forums where you can connect with others and gain valuable advice and information as to the next steps that need to be taken.

Help With Medical/Learning Issues

If you adopted a special needs child with your eyes open as to their medical conditions, then you will already have started dealing with them. However, if you were looking for a "normal" child and didn't expect any unusual problems, when they crop up, it can be devastating. There are obvious medical and learning issues that you can see with your naked eyes, and in some ways, these are easier to bear as they aren't hidden or attributed to other factors. Sometimes when there is a suspicion of problems but an unwillingness to consider a serious, permanent cause, many disparate things will get blamed, from the particular orphanage, to institutions in particular, even to customs and medical training in other countries. Try to resist the blame game and if indeed conventional fixes aren't working, keep in mind possible brain damage. And this is what I am referring to in this section, as brain damage is mostly hidden until it manifests in learning problems or behavioral problems.

One of the most common ones is Fetal Alcohol Syndrome (FAS). FAS is such a broad spectrum of brain damage that it can be quite difficult to diagnose. There are some similarities in severe cases with physical and mental manifestations that are predictable, but many cases are milder and much harder to diagnose. The bottom line in any case is that there is brain damage that has occurred and that is irreversible. There is no cure or therapy that can account for damaged neurons. There are some medications and therapies that can help one deal with the damage that was done, but the underlying damage is the same.

There are specialists in FAS, usually in more metropolitan areas, so if you are thinking this diagnosis fits your child, it pays to take them to someone who is well-versed in this. However, there could be other causes of brain damage that shouldn't be discounted. A child could have been the victim of other drugs of abuse while in utero, or could have been the victim of repeated physical violence and head trauma. Some older children could also have some damage from activities they themselves have pursued such as alcohol and drug abuse. Any of these scenarios could result in permanent brain damage.

There are also cases where such severe emotional and physical abuse can affect the brain of the child to the point where the child will stop growing and maturing. The brain, under so much stress, will stop producing growth hormone. While most cases of this will resolve with proper care and nutrition, it is possible that such severe abuse and neglect have taken place that the child had permanent brain damage and can't recover normal functioning.

Along these same lines are learning disabilities. Some learning disabilities can be overcome, but others will be life-long struggles and will need more extensive therapy and coping mechanisms. Unfortunately, medical problems that can't be seen, can be waved off as a result of an orphanage setting, lack of a consistent caregiver, or poverty, whether that is in a financial sense or educational sense.

It won't be until you have gotten home and started to deal with some of the perceived problems that you will realize they aren't responding as you think they should, or even at all. Multiple attempts at problem solving will leave you frustrated and really back at square one, needing to find help.

Any of the problems mentioned above will be devastating to you as an adoptive parent of a seemingly normal child. You will have to grieve for the child you have lost, the one you had anticipated. Then after giving yourself time, you will have to adjust to a new normal and seek help and services to best meet the needs of your child and your family.

Don't be afraid to share your story and seek the best help that you can. These problems are no reflection of your abilities as an adoptive parent. They aren't a reflection of the goodness of your child either. They are unfortunate facts of life that will have to be dealt with in order to allow both you and your family the best of outcomes. By hiding or being reluctant to share the truth, you will perhaps lead others astray and deny yourself the thorough support and help system you need.

Help with Family and Friends

We will all get various levels of support and acceptance from our family and friends, and while some is good, some might be unintentionally bad. Try to anticipate where you might have trouble. Cover with your family and friends ahead of time what your expectations should be with regard to their interactions with your new child. You won't be able to cover everything, but you will be able to head off certain problems. Don't feel bad about withdrawing from those that are not helpful to you. Your priority is you and your immediate family, including your new child. Sometimes others can be overly generous, giving gifts and presents that are inappropriately extravagant, or they can be overly permissive when you are trying to teach a new child limits and boundaries. Sometimes, children who have a disrupted sense of family, are not understanding of extended family relationships and will look to aunts, cousins, and grandparents for the guidance and help that needs to come from you as a parent. And sometimes, you will face downright disapproval for your actions. This can be the hardest to bear, as you will feel like you are losing part of your support system. Make sure you have someone you can talk to about this, whether it is a friend, or a counselor, or support group.

This brings up an important point, sharing of information. You need somewhere safe to share all the feelings and emotions that bubble up inside of you, both positive and negative. This needs to be in a setting without recrimination and with complete empathy and support. Many people have trusted friends or family members that can take on this role, but for others, they will need to seek out somewhere to be able to do this, especially if they have not been that type of person in the past to need a lot of outside support. A great place to start looking for support is on the internet. Even just reading the blogs and articles posted by other adoptive parents will help. But do so with a jaundiced eye. Usually the most vocal people are the ones with the most extreme situations or the biggest problems.

There are support groups out there for almost any kind of adoptive situation that exists and a great place to start looking is at www.adoption.org or www.adoptivefamilies.com. Finding other families that are going through similar type experiences or already have is very powerful. Don't be afraid to reach out, send an email. If you don't get a response, you really haven't lost anything.

Another great place to find support is through a support group. I joined FRUA which is an organization that is for families that have adopted from Russia and Eastern European countries. Meeting others that have gone through what I have has been great. Not everyone will share exactly the same experiences, but they will be close enough to help you. There are support groups that are run through state agencies, usually the Department of Children and Family Services.

Regardless of where you find it, find some kind of support. You need to be able to voice the not-so-pleasant thoughts that will be in your head, like "Why did I do this?" or "I have ruined my life," or "I can't say I love you one more time because I don't feel it right now." We all think these at one time or another, and they don't make us bad parents or bad people. They just show us that at the time we are thinking them, we need space, time, help, or all of these. We need to give ourselves a break and understand that we are attempting something difficult and emotionally taxing. There will be good and bad times. The key is to understand where the bad times come from and work on those root causes. When we can fix those, we will be left with nothing but good times.

Epilogue

We are at the one year mark with Alex now, getting ready for an A-day (adoption day) celebration to celebrate the date his adoption by us became official. We have gone through a move, his first Christmas with us, his first birthday with us, and the start of teaching him how to drive. Looking back over this first year, it is like he has always been with us.

The move to Seattle was actually one of the best things that happened to us. At first Alex was reluctant to leave Utah, his familiar piece of America. But once he understood that he was part of the family and his opinion of the house we chose was valued, he blossomed. Actually I have to give G4 most of the credit. With his obsessive compulsive ways, he was getting out of sorts with all the houses we were looking at. He started a system on his iPhone where we all had to give the house we had just toured a number from one to ten and then explain the reasoning for it. Then he would average the numbers together to get a final score for the house. Once Alex realized that his score was given equal weighting and his opinion valued, he got into the swing of it really quickly. It was also great practice for his English.

Then when we did finally all agree on a house, he and Amanda duked it out for which bedroom they would get. John tried to get involved, but I told him to step back and let them work it out on their own. In the end, Alex won, but it was a fair fight and he made several concessions to her. It was great to see them working things out together as normal siblings and both being happy with the outcome. Much better than a parent-imposed plan that everyone would resent.

Moving was a great leveler, as we all were new to the area and all needed to repaint our rooms, organize furniture, and make new friends. Nobody knew our family before, so they just accepted we always had three kids and treated us that way. We have chosen to share the fact that Alex was adopted to some, but to others we haven't. G4 and Amanda have been the greatest help to me. Never have they complained or fussed about Alex being brought into the family. There have been normal sibling issues, mostly with Amanda wondering why anyone would want brothers and why they are necessary in life, as they are smelly, messy, and obnoxious at times. But it is equally directed at both boys. G4 also feels sometimes like life as an only child would be preferable without little ones mucking up his carefully ordered academic pursuits. But again it is equally directed at both Alex and Amanda. And in contrast to the times they get on each others' nerves, there are plenty more times when you can find all of them jumping on the trampoline together, playing the Xbox together, or playing a board game together.

Alex and Amanda have gotten involved with the local teen homeschooling group and are making friends. They are an active group with plenty of outings and get-togethers. At first he was very shy, but after Amanda matriculated and made friends, he came out of his shell and has made friends as well.

Alex is involved in Capeoria, a Brazilian martial art, and enjoys taking lessons. His schoolwork has come along by leaps and bounds. Now on a regular basis he will come to me and insist that we do work. He is still doing Algebra 1, but we now are able to get three lessons done a week as he has caught up so much on the gaps he had before. This is a great leap forward from the beginning where it took us two weeks to do one lesson.

I am teaching both Alex and Amanda world geography and after those lessons every day, he does some English reading in an eighth grade textbook that deals with the subject we just learned about. This helps reinforce the concepts and visualize the words that he learned in the lesson. He also does copy work every week out of the same book, again to help reinforce the concepts. I have chosen not to formally teach English and let him absorb it through other subjects. Physics has been a hard subject to teach with the scientific vocabulary, but he requested it so we are plugging away at it very slowly.

He does work out of a third grade critical thinking book with synonyms, antonyms, and visual discrimination. It is below his level, but good practice work. Conversationally, he is fluent, but his academic vocabulary is still needing help. So I got a TOEFL book from a bookstore and every few days pick a word out of it and post it up on the refrigerator with the translation in Russian. It helps him learn English and expand his Russian vocabulary. Then everyone tries to use the word in their everyday conversation to help reinforce it. Today's word is "heinous" and already we have had too much fun using it!

I also found a grad student that has experience teaching homeschoolers and have hired him to teach Amanda and Alex a critical thinking/sociology class once a week. Amanda has more assignments and extensions that Alex can't do yet, but it is great for teaching him how to interact in discussions and think critically and analytically about subjects. They are using a college text that is very advanced, but I read it to Alex in small quantities. Even though much of it is above him, just the exposure to language and ideas has been great. He is really enjoying the class now and actively participates. I am hoping that in another six months or so, he will be ready to be in a larger group setting and will feel comfortable contributing.

The last bit of schoolwork is reading in Russian. I found a bookstore that carries books in Russian, and three to four times a week, he reads from a book in Russian. I like him to read about one book every two weeks or so. They are just fiction books, but hopefully they are enough to keep up his skills in his native language.

As far as keeping up with Ukraine, Alex blows hot and cold. There are times that he will suggest calling his Grandma and we allow it, but there are months that go by when he is not interested. Now, though, when he does call, he makes sure I am snuggled up right next to him and his arm is around me. He is more calm now after talking to his Grandma or stepmom and in fact the past several times, there have been no repercussions from the calls. Grandma is still asking for money of course, and we are sending some over when we can.

Alex has talked some about going back to Ukraine and picked up that I was a little reluctant. About two months ago he was going on and on about his stepmom and half sister and it was really irritating me. We were actually driving in the car to the library when I lost it and started crying.

He forced me to pull over and pulled me into his arms and asked me what was wrong. I told him that I was sick of hearing about his step mom. She wasn't that great if she beat him and it was just painful that he had allegiance and attachment to someone that was so damaging to him. I told him that I hated reminders that I was not always there for him and wasn't his real mom. I also shared with him that I was scared if we took him back to Ukraine that he would run from us and not want to come home to America with all of his ties there to friends and family.

He just held me as I blubbered all over him and told me that he understood. He told me that I wasn't his real mom, but then softened the blow by adding that he wished I was. He then told me that I never had to worry about him leaving me or the family, that he was with us forever and was a part of our family now. It seemed like that was a real turning point for him and me. My fears were allayed and he seemed so much more comfortable after that.

Alex seems more sure of our love and acceptance now. I think he truly believes that he thinks we are forever finally. While he hasn't left behind all his annoying habits, most of the worst have been extinguished and those that haven't, oh well, they are part of who he is. He will always like more violent video games than we like, but he is now equally accepting of fun E-rated games and the most violent ones have been forgotten.

He is still messy and lazy in the mornings, difficult to wake up and a cranky pants until about noon. But we have just learned that and adjusted our schedules accordingly. And when we can't, he gets with the program, reluctantly.

His tastes in music will always be a little different, but there are many artists that we all like and can agree on. He weaseled an earring out of us for a fifteenth birthday present, but he knows the tattoo is still a no go. He has been to his first concert here in the states. And the most momentous things: we took him to Disney World. There is nowhere else on earth that everyone has permission to be a kid and still be cool!

And speaking of being a kid. Alex is the most interesting mix of little kid and grown up in one person. He will charge around the house in shark slippers and a blankie tied around his shoulders at times and at others act like he is twenty-five. It is so clear that he never had a chance to be a child and is making up for lost time.

We still have our talks every once in a while, but for the most part, I know everything about his previous life now, so thank goodness, no more surprises. We now mostly talk about forward-looking things and his future. He is receptive to that and I think excited about his prospects for an education at a university and a career.

He still is moving back and forth through developmental stages. He had extinguished needing me so much, but just the other day he started needing me more again. It comes and goes and we have just realized that where as times there is something tangible that we can hang it on, many times there is nothing that we can point to as a trigger. We just realize that he is working through things in his mind and needs extra reassurance. One change, though: he has started getting this reassurance from other family members. If I am unavailable, he will go to Amanda first, and then to John. It isn't always me any more. And that does make me sad at times, but at others, I am so happy that he is finding his niche.

Around Christmas, he went through a period of being cranky and I figured out what it was. He was realizing that Ukraine was really, really slipping away. His memories are fading, but I still don't think he feels American enough. I talked to him and explained that he had to figure out who he was. I told him that being a teenager is all about trying on identities and finding the ones that fit. I told him that some of the identities at the beginning will be the opposite of us (meaning more Ukrainian and rebellious) but as he gets older and more mature they will become closer to the family. But I told him that only he can figure out how much he changes and becomes truly American. I told him this has nothing to do with where he lives or what language he speaks, but all about how his heart feels.

I told him not to worry about it now. Some days he will feel like Dima Supruncyhk, others Alexei (half and half) and still others just Alex. Letting go of Dima doesn't mean that he will lose him forever, as after all, that was who made him who is is today. Accepting Alex won't make Dima fade any faster either. It is a process that he has control over. There will be some fading of his Ukrainian self just because I can't keep it up with language and traditions as much as I would like. But we are willing to accept him no matter what hat he is wearing that day.

And if some day when he is out of school, he decides that Ukraine is the place for him, it will be done with us and we will be there for him as much as we can. Wherever he gets an apartment and a job and a wife, we will be an integral part of his life. The world is a global place and we will be his family no matter where he lives. He appreciated this talk and told me he thinks he will stay in America, but that he isn't sure.

I want Alex to feel that his future is a wide open door with unimaginable love and happiness on the other side, because that is exactly what he has given to us. Alex has given us so much love and laughter. We have been so blessed with his presence in our lives.

Just the other day, he reminded me that he very nearly didn't come to America for the hosting program, as he was being punished for some transgression or another at the orphanage. Then he slyly looked at me and said, "You never would have met me. You wouldn't have adopted me."

I shot back to him, "Oh, yes I would have. Did you know that God makes mistakes sometimes?"

He looked confusedly at me and answered back, "Of course he doesn't."

I replied, "Oh, yes he does. He mistakenly gave you to another mom and dad in Ukraine. It took me fourteen years to fix that mistake, but I did. Don't you think for a minute that you weren't meant to be ours. Even if you hadn't come with the other kids, I truly believe in my heart that I would have found you. I know I would have found you somehow and someway. It was our destiny for all of us to be together as a family." And then I placed my hand on his heart.

He looked at me for a moment digesting this bit of information and then reached out to hug me, answering seriously with, "I know."

References

1. **Big Brothers Big Sisters.**
   www.bbbs.org

2. **Congressional Coalition on Adoption Institute.**
   www.ccainstitute.org

3. Erikson, Erik. **Childhood and Society. New York,**
   W. W. Norton and Company, Inc. 1950.

4. Families for Russian and Ukrainian Adoption.
   www.frua.org

5. Harris, Diane. **The Cost of Raising a Baby. Parenting.**
   www.parenting.com

6. McKay, Katherine, Ross, Laurie, & Goldberg, Laurie. **Adaptation to Parenthood During the Post-Adoption Period: A Review of the Literature.** Adoption Quarterly, Volume 13, Issue 2 (May 2010): 125-144.

7. Senecky, Yehuda, Agassi, Hanoch, Inbar, Dov, Horesh, Netta, Diamond, Gary, Bergman, Yoav S., & Apter, Alan. **Post-adoption depression among adoptive mothers.** Journal of Affective Disorders, no. 115 (2009): 62–68.

8. Tuttle, Brad. **Million Dollar Babies: What It Really Costs to Raise a Child.** 2012.
www.business.time.com

9. Trzaskowski, Maciej, Dale, Philip S., & Plomin, Robert. **No Genetic Influence for Childhood Behavior Problems From DNA Analysis.** Journal of the American Academy of Child and Adolescent Psychiatry. no. 10 (2013.07.16).

10. **US Department of Immigration.**
http://www.us-immigration.com

11. US State Department. **The AFCARS Report.** No. 19. July 2012.
www.acf.hhs.gov/ programs/cb

12. US Department of Health and Human Services. **Adoption Tax Credit and the Affordable Care Act.** (2010)
www.hhs.gov

About the Author

Bethany M. Gardiner is a pediatrician, award-winning author, and seasoned mother of three, one of whom was adopted as a teenager from Ukraine. She is also a homeschooler with over a decade of experience homeschooling her own children and teaching co-op classes for other homeschoolers. Her first book, *Highlighting Homeschooling*, won 4 book awards, including being a finalist for the New Horizons Award for debut authors.

A National Merit Scholar that was accepted into the Honors Program at the University of Florida, she graduated in 1990 with a Bachelor's of Science in Mathematics and a Bachelor's of Arts in Statistics. Following graduation, she attended medical school at the University of Florida, graduating with honors in 1994. After completing medical school, Dr. Gardiner did her internship and pediatric residency at the University of Florida's Urban Campus. She also became an expert in sexual abuse, working with the Duval County Sexual Assault Response Team as a specialized pediatric examiner. Upon completion of residency, she joined Interlachen Pediatrics in Orlando, FL and became a board certified pediatrician and an internationally board certified lactation consultant.

After two biologic children left her unable to have others, Dr. Gardiner and her husband decided to adopt from Ukraine. They adopted a 14 year old boy and have chronicled the process and integration in their family with the blog, Dearest Dema. Currently, she lives in Seattle with her three children and is married to the same man she met as a freshman in college twenty-seven years ago. She enjoys traveling, reading, hiking, and writing.

Made in the USA
San Bernardino, CA
06 August 2014